BEYOND
CONFLICT

PETER R. BREGGIN, M.D.

BEYOND CONFLICT

▼ ▼

From Self-Help
and Psychotherapy
to Peacemaking

ST. MARTIN'S PRESS
NEW YORK

First published in the United States of America in 1992

Printed in the United States of America

ISBN 0-312-07654-1

Library of Congress Cataloging-in-Publication Data

Breggin, Peter Roger, 1936–
     Beyond conflict : from psychotherapy to peacemaking / Peter R.
Breggin.
          p.   cm.
     ISBN 0-312-07654-1
     1. Interpersonal conflict.   2. Social conflict.   3. Conflict
(Psychology)   4. Love.   I. Title.
BF637.I48B74   1992
303.6'9—dc20   92-4959
                                                              CIP

DESIGN BY SNAP-HAUS GRAPHICS
First Edition: September 1992

For my wife, Ginger Ross-Breggin,
who continues to inspire and enlighten me
with love in every sphere of life.

CONTENTS

▼ ▼

ACKNOWLEDGMENTS
AND RESOURCES

▼ ▼

As in all my work, my wife Ginger Ross-Breggin is the single most important and beneficial influence. She continues to inspire me to write in a more easily understandable manner and adds immeasurably to my awareness of the human condition. While I held my beliefs about love long before I met her, I genuinely doubt if I could have sustained them much longer without her. Love is a powerful idea; but so many forces in life, and too many within ourselves, act to discourage it. This book is a hymn to our "shared values," Ginger's concept that enriches the final chapter.

I am deeply grateful to my friends Leonard Roy Frank and Pam Clay, both of whom read the manuscript with great care and made many useful suggestions and necessary corrections. My neighbor, David Whitford, also carefully read the manuscript and made significant contributions.

Richard Rubenstein, my colleague at George Mason University in the Institute for Conflict Analysis and Resolution, offered important insights and much-needed encouragement as well. Without his original invitation to join the Institute, it's possible that I would not have been inspired to write this book. Another George Mason colleague, Frank Blechman, also made useful criticisms. In general, I want to thank all the members of the Institute and, in particular, Mary Lynn Boland, for making it all run smoothly.

Sharon Presley was especially helpful in directing me toward recent research in social psychology. Keith Hoeller also went through the book from beginning to end and found many ideas that needed clarification and elaboration. Emilio Viano and Robert Morgan not only helped with the manuscript, they provided lengthy, encouraging evaluations that helped inspire the finishing touches. In addition, I received a combination of moral support and/or criticism from David Cohen, David K. Hart, Larry Tirnauer, Craig Blaner, Yvette Ogle, Joann Robertson, Gerald Dubin, and Jean Ross.

Claudia Delgado has helped with innumerable office tasks surrounding the manuscript and Marilyn Cramer has come through as a consultant every time I've created a computer disaster for myself.

My agent for my recent books is Richard Curtis. He and his staff have done everything an author could hope for.

As I describe in the Preface, this book was completed only a few months after *Toxic Psychiatry*. St. Martin's is the publisher of both books, and I have been enormously pleased with the company and *all* its staff members. In the acknowledgments to *Toxic Psychiatry* I have already thanked senior editor Jared Kieling for his work on that book, which became an important step toward the publication of this one. Thanks again, Jared. Now I also want to thank his assistant, Ensley Eikenberg.

Simon Winder is the St. Martin's senior editor for *Beyond Conflict*, and it would be hard to imagine a more enthusiastic and appreciative supporter. Finally, authors do not usually get to thank their publicists in print because they don't know whether they want to thank them until several months after publication. Well, I have reason to thank the entire promotions office at St. Martin's, and especially Kate Kahn, for their efforts on behalf of *Toxic Psychiatry*.

For anyone who wishes to learn more about the burgeoning field of conflict analysis and resolution, many resources can be found at the Institute for Conflict Analysis and Resolution (ICAR), George Mason University, Fairfax, Virginia 22030-4444. ICAR offers masters degrees and doctorates in conflict analysis and resolution. It also houses two important national organizations in the field—COPRED (Consortium on Peace Research, Education and Development) and NCPCR (National Conference on Peacemaking and Conflict Resolution).

For people who wish to learn more about psychiatric reform, *Toxic Psychiatry* provides an appendix on resources.

I would also like to acknowledge Kenneth Boulding (1970, 1978) who has suggested a somewhat similar three dynamic analysis limited to the societal level, but with rather marked differences that do not so readily lend it to personal growth and conflict resolution theory. Boulding used the term dynamics or social organizers in his theory of human relationships and specifically described them as the threat system, the exchange system, and the integrative system. His theory helped to clarify the development of my own, but there are important differences. As one example, Boulding sees the integrative or love system as a form of exchange, while I envision it as unconditional love or gifting. This leads to both a different analysis and a different social ideal. Boulding does not relate the concept of dynamics or social organizers to basic human needs and does not apply his theory to self-development or interpersonal conflict resolution.

In addition, a variety of humanistic psychologists and psychiatrists have contributed to my thinking, as well as to basic needs theory in general. They include Erich Fromm (1956, 1976), Erik Erikson (1963), Gordon Allport (1955), Karen Horney (1945, 1950), Alfred Adler (1969), Ansbacher and Ansbacher (1956), and Abraham Maslow (1971).

PREFACE: FROM *TOXIC PSYCHIATRY* TO *BEYOND CONFLICT*

▼ ▼

Surprisingly, the two books that most fully present the twin aspects of my work have been published within less than a year of each other. First came *Toxic Psychiatry: Why Therapy, Empathy and Love Must Replace the Drugs, Electroshock and Biochemical Theories of the New Psychiatry* (1991), and now this book, *Beyond Conflict: From Self-Help and Psychotherapy to Peacemaking*.

While *Toxic Psychiatry* does describe caring, human service alternatives to conventional psychiatry, it is mainly a sweeping criticism of modern biologically oriented psychiatry. It exposes the politics of psychiatry and the damaging effects of drugs and electroshock. *Beyond Conflict* has a more positive thrust. It presents my approach to life as a practicing psychiatrist and psychotherapist, and a professor of conflict analysis and resolution. It is, in the words of one of my friends, a much more "uplifting" book.

Yet the themes of my life and work, as reflected in the separate books, are really inseparable. *Toxic Psychiatry* is an aggressive attack on the destructive principles, fraudulent claims, and dangerous technologies of modern psychiatry; but the spiritual energy behind it derives from the principles of liberty and love—my belief in human rights, the inviolability of every single human being, and the healing power of human caring. *Beyond Conflict* more fully articulates that spiritual energy. It proposes that love must become the guiding principle of human relationships in general, as well as the ultimate solution to the most severe personal, societal, and political conflicts.

The aim of both books has been to present scientific and philosophical ideas in a form available to any interested reader. They reflect my commitment to more holistic writing, accessible to any thoughtful person, and based on equal parts of thinking and feeling, scholarship and real-life experience. People need books that offer better principles through which to guide their lives. Toward that end, writing should be comprehensive *and* comprehensible. I have tried to meet that standard.

Part I

Understanding
the Three
Dynamics:
Love, Liberty,
and Coercion

CHAPTER 1

▼ ▼

From Self-Help and Psychotherapy to Peacemaking

Human values must be universal. In the past, narrow values have led to tragedy. As the twentieth century draws to a close, our values must be broad and deep. The question of the kind of life human beings ought to lead cannot be solved within the framework of accepted social commonplaces and mere common sense. This is true because man himself is not limited to a single society in a single country but is part of a chain connecting humanity, the natural phenomena of the whole earth, and the cosmos.
Daisaku Ikeda, Choose Life (1976)

We are the aware generation. Modern psychology and modern communications have enabled us to see conflict everywhere: within ourselves, between ourselves and others, on the world scene, and with nature. But we have not become so successful at seeing solutions—at finding ways of easing and resolving conflict within ourselves and our society.

In every aspect of life—from self-help and psychotherapy to peacemaking—we need better principles for resolving conflict and promoting harmony within ourselves and others. We need approaches that make personal *and* political sense, that connect us in a rational and caring manner to ourselves as individuals and to the world around us, including other people and nature. We need a viewpoint that helps us understand and heal the pain of human conflict.

A good set of healing principles should be useful in every aspect of living. Inner peace and world peace are, at root, one and the same. Complexity of course increases as we move from issues of personal growth to those of world community; but the principles, I believe, remain basically the same. This means we can deepen and fine-tune our understanding of life through self-examination and through studying society. We can apply one basic approach to self-help and to helping others, to resolving personal conflict and to ending social strife. This book attempts to provide such a holistic approach.

THE IMPORTANCE OF BASIC NEEDS

If we can understand basic human needs and how they become frustrated or satisfied, we will have made a critical step toward finding better ways of resolving all kinds of conflicts. The most severe conflicts often have to do with psychological and social needs, rather than physical or material ones. They can be resolved through improving human relations and, especially, through the collaborative satisfaction of each other's basic needs.

Human needs can be divided into three categories: love, liberty, and coercion. *Love* includes the whole range of motivation related to human bonding, from the infant's desire for holding to the adult's dependence on close friends, family, and community. *Liberty* includes needs associated with autonomy, independence, self-determination and freedom, such as the infant's first efforts to walk and the adult's later efforts to take charge of his or her own life. *Coercion* encompasses the need to use force, violence, and intimidation. It rears up in a small child's frustrated rage, in a man or woman's attempts to control a spouse, or in a politician's call to arms. Whether coercion and even violence are *basic* needs or purely learned responses remain controversial.

Human needs do not exist in a social vacuum. They develop and find expression through human relationships. A baby's smile at the sight of its mother is inseparable from the presence of a mother, and both mother and child interact to increase each other's tendency to smile. The desire for romantic love requires feeling passion toward another person, and it cannot fully mature without reciprocity. The development of feelings of esteem in a child depends upon those who encourage or undermine it, and even the most autonomous adults continue to respond to how others feel about them.

From infancy on, individual human needs cannot be teased out from the fabric of social relationships that satisfy or frustrate them. Indeed, it is impossible to conceive of an infant becoming a normal human in the absence of nurturing relationships. Babies don't learn to smile frequently without reciprocal responses from adults, and abandoned or neglected infants cannot by themselves grow into effectively functioning adults (see chapter 2).

THE PSYCHOSOCIAL NATURE OF BASIC NEEDS

Biological needs, such as sex or hunger, do not by themselves produce conflict. Conflict results from unfulfilled psychosocial needs, such as the desire for self-esteem, autonomy, or love. Both human beings and chimpanzees have needs for touching, nurturing, and companionship. Both humans and chimps compete for love in their communities and families, creating conflict among themselves, and both use loving gestures and overtures as a method of conflict resolution (see chapter 2).

Biological needs, such as sex, become sources of conflict through the psychosocial meanings or values attached to them. The rapist is no more out for "sexual gratification" by itself than is the lover. The one seeks power or revenge, the other tenderness or intimacy. The needs for power and for intimacy are the motivating forces, not physical sex.

Similarly, in typical marital disputes in my therapy practice, the man desires sex in order to feel respected or loved while the woman desires respect and love before she wants sex. Often sex becomes little more than the focal point for conflict over autonomy and control.

Some men and women suppress their sexual desires out of religious conviction, and still others seek sexual release without help from other people. In every case, the biological need for sexual pleasure or release is much less important than the psychosocial needs surrounding it, such as autonomy, self-esteem, or love.

The same is true of hunger or thirst. People are motivated by these instinctual drives to seek food or water, but are not necessarily driven into conflict with other people, even when they are starving to death or dying of thirst. For example, the social prohibition against killing people for food is rarely broken even under extreme circumstances. But when people associate hunger with injustice or other psychosocial or community issues, then it becomes a major source of personal and political conflict.

PSYCHOSOCIAL DYNAMICS

The word "dynamic" connotes energy, force, change, and progress. It suggests the capacity of human beings to overcome at least some of their biological constraints and cultural experiences to achieve a higher level of functioning based on rational values and loving principles.

Dynamic is most familiar through the term psychodynamic, a loosely defined concept indicating the internal forces and processes of the mind. Dynamic in this book refers to *psychosocial* experiences—interactions between an individual's needs and the social relationships that satisfy them. The love dynamic, for example, encompasses both the person's need for love and the kinds of relationships that stimulate and satisfy it. The liberty dynamic includes the individual's desire for autonomy and independence and how that is expressed or frustrated through relationships.

THE THREE DYNAMICS

The three psychosocial dynamics correspond to the three basic needs: love, liberty, and coercion. Each of the dynamics—love, liberty, and coercion—produces a very different kind of psychological and social experience. The feelings, thoughts, and actions that occur along each dynamic are different, and the outcomes for everyone involved are different as well. From each dynamic, we can identify a consistent set of unique principles to guide our actions and our lives.

Once we learn to identify each dynamic, we can more quickly and thoroughly grasp the implications of what is taking place within and among the participants. We can influence the quality and the result of a relationship or conflict depending on which approach we take toward others, and which approach we encourage them to take toward us. We can decide which principles to implement and to live by.

If a father, for example, has a conflict with a son, he has three basic options. He can force a solution on his child (coercion), he can create an environment in which his son has as much choice as possible (liberty), or he can solve the problem in a loving manner aimed at satisfying his son's basic needs (love). Or the father may try a mixture of all three approaches.

Similarly, if a nation is planning strategy for handling an international conflict, it again has three basic options—love, liberty, or coercion—and again, the outcome will be greatly affected by its choices. The nation can threaten war (coercion), seek to negotiate through diplomatic channels (liberty), or offer to collaborate with the adversary toward the mutual satisfaction of each side's basic needs (love).

People prosper psychologically and socially when they reject coercion and promote liberty and especially love in their lives. *People can improve their personal well-being and promote conflict resolution by identifying the three dynamics and by taking actions that limit coercion and promote liberty and love. This is true in personal as well as political activities.*

UNDERSTANDING THE THREE DYNAMICS

The following is a brief summary of the essential principles of each of the three dynamics:

LOVE (DYNAMIC I):

1. Nurturing, sharing, and giving gifts

2. Cooperative relationships

3. The generation of feelings of empathy, caring, and love

4. The abhorrence and rejection of force

LIBERTY (DYNAMIC II):

1. Bargaining, negotiating, or making voluntary exchanges

2. Competitive relationships

3. The generation of feelings of respect or esteem

4. Force limited to self-defense

COERCION (DYNAMIC III):

1. Forcing, threatening, bullying, and manipulating

2. Involuntary or oppressive relationships

3. The generation of negative feelings, such as hate, guilt, shame, anxiety, numbing, and chronic anger (These feelings will be identified as expressions of psychological helplessness.)

4. The arbitrary use of force

Attitudes toward force can be critical in identifying each dynamic and in understanding their outcomes. In love, force is abhorred. We do not wish to injure our loved ones even in self-defense. In liberty, we exercise the right to use force in self-defense, but we never initiate force. In coercion, we initiate force to satisfy our needs.

Love creates bonding on a personal and societal level. It is fulfilled through both caring personal relationships and through community. It encourages mutuality, sharing, and the equal worth of all people. Liberty encourages or produces independence in personal relationships and the free market in society. It encourages competition and ranking people according to a hierarchy of achievement or success. Coercion suppresses and injures people in authoritarian relationships and in the extreme produces totalitarianism in society. It fosters power and control on the part of the perpetrator and submission and helplessness on the part of the victim.

Notice that each dynamic has a both a personal and a political parallel:

Love generates personal bonding and human community.

Liberty generates personal autonomy and the free market.

Coercion generates personal oppression and totalitarianism.

Unhappily, coercion is too easily resorted to, especially in the handling of our most difficult personal and political problems. Too much of life is made up of dominators and dominated. Meanwhile, the competition generated by liberty too easily deteriorates into winners overpowering losers. Love is required to reject coercion and to soften the competition of liberty. But love itself can become as elusive as a mirage in a desert, a distant vision maintained only by our sheer thirst for it. We frequently seem unable to love our immediate family and friends, let alone other members of our society, foreigners, nature, and the earth.

The three-dynamic approach encompasses all the ways human beings try to resolve their conflicts. In a broader sense, it also encompasses the whole range of human relationships. Thus it provides guidelines not only for resolving conflict but for personal growth and human progress in general.

Progress, however, is no longer a concept that can be glibly used. It cannot uncritically be identified with industrial or technological development, with an increasing gross national product, or a higher material standard of living. In our personal lives and within society, progress must take into account the *quality* of life, including the quality of our inner life, our relationships with other human beings, nature, and the earth itself. Human beings must learn to value nature and the earth as they would ideally value each other—with unconditional love.

NEEDS AND VALUES

All individuals probably begin with somewhat similar "human nature" or biological capacities to feel. How these capacities are inhibited or channeled into psychosocial needs will depend upon individual personality, varying social roles and culture.

When needs are assigned negative or positive worth, we call them *values*. Love begins as a biologically based potential for having feelings toward other people, becomes expressed as a psychosocial need, and then, with the aid of human consciousness, it is recognized as a positive or negative value.

INSTITUTIONS AND IDEOLOGIES

Needs become values, and then values become further elaborated into philosophies, religions, and ideologies; and these in turn become embedded in social institutions, such as the family, schools, churches, or governments. Love, for example, is transformed by culture into love of school, country, or God. It may even become corrupted by coercion in religious or patriotic wars.

Even among chimpanzees, love is embodied in an institution, the chimpanzee family consisting of the mother and her offspring, and their extended relationships within the group. Like human children, young chimps learn to love, or fail to do so, depending upon their upbringing. An elderly, failing mother chimp may produce an offspring who is "spoiled," lacking in both self-control and a sense of being loved. Similarly, both humans and chimps learn, or fail to learn, loving conflict resolution through their familial and social experiences (Goodall, 1986; de Waal, 1989; [see also chapter 2]).

We will at different times focus on feelings, needs, values, ideologies, and their institutional and societal embodiments, such as religion and the state. It is important to remember that they are one package seen from different perspectives, and that basic human needs are at the root of it all.

THE ALIENATION OF VALUES FROM THEIR ORIGINAL NEEDS

Unfortunately, values and ideologies can easily become divorced from the underlying basic needs. People end up competing and fighting over values and ideologies that have taken on a life of their own. The conflict cannot be resolved because all involved have lost sight of their underlying needs.

A married couple quarrels over money with no awareness that the struggle originated over feelings of financial insecurity or the need for power and control. Or they fight over sex without discussing the underlying issues of love and self-respect. A parent and child struggle over bedtime or homework without recognizing and resolving conflicts between the child's need for autonomy and the parent's need to fulfill a parental role.

Cultures and nations similarly go to war and slaughter each other over slogans and ideologies that have long ago become estranged from their underlying basic needs. Political leaders often take advantage and generate "patriotic" wars to distract citizens from their frustrated needs for economic security or cultural identity. They foment outrage over fabricated atrocities in order to motivate people to support violent solutions to conflict. For conflict resolution to take place, people must be redirected to their basic needs and to principles and methods of satisfying them, often in collaboration with their supposed enemies.

THE CHILDHOOD ORIGINS OF CONFLICT

More confusing, the origins of the conflict may extend back into the childhood of one or more of the participants without their being aware of it. A woman may persistently ridicule her girl-friends without realizing that she is compulsively reacting against the humiliation she received as a small child from her older sister. A man may feel compelled to dominate a woman without knowing that he is responding to the shame and "unmanliness" he feels over being sexually abused as a child. In both instances, resolution of the earlier conflict can ameliorate the more recent ones.

The childhood origins of the harmful behavior should not be used to excuse or condone it; but understanding the origins can help the perpetrator control the impulses (see chapters 4 and 5). In the meanwhile, the oppressive conduct should be controlled by the individual, and if necessary by others, regardless of the compulsion behind it.

A SUMMARY CHART OF THE THREE DYNAMICS

The essential qualities of the three dynamics are summarized in the following chart. It focuses on the differences among the three dynamics in regard to eight important factors:

1. How people are viewed;

2. How people obtain value;

3. How force can and should be used;

4. The nature of relationships;

5. The nature of attachment;

6. The degree of honesty;

7. The kind or quality of emotions, and

8. The effect on conflict resolution.

Remember that each dynamic represents a group of psychosocial needs and their method of expression through other people. The chart should become increasingly meaningful as the reader progresses through the book.

The Three Dynamics

	I. LOVE	II. LIBERTY	III. COERCION
1. PEOPLE:	persons, beings	agents, doers	objects, subhuman
2. VALUE:	unconditional	earned, acquired	assigned
3. FORCE:	abhorred, rejected	in self-defense	arbitrary
4. RELATION-SHIP:	gifting, sharing	voluntary, competitive	involuntary, coercive
5. ATTACH-MENT:	interdependent	independent	detached
6. HONESTY:	maximized	contractual	restricted
7. EMOTIONS:	love, joy	esteem, respect	helplessness, emotional pain
8. CONFLICT:	prevented, resolved	barely controlled	suppressed, exacerbated

Three dynamics typically occur in combination within both individuals and institutions. A person or a religion, for example, may express a mix of themes based on love, liberty, and coercion all at once. The goal is to identify the dynamics, to understand their characteristics and consequences, and, if possible, to encourage shifts toward liberty and ultimately toward love.

THE THREE DYNAMICS AND CONFLICT RESOLUTION

Love, with its abhorrence of force and inherent valuing of the other, is the ultimate route to conflict resolution. The deepest conflicts can rarely be prevented or resolved without empathic love for those with whom we are in conflict. Only when people treasure each other and care about *each other's* basic needs can conflict be turned into mutual cooperation with lasting peace or harmony.

Love is the ultimate source of conflict resolution in every aspect of our lives. To resolve inner or psychological conflict, we must learn to love ourselves; to resolve interpersonal conflict we must learn to love ourselves *and* those with whom we are in conflict; to resolve global conflict we must learn to love ourselves *and* all other human beings; to end our abuse of nature, we must learn to love ourselves and the earth as well.

Liberty, with the use of force limited to self-defense, is an important stage in conflict resolution. The principle of equal rights provides the safety people often require before they will dare to become intimate and loving. The principles of reason, self-determination, and equal rights encourage bargaining and mediation. Too often, conflict resolution is based on these Dynamic II concepts of liberty without aiming at the more profound level of mutuality and love.

Liberty without love results in more superficial and temporary solutions, with the regeneration or recycling of conflict at a later date. A married couple bargains over where to go on vacations, and each year one of them is less satisfied with the choice than the other. Annually they must go through tense and competitive negotiations over how to spend their two weeks together. Conflict resolution occurs when they love each other sufficiently to take joy in each other's happiness. They become as delighted with their partner's pleasure as with their own, and now help each other find their ideal vacation spot. When people in conflict work together to identify and to fulfill each other's needs, the result is always a more lasting and profound conflict resolution.

The same is true on an international level (see chapters 9–11). To create a war, a leader must stir up hatred for the enemy. To bring lasting peace, as between the United States and Canada, people must feel affinity for each other. They must seem so alike to each other in terms of their common humanity that they would not dream of resorting to violence to solve their problems.

The most successful policies of the United States—for example, the Marshall Plan that helped reconstruct postwar Western Europe or Douglas MacArthur's successful efforts to bring democracy to Japan—have been based on the principle of empathic caring. In each case, the United States helped other nations fulfill their basic needs in ways they could not have done alone. Having been joined together in this mutual effort, the possibility of war between the United States and its old enemies now seems remote.

Coercion all too often seems the preferred method of conflict resolution, but it only leads to suppression, and ultimately to the creation of more severe, long-lasting conflicts. Coercion, as we shall see, has negative consequences for the perpetrator as well as the victim in both the personal and the political arena (see chapter 4).

REJECTING OUR COMMON HUMANITY

Nothing causes and perpetuates conflict more than the notion that our adversaries are by their very nature different from us and from other more valued human beings. This rejection of the equal humanity of our adversary is among the greatest impediments to conflict resolution. It justifies and intensifies conflicts between parents and children, husbands and wives, different races, conflicting cultures, and hostile nations. In each case, at least one party to the conflict has decided that the other is "inferior," "less worthy," "more dangerous," "basically untrustworthy," or otherwise alien to the human race. Too often, *all* parties to the conflict think this way about each other. To grasp this problem, and the road to its solution, it is useful to envision "the conflict tree."

THE BASIC NEEDS CONFLICT TREE

The metaphor I call the Conflict Tree describes how we lose track of our ties to each other as human beings as we become separated by our values, cultural views, special interests, and the ideological commitments of our groups and leaders.

The common root of the tree is our human nature with its basic needs. This reflects the fact that our brains and bodies do not significantly differ on a racial, national, cultural, or other basis. Unfortunately, this single human root lies below ground and takes imagination to envision.

Immediately above ground, the trunk quickly begins to divide into the varying *expressions* of our basic needs. While all people have more or less the same underlying needs, the needs are manifested and satisfied somewhat differently from individual to individual and culture to culture.

Above the already diverging basic needs, the trunk further divides into branches called values—the conscious awareness and expression of the basic needs. These vary according to temperament and upbringing. Special interests and ideologies are next on the now broadly diverging canopy of the tree. Some of these are personal: my family, my job, my gender, my money, my property. Some are more societal: my country, my religion, my political party, my ethnic group, my race. The differences and potential sources of alienation and conflict are becoming infinite.

As the tree spreads, leaving our common root of human nature further and further below, values and interests tend to become rigidly embodied in social institutions, political ideologies, and the leaders of contending groups and viewpoints. In the last stages of alienation, the conflicts become directed by leaders with their own special interests, ideologies, and institutional commitments.

In order to drive a greater wedge between their peoples, the leaders often hurl epithets at each other. George Bush is the devil; Saddam Hussein, the madman. For the Iraqi, the ultimate insult is a religious condemnation; for the Americans, it's a psychiatric label. That tells us something about which institution has the greatest moral authority in each of the societies: religion in Iraq, psychiatry in America (see chapter 7). Either way, devil or madman, the citizens of Iraq and America are encouraged to reject their common heritage as members of the human race.

The Conflict Tree metaphor dramatizes how human beings start with much in common—their human nature and basic needs—and too often end up locked in mortal conflict with adversaries whom they see as wholly alien from themselves. Consider the tragic image of the spreading branches and dividing trunks flailing about in violent clashes with each other, with no realization that they come from the same root.

Conflict resolution attempts to help people "climb back down" the Conflict Tree to reach and recognize their common origin. There, at the foot of the tree, they can meet on common ground—their shared human nature and basic needs—while appreciating the tree of their cultural differences.

When people realize that their inherent differences as humans are negligible, the conflict tree can blossom into an appreciation of cultural differences. Its canopy of branches with its leaves, flowers, and fruit becomes a source of inspiration instead of mortal conflict. This is true whether we are attempting to "climb back down" the tree with someone we love, or whether we are trying to grasp the common humanity of all human beings. When we become aware that all people are made of the same biological and psychospiritual stuff, we have begun to love humanity.

The metaphor may be extended to the whole of existence—the entire animate and inanimate universe that supports and interrelates with this human tree. The tree exists in relation to the earth, air, and water, and all its inhabitants. The roots draw life from the earth and the leaves draw it from the sun and the air. Life becomes our tree; our tree becomes life.

THE THREE DYNAMICS TABLE

The Three Dynamics Table (see p. 12) expands on the summary chart (see p. 11) and provides a more extensive overview of the theory. The reader might wish to glance at it now and perhaps on occasion later in the book as the concepts are further developed. The table is, to say the least, a simplification. The catchwords and phrases are intended to help the reader to scan the salient points, especially the principles and qualities of relationship and life associated with each of the three dynamics. The table is not presented as a philosophic blueprint or final word on the subject of the three dynamics.

PROCESS VERSUS SOLUTIONS

Keep in mind that the principles of conflict analysis and resolution, as well as those of self-help and psychotherapy, do not prescribe specific outcomes for individuals, institutions, or societies. Instead they suggest ideal approaches for resolving conflict through actions based on liberty and love.

There are several generally accepted principles that are characteristic of modern conflict resolution as a growing discipline (Burton 1987, 1990a, 1990b; Coate and Rosati, 1988).

1. The process is voluntary.

2. The parties do not resort to power.

3. Basic needs and vital interests are identified and addressed.

4. The benefits of ending the conflict are weighed against the negative costs of continuing it.

5. Collaborative analysis and problem solving are encouraged toward the development of mutually satisfying solutions, including those that benefit both parties. Win–lose conflicts are redefined, when possible, into win–win conflicts. Competition is replaced by cooperation.

6. Alternative options are generated that satisfy the basic needs of all the participants.

It is frequently thought in the field of conflict resolution that the facilitator or conflict resolver should be neutral (Burton, 1990a). Instead of neutrality, I favor a strong, personal, caring commitment to the interests of both parties (see chapter 6). It is more realistic to try to care about both parties than to try to be neutral about them. Similarly, I believe that the therapist or conflict resolver should be loving rather than merely objective and analytic. Ultimately, he or she should facilitate empathy for each other among the adversaries. While love is the key to thoroughgoing conflict resolution, it is rarely discussed as a principle in the practice of psychotherapy and conflict resolution.

When individuals relate freely and lovingly, they function creatively and will bring forth new and often unexpected approaches and solutions to life's problems. While no one can predict the specific outcome of these efforts, certain trends can be expected. These are reflected in the scheme of values in the Three Dynamic Table. The principles of liberty and love enable people to satisfy their basic needs and to develop their human potentials *from their own viewpoint* and *to the best of their ability.* When people combine liberty with love, conflict will be more easily prevented and resolved *to everyone's satisfaction.*

In helping individuals, groups, and societies live by the principles of liberty and love—we can anticipate the best for them, without knowing what their best will be. We cannot predict the exact results of living by better principles—other than that they will be better from the viewpoint of the participants.

At present there are few state or community resources for conflict resolution. There are few institutional mechanisms for effectively addressing basic needs within the family and society. Can social and governmental institutions be developed for the purpose of satisfying basic needs and resolving conflict within the family and community? In the words of Richard Rubenstein, "Can the state become a conflict resolver instead of a power broker?" Can governments and other social institutions assist conflicted parties in identifying and satisfying their basic needs through cooperative activities without the coercive use of power?

The flow of the book will take us through love, liberty, and coercion, in that order, in the next three chapters. Then we will look at psychological or inner conflict, interpersonal and family conflict, the role of psychiatry in conflict resolution, and liberty and love within business corporations. In the final three chapters, the perspective is further broadened to include societal conflict as illustrated by recent events in the former USSR and Eastern Bloc nations, and international conflict as exemplified by recent events in the Middle East. Finally, the book concludes with basic principles for building a more loving personal and community life, including an emerging group of "shared values" within contemporary reform movements.

Because it is so key to conflict resolution, we now turn to the subject of love.

CHAPTER 2

▼ ▼

Understanding Love

*I am ready to say to every human being "thou art my brother"
and to offer him the hand of concord and amity.*
Thomas Jefferson, letter (1819)

*I can never be what I ought to be until you are what you ought
to be, and you can never be what you ought to be until I am
what I ought to be. This is the interrelated structure of reality.*
Martin Luther King, Jr., Strength to Love (1963)

*We are members one of another; so that you cannot injure or
help your neighbor without injuring or helping yourself.*
**George Bernard Shaw, "Why Not Give Christianity a Trial?"
Preface to Androcles and the Lion (1912)**

*But whatever may be the cause of sympathy, or however it may
be excited, nothing pleases us more than to observe in other men
a fellow-feeling with all the emotions of our own breast.*
Adam Smith, The Theory of Moral Sentiments (1759)

Many people believe that love can prevent or resolve *personal* conflicts, but few seem to believe it can do the same for *societal* or
political disputes. The premise of this book is that love is the best
and most effective approach to conflict resolution on every level
from the personal to the political.

LOVE IN THE JUDEO-CHRISTIAN TRADITION

While rarely invoked within the academic community, love holds
an honored place in the Judeo-Christian and Western tradition and
in the spiritual life of millions of people throughout the world. In
Leviticus the Hebrews are instructed, "Thou shalt love thy neighbor as thy self (Hertz, 1960)." Drawing on ancient Hebrew

wisdom, in the New Testament Jesus makes clear that love is the central theme of his teachings, and he reaffirms the Golden Rule as "Do unto others as you would have others do unto you."

In *The Good Society* (1937), Walter Lippmann notes that the Golden Rule, in its positive or negative form, has been "enunciated among many peoples widely separated in time and space," (p. 376):

> *In the Upanishads of Indian Brahmanism it is said: "Let no man do to another that which would be repugnant to himself. . . . In refusing, in bestowing, in regard to pleasure and to pain, to what is agreeable and disagreeable, a man obtains the proper rule by regarding the case as like his own." "My doctrine," says Gautama Buddha, "makes no distinction between high and low, rich and poor. It is like the sky. It has room for all, and like waves it washes all alike. . . . to him in whom love dwells, the whole world is but one family." The rule appears again and again in Confucius: "When one cultivates to the utmost the capabilities of his nature and exercises them on the principle of reciprocity, he is not far from the path. What you do not want done to yourself, do not do unto others." (pp. 376–377)* [Ellipses in original.]

To exclude these religious teachings from our analysis on the grounds that they are not "scientific" is to ignore how profoundly they influence Western thought. Such an exclusion also ignores the reality that the psychosocial sciences themselves are fundamentally ethical in nature. Neither their methods nor their aims can be divorced from values.

That religious institutions too often fail by their own standards and frequently foment hatred is not the issue at hand (see chapter 11). What matters at this point is the ideal—that many religions recognize love as the guiding principle of life.

THE NATURE OF LOVE

Before examining relevant scientific research involving animals and humans, I'll first discuss the concept of love in general. The time-honored word "love" will be used to describe all of the

Dynamic I psychosocial needs, variously described in the conflict resolution literature as nurturing, caring, bonding, affiliation, recognition, and valued or meaningful relationships. Love is the more generic word, and it grounds us in everyday life and language.

Love encompasses two related phenomena—human *bonding* in general and, more specifically, a *joyful awareness and treasuring* of other people, personal activities (such as work and play), nature, or life. Bonding and joyful awareness are inextricable. A well-loved infant experiences joy in the bonding or strong connectedness it shares with its parents. Within weeks after birth, smiling, body wriggling, and other signs indicate the child's joyful recognition of other human beings. With growing maturity, these feelings can become a way of life.

Conversely, when bonding fails to occur between infant and parent, the social capacities of the growing child are hampered. A joyless attitude toward all of life, and even withdrawal and death, may result (see p. 44).

The concept of love is not rarified and abstract. Love is a biological and social phenomenon—a dynamic. It emanates from the whole human organism as a basic need and finds its expression through other people, nature, and an infinite variety of creative activities.

The capacity for love is present in all at birth. As children and adults with developmental retardation exemplify, love is more deeply ingrained in us than intelligence and can flourish in people who function intellectually below normal. Love also plays an important role in the life of animals, and in relationships involving humans and animals. Many people experience the high point of love in their daily lives when they return home to be greeted by a dog that wildly wags its tail, barks in ecstasy, jumps and whirls about, and otherwise communicates a joyful greeting. Chimpanzees routinely hug, kiss, and display other signs of affection for each other when they get together or settle conflicts.

Love is an attitude and feeling that can be found to some extent in every human being. Few people are wholly devoid of positive connections to people or other aspects of life. Clinically, a person with no experience of joyful awareness would be withdrawn, living in a lifeless world of objects. Psychosis often reflects the breakdown of all connectedness to other human beings, and a loving relationship is the most therapeutic intervention (Breggin, 1980, 1991).

Love can be viewed as the experience, conscious or unconscious, of being drawn toward and valuing others. It is a connection to others that is fundamental to our social life, an essential connection. It binds mothers and fathers to their offspring and to each other. It binds friends, family, and society.

In spiritual terms, we would say love reaches from essence to essence, from soul to soul. In psychological terms, we would say it reaches from person to person. In more social terms, love is the evolutionary force that nourishes the psychosocial growth of the infant and creates community and culture. It is Dynamic I, the primary motivator of social life.

Love exists along a continuum of intensity and of specificity for particular individuals (Schneider, 1964). In the most general sense, it designates the need people have for human contact of any kind. This is a profound aspect of ourselves. Not only are we literally formed as infants and children by our contacts with other people, as adults we tend to unravel without them. The worst punishment of all is solitary confinement. People in isolation can become psychotic—their very minds coming apart in the absence of social contact. As a patient of mine said, "When I get too isolated, I start to hallucinate."

Love can also focus on specific persons. In romantic love, it can become an intense desire for sexual merger with one particular human being, to the exclusion of all others. The underlying experience is the same—a fundamental valuing of other people (Breggin, 1987; Ellis, 1937). What varies is the intensity and the specificity for one or another particular individual.

Love is at root a happy feeling. The radiant connection between mother and child is pleasurable, as is the warmth we feel in good company. It feels good to be with other people, to openly love them, and to express passion for them. But because human beings are so vulnerable to each other, and so often have a history of severe injury at each other's hands, love can become chronically associated with pain. Because people need each other so much, they can become afraid of the potential loss associated with love. Yet love itself is a positive, joyful feeling.

Love, as noted, involves the placement of value on others. At times, their value to us may approximate or even exceed our own.

A parent, for example, may sacrifice his or her life for a child. Similarly, a lover may willingly die in defense of his or her loved one. I have known people who have risked their lives for beloved pets. I recall a young boy who drove a large, vicious dog out of his yard when it was threatening his crippled cocker spaniel.

There can be less noble motives, such as guilt and fear, that cause people to "sacrifice" for each other. But in loving relationships, people do not experience altruistic actions as sacrifices. It is no sacrifice to risk one's life for another life of equal or greater value.

LOVE AND EMPATHY

Mutuality, sharing, and sacrifice depend upon empathy—a caring awareness of the viewpoint and condition of another or others. Empathy is essential to love and in many ways epitomizes it.

Empathy first appears in an undeveloped form in infants and in more mature forms in small children. It is a part of human social life from the start. There is even some evidence that infants *in utero* respond selectively to their mothers' voice.

Even though love is fundamentally a joyful feeling, empathic love can end up eliciting emotional pain. But if people experience the same intensity of pain as their injured loved ones, they may become helpless and lose their effectiveness as helpers. In psychotherapy or surgery, in coming to the aid of a pet or friend, in helping to resolve painful marital conflicts, individuals must not become overwhelmed with the suffering of others.

If caregivers do become overcome by empathic pain, they can worsen the situation. They can lose their rationality and self-control. They can end up resenting the sufferer for inducing pain in them as well. To protect themselves from further pain, caregivers may withdraw from those who are suffering or even deny that they are in pain.

If the person offering help shows signs of becoming overwhelmed, the original sufferer may be made to feel more helpless. If a the potential helper cannot handle the suffering of the victim, how can the victim expect to survive it? The victims may also end up feeling guilty about the suffering they are causing. This can lead them to hide their pain or to avoid seeking help.

EMPATHY AND CONFLICT RESOLUTION

Empathy is an essential ingredient to conflict resolution in children and adults. It is the most powerful force in leading us to care about the basic needs of others and to seek ways of satisfying them. Thus empathy can be viewed as the essential element or principle of love that most directly affects conflict resolution.

Love, with its special empathic quality, tends to render meaningless the distinctions between self-interest and the interests of loved ones. When a parent loves a child, or a lover her loved one, the other's needs, well-being, and happiness become of great importance. The parent wants the infant to thrive, even at the parent's expense. On the other hand, she knows that she must thrive in order to help her infant do so. Needs become mutual rather than individual. Instead of being in competition, the other's needs approximate and dovetail with one's own.

Thus empathy transforms self-interests into joint interests, individual needs into mutual ones. This is why love is the ultimate avenue to conflict resolution. Love transforms conflict into cooperation and mutual aid.

Adam Smith is best known as the leading Eighteenth-century advocate of competition and the free market; but in his 1759 book, *The Theory of Moral Sentiments* (1976), he provides one of the most thorough arguments for the necessity of empathy in the good society. For Smith, "fellow-feeling" ameliorates bitterness and competition, and cements loving community. He declares, "The bitter and painful emotions of grief and resentment more strongly require the healing consolation of sympathy," (p. 87).

Smith considered empathic, unconditional love to be an essential principle in human beings:

How selfish soever man may be supposed, there are evidently some principles in his nature, which interest him in the fortune of others, and render their happiness necessary to him, though he derives nothing from it, except the pleasure of seeing it. (p. 47.)

Love can play a key role in resolving conflict even when those in conflict do not feel love for each other. Adversaries can find a common interest through their love for *other* people or things.

Couples who are separated or divorced can be motivated by love for their children to resolve their conflicts. People who feel little for each other may join together in their love for animals, the environment, or the whole earth. Even the love of liberty can bind people into common action. Indeed, the love of seeming "abstractions" such as God, country, or liberty frequently brings people together to make a common cause.

LOVE AND THE ABHORRENCE OF VIOLENCE

Because empathy and love encourages people to feel one-and-the-same with those whom they love, the use of force within a loving relationship becomes abhorrent. The pain they might cause their loved one afflicts them as well. There is a reluctance to use force in self-defense if it means hurting a loved one. Thus the principle of self-defense, which is so critical to liberty (see chapter 3), may be rejected in a caring relationship.

Love does not lead to a masochistic way of life in which people seek out or luxuriate in suffering. However, when people love, they wish to protect and nurture their loved ones even if it means accepting some increased risk of personal harm or suffering. Nonetheless, loving people can exercise judgment about whether or not to remain in a chronically conflicted or threatening relationship.

When people are loving, they will in fact be more aware of when others are oppressing them. The ability to love makes people more aware of when their own needs are not being met or are being thwarted by coercion and rejection. The more loving an individual is, the more likely he or she will be sensitive to the lack of it in others. The loving person will more easily recognize and seek similar companions.

The salutary effect of love on violence is extremely important for conflict resolution and provention. Caring relationships produce an environment in which violence is abhorred and sometimes totally rejected. When touched by love, people feel motivated to resolve conflicts through cooperation and mutual aid, and by actions that, in the absence of love, might be labeled self-sacrifice.

THE LIMITS OF SELF-LOVE

In modern popular psychology there is an axiom that one must love oneself first and foremost. In reality, people who attempt to live by this principle are likely to be profoundly unhappy and socially incapacitated.

Human beings are born into a world in which people are designed by genetic and cultural evolution to take care of and value each other, and especially to lavish attention on infants. Ideally, the wholly dependent, helpless infant is nurtured by a parent who in many ways may value the life of the infant above his or her own. A typical mother will feed her infant ahead of herself and defend it at the cost of her own life. A father and mother will often sacrifice sleep for months to comfort a colicky infant. In a similar vein, modern parents may work hard to put their children through school and provide for them as they grow, and if necessary may defend them with their lives.

Humans often take action to help others outside their immediate family. Most disasters produce stories of individual heroism. Many people choose occupations or volunteer jobs that pay little or nothing financially but which greatly benefit society. To live a happy, full life usually means daily decisions that constantly put other people and values ahead of our immediate interests and needs, and sometimes ahead of our long-term ones as well.

As we have seen, the human being is a fundamentally social creature who, starting from infancy, learns to love through being loved. The infant has the inborn capacity to love, much as it has the innate capacity to experience itself as a unique individual; but love and self-awareness are developed through the infant's and child's relationships with others. The infant does not learn to "love itself" first. The infant experiences *being loved*. Without that, the infant may not thrive at all. He or she may not survive.

Out of the experience of being loved develops our social capacity, including our later ability to relate and to love. People feel loved and loveable, and in the process they learn to love. We learn to feel loved and loveable through the gift of love from other people.

In my clinical practice, I frequently find that people can love others despite grave deficits in loving themselves. Often we love our children more than ourselves, devoting ourselves more to their happiness than to our own. I do not advocate this, but note it.

Can the isolated, unloved person learn to love himself or herself? Despite modern notions of "self-sufficiency," I doubt it. The nearest example might be that of reclusive mystical ascetics who learn to love themselves through God's love for them; but again the source is envisioned as coming from outside oneself.

Perhaps the emphasis on the primacy of self-love is the product of a hierarchical male society in which men—having alienated themselves from each other, from women, and from children—turn to their "inner self" for love. Whatever sense of power this apparent self-sufficiency endows us with, it does not give us a feeling of being truly loved.

A feeling of being loved is not something one can give to oneself. Efforts to do so result in tragic aberrations such as autistic withdrawal or mania. A rejected, abused child—rocking and stroking himself or herself in the corner of an institution—exemplifies a last ditch effort at self-love. It is self-destructive to turn our social nature on its head, claiming that we must love ourselves before we can love others.

Once we have learned to love, we can then become capable of maintaining the feeling toward others in an independent, self-sustaining manner. We can generate unconditional love—a joyful, positive valuing of another that can withstand the vicissitudes of relationship, including rejection and betrayal. In most of our roles in life—as parents, spouses, friends, colleagues, and contributing members of society—we are likely to undergo rejection, betrayal, and other threatening experiences. We sustain ourselves and sometimes our relationships by maintaining our ability to love through the ups and downs. Deep-rooted conflict resolution often requires unconditional love on the part of all those involved.

LOVE, REVERENCE, AND BEINGNESS

Reverence reflects respect for the intrinsic worth of another. It has a spiritual connotation that suggests a holiness to the value placed upon the individual. After years of searching within the traditions of the East and the West, Albert Schweitzer finally summed up the essence of his philosophy in the phrase "reverence for life." (See chapter 11 for further discussion of Schweitzer's views.) In *My Life and Thought* (1933), he declared:

The ethic of Reverence for Life is the ethic of Love widened into universality. It is the ethic of Jesus, now recognized as a necessity of thought.

For Schweitzer, reverence for life was divinely inspired, and extended itself to all life forms, to the "mysterious value" of life itself. Anecdotes about Schweitzer abound concerning the sincerity of his devotion to all life. He would turn down his reading lamp at night rather than singe an occasional flying insect; he would not dip fence posts into insecticides for fear of harming individual termites.

In *I and Thou* (1923), theologian Martin Buber, whose work influenced interpersonal psychology and psychiatry, infused all human relationship with sacred meaning. He distinguishes "I–Thou" relating from "I–It." In I–Thou relating "the whole being" of the individual is in the relationship. I–Thou relating involves "revealing" the divine in each other, a standing in the presence of that divine, rather than a simple feeling between people. I–It relating separates us from the other and his or her spiritual worth. It enables us to reject or coerce the other.

Humanists often view love for humanity as central to their philosophy and their words communicate a secular holiness. In the *Philosophy of Humanism* (1949), atheist Corliss Lamont rejects "brute egoism" as well as one-dimensional motivational systems based on economic self-interest, sexual pleasure-seeking, or self-interest in general. He states:

On the ethical and social side Humanism sets up service to one's fellowmen as the ultimate moral ideal. It holds that the individual can find his own highest good by working for the good of all, which of course includes himself and his family. . . . It insists on the reality of genuine altruism as one of the moving forces in the affairs of men.

There is a reverent ring to Lamont's discourse on how humans should be guided by altruism as a moral imperative. I can find no satisfying logical argument for this view within his writing. Love inevitably remains something of a mystery. It is so deeply and completely rooted in our nature that we stumble over analyzing it as something separate from ourselves. We try to make an abstraction or principle out of that which simply *is*.

Erich Fromm places love at the center of his secular philosophy. In *The Art of Loving* (1956), he sees love as "the answer to the problem of human existence":

The awareness of human separation, without reunion by love—is the source of shame. It is at the same time the source of guilt and anxiety.

The deepest need of man, then, is the need to overcome his separateness, to leave his prison of his aloneness. The absolute failure to achieve this aim means insanity. . . .

From the theologian Buber to the secular psychoanalyst Fromm, there is an attitude toward the human as a *being* rather than a thing or an "it." To say people are beings is to invest them with sacred meaning—with special, *inviolable* importance.

There is a growing tendency among environmentalists and ecologists to view the earth itself as a living being, sometimes called Gaia. What some people would call a thing becomes invested with an aura of inviolability.

UNCONDITIONAL LOVE AND INTRINSIC WORTH

To love humans—to experience them as beings—means recognizing their intrinsic worth. Love, as I am defining it, is therefore *unconditional*—not contingent on anything particular about the individual who is loved. Rather, love reaches to the essence of the individual, the beingness, and sees the inherent value.

Since this value is inherent, it is not earned. Rather, it is made visible by the individual or recognized by someone else. Thus, love differs drastically from respect and esteem, which are barometers of how we judge or evaluate another's ethics or accomplishments. Esteem plays a necessary role in human relationships, but it should not be confused with the much more fundamental experience of love (see chapter 3). Lacking the more basic sense of feeling love-able and loved, many people compulsively seek to be esteemed and respected, while finding little or no peace in the process.

The concepts of intrinsic worth and unconditional love are at the center of this book. They extend not only to people, but to all life forms, and to life itself. The concepts of intrinsic worth and un-conditional love must reach toward the physical earth as well and may be required for the survival of life on the planet.

The question of the intrinsic worth of people is a very important one in everyday living and therefore in self-help, psychotherapy, and conflict resolution in general. When we accept that people have intrinsic worth, then our conflicts with them take on a rev-erential, caring aura. We cherish or treasure the people with whom we are dealing and find their well-being inviolable, even as we seem locked in deep-rooted, severe conflict with them.

FALLING INTO FEAR AS WELL AS LOVE

Sometimes we find it easier to recognize the intrinsic worth of animals. We may love a dog or cat, for example, who has little practical value to us and who has done little to earn our respect or esteem. Instead we feel a connection to the "life force" or "being" within the pet. We become happy feeling love for and feeling loved by our pet. In my home, a small Eastern-Painted turtle is often the center of attention and genuine love.

I am reminded of a patriarchal male, a high-ranking military officer, who always severely judged the women he had known, including his current wife. He seldom praised them and always tried to make them over into his compliant ideal. In couples ther-apy, he acknowledged only one regular experience of sheer, un-adulterated, nonjudgmental delight in a being. It was felt toward his now-deceased cat for whom he felt a special love.

Similarly, we feel love for infants before we can claim to respect their individuality or to admire their unique properties. People who wish to adopt newborn infants, for example, are sometimes advised not to let their natural mothers see them, even for an instant, for in mothers, as well as lovers, there can be an element of "love at first sight."

Love for plants or for nature also indicates an impulse toward something essential and inherent in that which we love. We may feel peace in being "at one with nature" and we may feel joy at the sight of a lovely bird or a beautiful sunset. Sometimes apparently mundane aspects of nature—a pebble or a cloud—may evoke delight in us. This delight or joy in awareness is the essence of love. I sometimes define love as nothing more nor less than *joyful awareness and treasuring*.

Why can we more easily express unconditional love for infants, pets, or natural phenomena? Because it feels more threatening to love adult people than to love infants, animals, or nature. None of us are tough when it comes to our innermost selves and innermost yearnings for closeness or oneness with other people. Our souls are wrapped in tenderness.

It would fill volumes to survey the ways in which people fear being hurt by other people, from accidental loss through death to willful betrayal. I tend to doubt if someone is falling in love if they are not falling into fear as well.

THE SELECTIVITY OF LOVE

If love reaches toward essences, and if all people are equally valuable, then why do we love one person more than another? I am tempted at this moment to fall back on the notion that love is a mystery. But there's more to say than that. Love is a blessing, a form of "gifting"—of giving that which no one feels they really or wholly deserve. When a person feels truly loved that person feels grateful. We often doubt that our true value can match the value assigned to us by those who love us most profoundly.

It is often difficult to understand why people single out each other to love, but to some extent it has to do with visibility, with how easily we can see the "essential humanity," the spirit, beingness, or inherent worth of another. Some people are more visible or psychologically available to us, and we love them more easily. They may be more available because of their own traits: they are more open, communicative, or loving. We can also esteem them for the work it takes to reach such a spiritual state. Or they may seem to meet some standard of beauty or status that then allows us to overcome the fear or shame surrounding love. We may even think we love them because of their beauty or status, when in reality those qualities have merely provided us the "window to the soul." The socially approved qualities have given us permission to love.

Often we allow ourselves to love others because of their weaknesses or negative traits. More precisely, their vulnerabilities or personal problems enable us to love them. Many people, for example, are drawn to love members of the opposite sex who seem weak or ineffectual. This often puzzles those who view the relationship from the outside. Because of their own fears, people often feel safer in the presence of weakness in another person. They may feel the other person less likely to hurt or reject them. They may hope that the other person will be more in need of them. Even though its expression depends upon the vulnerability of the other, the love can be genuine. The nature of the pairing, based in part on emotionally injured aspects of the partners, may become an increasing problem in the relationship, and may even doom it; but it does not necessarily render the love less real. The need and desire to love is no less pure because the individual can only express it within the confines of a seemingly safe relationship.

If love reaches toward intrinsic values, then can we love all people—and perhaps even love all people *equally?* Is that absurd or utopian? I believe it is *impractical,* given the limitations we have as human beings and the constraints under which we live. To love all people equally, an ideal maintained by some mystics and encouraged by Jesus, also deprives us of the special joy of focusing our attention and deepening our knowledge of one single person or family. To *pretend* to love all people equally can even become a defense against loving one person or one family fully, with all the fears and responsibilities entailed in personal relationships and domestic life. Mystical love for humanity may indeed reflect escapism from the realistic needs of the people in their lives, including husbands, wives, and children. Women, needless to say, have not generally been permitted this luxury, nor would they tend to choose it at the expense of their dependent children. Some women end up choosing a professional career over marriage and family because they cannot find a husband to share homemaking with them.

Despite these caveats, psychotherapists and others in helping professions need to empathize with and even to love each of their clients, or else they are likely to fail in their healing work. As I will discuss in chapter 6, a deeper understanding of love can help the therapist open his or her heart to increasing numbers of people.

While we may not be personally or practically capable of loving all people, recognizing the possibility—confirming the inherent worth of all people—remains an important concept for guiding our actions. Only through the growing extension of our love to all people will we eventually end deep-rooted, murderous conflict on earth. Only by extending love to the whole earth are we likely to prevent its demise as a liveable planet.

ROMANTIC LOVE

Some authors have linked romantic love directly to liberty and have claimed that it could not truly exist until the flowering of individualism in Western Europe (Branden, 1969). While the widespread cultural acceptance of romantic love does seem to be a relatively modern phenomenon, examples of it can be found in ancient mythology and religious literature, including the Hebrew Bible (see Breggin, 1987).

Romantic love is among the most intense expressions of love experienced by most people. It is a realm in which mystery and spirituality truly abound, and in which cynicism and skepticism often set in. In the story of Cupid and Psyche, a god, Cupid, falls in love with a mortal, Psyche, whose name means butterfly . . . or soul. Eventually, Cupid and Psyche are married, but first Psyche is made an immortal. In this great love story, the model for many others, including Shakespeare's *Romeo and Juliet*, the romantic and the spiritual are wholly intertwined, and love ultimately endows a human with divine qualities (see Breggin, 1987).

Not everyone accepts the mystery that shrouds romantic love. Not everyone believes in romantic love as a viable way of relating. The great American psychologist William James, in *The Principles of Psychology* (1890), diagnosed romantic love as a form of insanity or "monomania":

The passion of love may be called a monomania to which all of us are subject, however otherwise sane. It can coexist with contempt and even hatred for the "object" which inspires it, and whilst it lasts the whole life of the man is altered by its presence.

To confirm his viewpoint, he presented the case history of man driven to "frenzy" and "melancholy" by a humiliating attachment to a woman.

James's viewpoint seems rooted in a misogynous fear of women. The lover in his vignette struggles to possess the *object* of his desires, a woman deemed inferior to him, and suffers the humiliation of failing to have his way.

Ironically, James invested mystical union with God with the intense romanticism that he denied to human relationships. In *The Varieties of Religious Experience* (1929) he criticized "medical materialism" in regard to religious devotion to God, but not in regard to love for human beings. He promotes a deep, mystical connection to God as a route to the fulfillment of our innermost personal need for completion. His descriptions parallel closely that of romantic love.

James, like so many other men, rejected passionate down-to-earth relating to women in favor of something else—in this case, the mystical experience. His philosophy embodies what many feminists, including Marilyn French in *Beyond Power* (1985) and Kate Millett in *Sexual Politics* (1978), have described as a hierarchical attempt to transcend relationships with women. This transcendence involves the rejection of love between equals in favor of "power over" and control, or escapism.

In many ways Freud's position paralleled James's, especially in its rejection of love for women. Like James, he viewed love as a form of insanity, a "narcissistic" derangement. However, instead of directing his passionate, spiritual desires toward God, Freud utterly rejected the validity or worth of these feelings. As many critics have confirmed, he denigrated women in the process.

Freud's disciple, Alfred Adler, who later broke with him, had a wholly different vision. He found human beings motivated by "social interest" and the desire to have meaningful relationships with each other.

LOVE THAT LEADS TO BAD OUTCOMES

Love can be misdirected or manipulated toward bad ends. This is perhaps most obvious within the family. As Susan Moller Okin has documented in *Justice, Gender and the Family* (1987), patriarchal philosophers have long argued that love, rather than justice, should be primary in family life. They have done so in the interest of maintaining male dominance and the subservience of women to the needs of others. On a more personal level, men who batter women almost always state that their attempts to control their victims are motivated by love; and adults who sexually abuse children frequently profess love for them.

Whether or not abusers actually feel the love they profess, their oppressive actions are typically motivated by their own personal feelings of helplessness and inferiority, expressed through culturally sanctioned attempts to overpower women and children. Furthermore, their actions actually suffocate love. Coercive relationships breed dishonesty and manipulation in both the perpetrator and the victim, and tend to be incompatible with love (see chapter 4).

Love is also used outside the family to justify the abuse and control of other human beings. Dictators give speeches about how much they love the victims of their totalitarianism; slave owners profess love for their chattel; and institutional psychiatrists claim to care about the inmates they confine and otherwise abuse.

The need for love can motivate a person to submit to coercion. The German people, for example, were motivated in part by "love for the Fatherland" in joining the Nazi party. Hitler became a beloved father figure for many of them. Similarly, love for a cult leader or fellow members of the cult sometimes helps to motivate destructive activities. There may even be meaningful and sometimes joyful bonding among the participants or conspirators, despite the other disastrous consequences. Often there is a sense of purpose, identity, or recognition as well. Thus love can resolve conflicts within a group while nonetheless bringing forth hideous consequences for others outside the group.

Because of the potential victimization of women, romantic love as a principle has been criticized by some feminists as a snare for women. The trap may be subtle, as in the submissiveness inherent in what Betty Friedan has called "the feminine mystique," or it may be more brutal for women who remain in battering and abusive relationships. While it is true that many other forces, including male domination and control, influence women to stay in these relationships, many women feel that love for the man plays a significant role.

Love should not be used as excuse or rationalization for infringements on liberty. While love can surmount almost any obstacle, it is most easily achieved and expressed within a context of liberty. Liberty and love, properly understood, supplement and support each other. Love finds inherent worth in whomever is loved; the principle of inherent worth leads logically to equal rights, justice, and liberty. Dr. Martin Luther King, Jr. was especially adept in politics at making the connection between the Christian ideal of the equality of all souls and the Western ideal of equal rights (see chapter 10). Indeed, the Declaration of Independence connects the ideal that all people are "created equal" to the principle that they are "endowed by their Creator with certain inalienable rights."

Love *requires* liberty as a context or it risks becoming an excuse for oppression. The interaction between liberty and love, as complex as it is, remains critical to human well-being on both a personal and political level. Liberty—addressed more thoroughly in chapter 3—remains primary in establishing a just (and hence, safe) context for the expression of love.

The reader might wish to take a moment once again to review the Three Dynamics Table (see p. 261) that compares the attributes of Dynamic I: love and Dynamic II: liberty. It is discussed in chapter 1.

LOVE IN SOCIETY AND POLITICS

Throughout Western philosophy and even political theory, love has frequently reappeared as a guiding principle. In recent centuries it can be found in one form or another in such diverse sources as Adam Smith's *The Theory of Moral Sentiments* (1759) (see p. 24) and in Karl Marx's *The Economic and Philosophic Manuscripts of 1844*, where "alienation" from work and ultimately from society is seen as the unacceptable cost of capitalism. Citing Leo Tolstoy's *The Kingdom of God Is within You* (1894) and John Ruskin's *Unto This Last* (1860), Mohandas Gandhi saw love as the ultimate source of truth and of power. Later, Martin Luther King, Jr. would follow in his footsteps (see chapter 11 for a discussion of Gandhi and King).

In modern times, economists have begun to emphasize that something more than self-interest fuels human society. In *Ecodynamics* (1978) Kenneth Boulding has described affiliation or love as one of three moving forces or social organizers in our socioeconomic life. Drawing on John Kenneth Galbraith's *The Affluent Society* (1958), as well as on Boulding and others, modern writers have increasingly tried to escape the confines of economics based solely on self-interest.

Amitai Etzioni, in *The Moral Dimension: Toward a New Economics* (1988), has proposed that individuals, operating in the economic and political realm, are motivated by two sometimes-conflicting paradigms. One is the "utilitarian, rationalist, and individualist paradigm" of self-interest and competition. The other is unselfish morality—"a sense of *shared* identity, and commitment to values, a sense that 'We are members of one another.' " He believes that individuals are motivated in part by a spirit of cooperation based on an altruistic concern for others.

LOVE IN PSYCHOLOGY AND PSYCHIATRY

As a principle in personal living, love dominates popular music, romantic novels, and some popular psychology. It has only occasionally been addressed as a guiding principle by more academic psychologists. There's no mention of love as a healing principle in the commonly used textbooks of psychiatry, and there is merely passing mention of it in reference to "rapport" or "positive reinforcement" in most psychology textbooks (see Breggin, 1991).

However, two psychiatrists have made love the central theme of their work, and each resonated sufficiently with the public to attain substantial popularity. Both have drawn on a combination of psychotherapeutic and religious insights.

Psychiatrist Smiley Blanton was a close associate of Norman Vincent Peale, and Blanton's own book, *Love or Perish* (1956) clearly draws on Peale's somewhat simplistic concept of "the power of positive thinking." Blanton's psychoanalytic and religious background leads him to conclude that all human beings must struggle within themselves between love and hate. In religious terms, it is the conflict between good and evil; in Freudian, eros (the life instinct) and thanatos (the death instinct). Much more idealistic and optimistic than Freud, Blanton declares:

Love has reached across the ages to bind men together in an ever-widening circle of humanity. It has served to construct the essential fabric of most the world's great religious and ethical teachings. (p.12.)

Consistent with my own views, Blanton sees love as a "universal need," (p. 3) that is expressed through all of human life:

Love is born when the child rests in its mother's arms. From this beginning, love grows until it includes the love of family and friends, of school and country, and ultimately of all the world. . . . Love is all of one piece—from the love of mother and child to the love of sweethearts, husbands and wives, and friends. It is present, too, in the laborer's devotion to his work, in the teacher's solicitude for her pupils, in the physician's dedication to his art. All that heals, cultivates, protects, and inspires—all this is part of love. (p. 2.)

More recently, psychiatrist M. Scott Peck has written an enormously popular book, *The Road Less Traveled: A New Psychology of Love, Traditional Values and Spiritual Growth* (1978). Again drawing on both psychotherapy and religion, Peck declares "Love is too large, too deep ever to be truly understood or measured or limited within the framework of words," (p. 81). His own attempted definition of love is "The will to extend one's self for the purpose of nurturing one's own or another's spiritual growth," (p. 81). Love, for Peck, is key to normal child development and to psychotherapy:

For the most part, mental illness is caused by an absence of or defect in the love that a particular child required from its particular parents for successful maturation and spiritual growth. It is obvious, then, that in order to be healed through psychotherapy the patient must receive at least a portion of the genuine love of which the patient was deprived. (p. 175.)

LOVE AND EMPATHY IN EVOLUTION

Is there an inborn capacity for love, cooperation, or some other closely related social instinct? Behavioral scientists steeped in the theory of evolution, including Herbert Spencer (1916) and contemporary sociobiologists, such as Edward O. Wilson (1978), believe in an inborn drive toward the pursuit of self-interest that leads us to compete *against* others. But as early as 1902 in *Mutual Aid* and then in *Ethics: Origin and Development* (1924), Petr Kropotkin analyzed the tension between individual striving (liberty) and mutual aid (love). He demolished the attempt of the social Darwinists to impose on human society a constant struggle for supremacy and the survival of the fittest. Kropotkin found that human beings and animals alike survive and thrive through mutual aid—benevolent sharing. He cited many examples of animal and human society in which social cooperation is the most pro-survival activity of all.

Empathy, as we shall see, is closely related to human relations in general and more specifically to love. Robert Plutchik has reviewed the "evolutionary basis of empathy," (1987). He believes that empathy is a "widespread phenomenon in the animal world" as implied in a wide variety of behaviors, including "schooling behavior of fish, flocking and mobbing behavior of birds, and herding behavior of mammals." He cites alarm calls as an example of empathic behavior, "the communication of an emotional state from one organism to another." He also finds empathic behavior in animal play that requires "mutual affective signaling" to make clear that no real hostility is intended. He lists a variety of display behaviors that are both social and empathic in animals. These displays are found in greeting or recognition, courtship, mating, dominance, submission, alarm, challenge, distress, feeding, and food-begging.

Courtship displays, Plutchik points out, are "designed to overcome aggressive and fearful barriers that might normally exist between males and females." This pertains to an issue we shall examine further—the tension between liberty (self-defense) and love. Even in the animal kingdom, love in the form of mating must overcome aggressive tendencies to defend oneself. Most or even all social animals have built-in protective mechanisms to separate and protect themselves not only from outsiders but from members of their family and species. Thus our two Shetland sheepdogs will at times nip at each other to maintain their own "space" when one or the other doesn't feel like playing.

Plutchik summarizes:

Empathy may also be thought of as a component of affective communication and is triggered by the large number of display behaviors seen in animals. The available evidence suggests that empathy can be inferred in both young and mature animals and that it is probably based on innate schemata that are genetically determined. As with all behaviors that have genetic components, there is reason to believe that experience and learning may also influence the intensity and frequency of empathic behaviors.

From an evolutionary point of view, empathy has important survival value. . . . It assists individuals in gathering and hunting for food, detecting predators, courtships, and ensuring reproductive success. (pp. 44–45.)

The potential for love is innate. Aspects of love are apparent in the infant from birth, and without love, the individual cannot develop into a social being capable of autonomous activity or mutuality and cooperation.

INFANT SOCIALIZATION AND EMPATHY

Research has begun to confirm what mothers have always known—that the infant is a social being from birth. Ross Thompson (1987) reviews research indicating that infants react by crying in response to the crying of other infants as early as one to four days after birth. This may well reflect the rudiments of empathy. According to Thompson:

First, it is clear that from early in the first year, infants are capable of emotional resonance or contagion—that is, of sharing the same emotion as a consequence of another's emotional display. Although these responses are not empathic in quality since they do not derive from knowledge of the other's situation or condition, they are probably important precursors of empathy. Second, responses to another's arousal that are more clearly empathic in quality begin to appear midway through the second year of life. (p. 125.)

By the age of two to three months, Thompson and others point out, infants will involve themselves in face-to-face play with their mothers in a "nonverbal conversation" or "behavioral dialog" in which their responses influence each other. By two to five months infants are able to discriminate emotions from facial expressions and soon after they are able to use "social referencing," checking their mother's expressions before responding to situations positively or negatively. By one year of age, many children will respond with help-giving behavior, such as pats and concerned attention, to distressed children. Thompson believes that there is strong evidence for "the emergence of empathic responding midway through the second year and its role as a motivator of prosocial initiatives," (p. 133).

Randy Lennon and Nancy Eisenberg (1987) distinguish among three types of human responses to the situation of another: (1) personal distress, (2) emotional contagion, and (3) genuine concern or sympathy for another. They too find that empathic or sympathetic prosocial actions, such as "patting or touching the victim," begin in the second year of life.

In an article entitled "The Contribution of Empathy to Justice and Moral Judgment," Martin Hoffman (1987) takes the position that ". . . empathy contributes to caring and most principles of justice through empathic identification with victims and potential victims of society and its institutions," (p. 71). This is similar to my viewpoint, expressed in the *Psychology of Freedom* (1980), that empathic love for others is a cornerstone for most people's commitment to human rights and liberty.

More than two hundred years ago, as already noted, Adam Smith voiced a similar principle, that fellow-feeling or sympathy for others leads people to act generously on behalf of others. He also found that the reward of being loved motivates people to live justly:

What reward is most proper for promoting the practice of truth,
justice, and humanity?—The confidence, the esteem, and the love
of those we live with. **Humanity does not desire to be great, but**
to be loved. *(p. 276.) [Emphasis added.]*

That concern for human rights is a function of love was confirmed by Oliner and Oliner (1988) in their study of the personalities of individuals who risked their lives to protect and save Jews
during the Holocaust. They observe:

What distinguished rescuers was not their lack of concern with
self, external approval, or achievement, but rather their capacity
for extensive relationships—their stronger sense of attachment to
others and their feelings of responsibility for the welfare of oth-
ers, including those outside their immediate family or communal
circles. . . . They remind us that such courage is not only the
province of the independent and the intellectually superior think-
ers but that it is available to all through the virtues of connect-
edness, commitment, and the quality of relationship developed in
ordinary human interactions. (p. 249, 260.)

The human being is a social creature from birth onward and very
early in life the infant develops the rudiments of what will become
genuine empathy. The love dynamic is fundamental to human
nature and to the development of human values, such as empathy,
caring, and even abstract principles, such as justice and human
rights. It is the primary source of what Oliner and Oliner identify
as "moral heroism."

LOVE, CARING, AND NURTURING

Love often colors relationships with caring and nurturing. The
feeling of empathic love and the activities of caring for and nurturing are probably at root one and the same, both originating in
the parent-infant bond. Nurturing is the critical activity through
which lessons of human relationship are initially learned. The

mother socializes the child through feeding, bathing, changing diapers, burping, stroking, cooing, smiling, face-to-face play, and myriad other activities, conscious and unconscious.

Among our primate cousins, grooming is a critical expression of their social bonds, and it is also a primary method of conflict resolution among adult chimpanzees. (At the same time, of course, it helps keep the animals rid of parasites. The one function does not exclude the other.) In *Touching: The Human Significance of the Skin* (1978), Ashley Montagu suggested that touching, including caressing and cuddling, is a "basic need." He concluded:

. . . adequate tactile satisfaction during infancy and childhood is of fundamental importance for the subsequent healthy behavioral development of the individual. The experimental and other research findings on other animals, as well as those on humans, show tactile deprivation in infancy usually results in behavior inadequacies in later life. (p. 318.)

When love and direct, physical nurturing become separated, something is lost. This is exemplified by those men (and sometimes women) whose capacity to love is inhibited by their unwillingness or inability to nurture. They defend their love as real even though it is not expressed through tender actions; but however real it may seem to them, it impacts relatively little on their lives or on the lives of those around them. Often they are unable to touch or to embrace their children or to use the word "love." Typically, their families speak of them as "distant," "unemotional," or "unapproachable."

When fathers become more involved in nurturing their offspring, they generate more love with their wives as well. I have enjoyed observing the process on a weekly basis when a couple with their newborn infant continues in therapy with the baby. The men in these sessions, much more involved with daily nurturing than typical males, also share a more radiant love with their wives. Instead of competing for their wives' affections, they bask together in the glow of mutual love.

THE LESSONS OF FAILED NURTURING

Recent research discloses that the infants of depressed or withdrawn parents quickly begin to reject their own parents and to withdraw socially. Byron Egeland and Martha Farrell Erickson (1990) have been studying the effect on infants of parental failure to nurture and support them. Their conclusions are based on direct observation of parents and infants. They summarize:

> *We know also that infants who are not nurtured or comforted during times of distress will develop an avoidant pattern of attachment with their caregiver. At times of distress these infants avoid their caregiver because they have learned that their caregivers will not provide them with the needed comfort or support. We have found that avoidant babies continue to avoid close relationships as they get older. (p. 32.)*

Egeland and Erickson's empirical research bolsters the earlier observations of psychoanalysts, such as Bowlby (1973), who found that infants fail to thrive and become depressed when deprived of maternal love. Mahler, Furer, and Settlage (1959) reviewed the early literature on infants and small children subject to maternal or institutional abandonment, and described the devastating impact, including severe withdrawal and depression, psychosis, and death. When mothers fail to relate to their infants, the children can become autistic, displaying "a spectacular struggle against any demand of human—of social—contact," (p. 825).

Spitz (1946) studied the impact on children of being institutionalized and removed from their mothers for a period of two or three months at the age of six to eight months. The final result in many cases was a complete withdrawal, obvious dejection, and an expressionless face. If the mothers were restored, recovery took place. If not, the infants deteriorated and a large percentage died.

John Bowlby (1973) has also presented evidence and reviewed the literature on anxiety generated in small children by removal from their parents, even into the best of circumstances. The responses of the children were characterized by "*intense* protest, followed by despair and detachment," (p. 22). These responses, including "sadness, anger, and subsequent anxiety," (p. 22), were seen most dramatically in children two years and older, but less intensively in younger ones as well. Similar responses could be elicited by parents who were physically present but emotionally withdrawn or absent. How much children subsequently recovered depended largely upon how loving their environment later turned out to be.

The original studies on children suffering from infantile autism, a severe state of withdrawal, identified their parents as typically emotionally cold and unable to relate (Eisenberg and Kanner, 1958). Often these parents encouraged their children to do without human contact, attention, and loving support. It was then no surprise that these youngsters then went on to treat other people as if they did not have human qualities, often banging into them or staring through them as if they were inanimate objects. While modern biopsychiatry has tried to dismiss these early studies and to claim that autism is genetic or biological, they have no substantial evidence to support their claims (reviewed in Breggin, 1991). Thus clinical and empirical research confirms the existence of basic needs for love in the form of nurturing, comfort, and emotional support, and finds that the failure to fulfill these needs leads to psychosocial disorders.

Animal studies in the wild have confirmed the human research. Chimpanzees observed by Goodall in *Chimpanzees of Gombe* (1986) and mountain gorillas observed by Dian Fossey in *Gorillas in the Mist* (1983) have displayed profound mourning reactions, including what psychiatrists might label "clinical depression," in response to psychosocial losses and deprivation. Depending on their age and maturity, young orphans may or may not be able to bond again with another chimp or gorilla. If they are too young to bond after the loss of a parent, they may stop eating and caring for themselves, and die. Fossey describes feeding and stroking an orphaned baby gorilla back into health. Goodall also describes how chimps are capable of generosity and altruism toward each other, including sick or feeble relatives and friends. In *Toxic Psychiatry* (1991), I reviewed these primate studies and compared the responses of the animals to those of humans under similar circumstances, and found them largely indistinguishable.

It must be concluded that love is a basic need. In the infant, love may be the *most basic need*, because the infant cannot thrive without receiving it. It is more primary in some respects than food or water, because the unloved infant (human or primate) may refuse both and die. It is certainly the most basic need in terms of normal psychosocial development. Without being loved, and subsequently learning to love, an infant and child cannot grow up to function well as an adult.

LOVE AS A BASIC NEED IN CONFLICT RESOLUTION LITERATURE

In the literature of conflict analysis and resolution, we find an increasing awareness that people have basic needs for love, nurturing, affiliation, and meaningful relationships, and that these love needs must be satisfied to achieve more harmonious living on earth.

Among basic needs, John Burton (1990a) includes "bonding," "valued relationships," and "recognition." As an ideal, he promotes a "sharing society" with "close bonded relationships," (p. 50). Others of his basic needs or values, such as autonomy and control, would seem more related to the liberty dynamic (see chapter 3) than to love; but as we shall see, the development of autonomy, social role, identity and similar capacities requires some degree of prior fulfillment of the need for nurturing and love.

In "The Existence of Human Needs" (1988), James Chowning Davies speaks more directly of "the social-affectional or love needs." He places them second in a list of four basic-need categories that also includes, first, "the physical needs;" third, "the self-esteem or dignity or equality needs," and fourth, "the self-actualization needs."

Consistent with viewing the human being as a "social animal," Davies finds that love plays a crucial role in regard to the fulfillment of all other basic needs:

. . . the love needs form a continuously traveled bridge between a human being's most elemental physical needs and his/her more distinctly human needs as a unique individual. A person's demands for everything from food to recognition of his/her unique creativity are all transacted with other human beings. (p. 27)

Davies notes that chimpanzees and humans cannot develop normally without love and nurturing. He further believes that individuals require a loving upbringing in order to move on to self-actualization, and even as adults must return to socializing in order to recuperate or reenergize for the task of self-actualization.

In *Peacemaking Among Primates* (1989), Frans de Waal describes the tension between cooperation and aggression in chimpanzees, pointing out that both dominant and submissive animals actively promote reconciliation through vocalizations, facial expressions, posturing, grooming, and even hugging and kissing. Often acts of aggression end in reconciliations that tighten the bonds between animals.

Chimpanzee life is hardly a survival of the fittest struggle among the animals; rather it is a complex social enterprise involving a shifting balance between competition and cooperation between individuals and coalitions. While conflict frequently occurs, it rarely escalates to the point of social disintegration or lethality, in part due to a wide variety of conflict resolution techniques, including individual reconciliations and third party interventions on behalf of peace and cooperation. As de Waal cleverly puts it, "The law of the jungle does not apply to chimpanzees," (p. 49).

THE LOVE OF SCIENCE, TECHNOLOGY, AND KNOWLEDGE

The escalating development of science and technology is usually attributed to (or blamed on!) liberty rather than love. However, love for their work or the subject they are studying is extraordinarily important in motivating most scientists and technologists, as well as artists, historians, philosophers, social scientists, and others who contribute to human knowledge. Love for the pursuit of knowledge also helps to establish the international community of these individuals in their various specialties.

Albert Einstein's life and work illustrates the role of love in science. It is well-known that he viewed his theoretical work in part as an attempt to understand God's universe. The passionate, loving enthusiasm that he gave to these pursuits is captured by Ronald Clark in *Einstein: The Life and Times* (1984). Clark quotes a friend who witnessed Einstein's meeting with fellow physicist Hendrick Lorenz:

Lorenz sat smiling at Einstein completely lost in meditation, exactly the way a father looks at a particularly beloved son—full of secure confidence that the youngster will crack the nut he has given him, but eager to see how. It took quite a while, but suddenly Einstein's head shot up joyfully; he "had" it. Still a bit of give and take, interrupting one another, a partial disagreement, very quick clarification and a complete mutual understanding, and then both men with beaming eyes skimming over the shining riches of the new theory. (p. 240.)

Notice that the men are not only joyful about each other in the process of scientific analysis and discovery; they also cherish the product of their work.

In his book, *Therapeutic Studies* (1985), in a section entitled "Einstein; thinking and loving," psychiatrist Kenneth Artiss declares:

Now it is possible to compare the openness of Einstein's mind with that of the lover's. We are surprised by some similarities.

Artiss follows the discussion of Einstein's passion for truth with a few trenchant paragraphs headed "Freedom to Love." He declares that to love someone or something is to desire and to search for complete knowledge of the loved one's uniqueness. He quotes Goethe's maxim, "A man doesn't understand anything unless he loves it."

We shall return to the theme of love and knowledge as we further examine the role of love in conflict resolution. If love is indeed a path—and perhaps *the* path—toward understanding, its importance in conflict resolution becomes further magnified.

Einstein has not been alone in being motivated by a passionate love for knowledge. His predecessors—such as Copernicus, Brahe, Kepler, Galileo, and Newton—were motivated by a passion for science and understanding, and not purely by self-interest or competition. Some of them risked their careers and even their lives.

The community of scientists, as well as other truth-seekers, exists as a continuum in time that spans the ages. Einstein felt a strong affinity for his predecessors and was drawn to ancient institutions where they had studied and taught. The feeling we often have for those who have paved our intellectual way often transcends simple respect. It becomes loving and reverential. I am reminded of how one of my philosophy professors felt toward Plato and Aristotle. His feeling toward the old masters reached beyond the analytic, comprehended their flaws, and nonetheless took delight in them.

Often these communities of truth-seekers reach into the future as well, not only revering those who crèated the traditions of the past, but enjoying the prospect of contributing to the future. Einstein also expressed his love for future generations through his work in support of international peacemaking.

Through his biography of Einstein, Clark also documents how the community of scientists attempted, before and after World War II, to maintain itself across national borders despite the hatreds generated by war. To this day, international scientists frequently see themselves as members of a community that transcends individual and national interests.

THE HOPE OF LOVING COMMUNITIES

It is relatively easy to understand how love bonds and motivates people in families and in local community organizations, such as the many volunteer groups that serve the needs of Americans. A recent TV movie based on the rescue of baby Jessica McClure from a well shaft in Texas was described in its subtitle as a story of volunteerism and love. Unfortunately, love does not sufficiently motivate us in regard to the vast but more commonplace suffering found in our local communities, for example, among the poor and minority groups. But notice that, in the absence of love, we usually fail to come up with any benevolent, workable solutions.

Love also plays a role in many divergent worldwide movements aimed at solving our most difficult global problems, including the destruction of our environment and the increasing disparity between the rich and the poor of the world (see chapter 11). Here I want to emphasize that love can reach across national boundaries through a variety of organizations based on social justice, religion, shared cultural values, philanthropy, and common interests such as science and the arts. Often the individuals involved also see themselves as a part of a larger community extending through time, even into the future where they anticipate the good effects of their contributions.

Love is rooted in the whole human being—the biological, psychosocial, and spiritual—and binds human beings in positive, valuing relationships from the most superficial to the most intimate and intense. The capacity for love is inherent in the newborn infant, but it must be brought forth through nurturing. The infant requires love in order to thrive and then in order to join society as an adult. Love is *the* most basic psychosocial need; the individual cannot function autonomously or socially without a loving introduction into life.

The feeling associated with love is positive and, at its best, joyful. It inspires attitudes and activities of caring, nurturing, cherishing, and reverent treasuring. It encourages liberty and justice, sympathy and mercy. Empathic love transforms individual self-interests into mutual interests and becomes the final common pathway for those values leading to the resolution and prevention of deep-seated conflicts in the personal and political spheres alike.

CHAPTER 3

▼▼▼▼▼▼▼▼▼▼▼▼▼▼▼▼▼▼▼▼▼▼▼▼▼▼▼▼▼

Understanding Liberty

*But we assure the socialists that we repudiate only forced orga-
nization, not natural organization. We repudiate the forms of association that are forced upon us, not free association. We
repudiate forced fraternity, not true fraternity. We repudiate the
artificial unity that does nothing more than deprive persons of
individual responsibility. We do not repudiate the natural unity
of mankind under Providence.*

Frederic Bastiat, The Law (1850)

Property rights are *human rights, and are essential to the human
rights which liberals attempt to maintain. The human right of
free speech depends upon the human right of private property in
newsprint.*

Murray Rothbard, For a New Liberty (1973)

*I suggest that the greatest threat to the exchange system [the free
market] is the claim that it can do everything. This leads to the
equally absurd claim that it can do nothing. The real problem
here is to appraise it in its setting and to get the right kind of
setting for it.*

Kenneth Boulding, Beyond Economics (1968)

*Whether complete identification of human nature with individu-
ality would be desirable or undesirable if it existed is an idle
academic question. For it does not exist. Some cultural conditions develop psychological constituents that lead toward
differentiation; others stimulate those which lead in the direction of the solidarity of the beehive or anthill.*

John Dewey, Freedom and Culture (1989)

Love grows best in the soil of liberty.

Leonard Frank, unpublished letter (1991)

From the dawn of humankind, communities have probably been
aware of their freedom and the need to protect it; but personal or

individual freedom is a more recent concept. It is not yet accepted in many cultures and nations of the world, especially for women, children, and minorities. In their personal lives, even in the United States, many people have little or no concept of how to exercise their own personal freedom.

THE IDEAL OF LIBERTY IN PERSONAL RELATIONSHIPS

In our personal lives we can determine to conduct ourselves with a maximum amount of respect for the rights of others. We can, with some success, make sure that our most intimate relationships are strictly voluntary in spirit and in fact (Breggin, 1980; see also chapter 6). I can, for example, decide on my own never to threaten or deceive my family or friends. I can also try not to exercise my advantages as a male when bargaining with my wife about matters such as domestic chores, money, or career. When we then sit down to discuss the division of labor within the family, there is some hope that the outcome will reflect, at least in part, a genuine bargain, a voluntary exchange.

The problem is of course more difficult for women, especially if they choose to raise children within a typical family. Their choices may be vastly limited compared to men's. Nonetheless, even in this arena there is a beginning awareness of the need for equal rights.

In personal and political relationships, and in conflict resolution, the aim is to maximize the voluntary nature of relationships, and within them, to maximize the mutual fulfillment of needs. To some extent, this is a three-step process from coercion through liberty to love.

To the extent that the principle of liberty can be built into relationships, it establishes the first step or initial context for the development and survival of love (see chapter 6).

WHAT IS LIBERTY?

Liberty can be understood and justified in many ways, including theories of natural or divine rights, human nature, property rights, or constitutional law. The subject has attracted volumes of attention over the centuries. I will not at this point examine the many debates concerning liberty, such as the validity of equating personal freedom with the right to own private property. My aim is to develop a narrow definition of liberty for use in contrasting it to coercion and to love.

Liberty will be defined in terms of "freedom from" rather than "freedom to." That is, it will be limited to the right to defend oneself from external oppression or control, rather than the right to have one's other needs fulfilled, such as those for food or medical care. These more complex issues will be taken up in the chapters that deal with business corporations, society, and international politics.

For many advocates of liberty, *self-ownership,* including the ownership of property and other presumed products of one's labor, is the basic axiom from which all other rights are derived. In *For A New Liberty* (1973), Murray Rothbard adopts as his "primary axiom" the "universal right of self-ownership, a right held by everyone by virtue of being a human being." Self-ownership further justifies the right to pursue one's own interests free of outside restraint:

Since each individual must think, learn, value, and choose his or her ends and means in order to survive and flourish, the right to self-ownership gives man the right to perform these vital functions without being hampered and restricted by coercive molestation. (p. 27.)

In the epilogue to the *Psychology of Freedom* (1980), I cited self-ownership as a fundamental ethical and psychological principle:

You own yourself; you possess yourself; you belong to yourself. You are your own natural resource, your own and sole source of life energy. You have complete rights to yourself. (p. 237.)

But self cannot so easily be separated from others, and I went on to describe love for others and for life as the highest expression of self-ownership.

Liberty can also be defined in terms of the "non-aggression axiom." According to Rothbard, "no man or group of men have the right to aggress against the person or property of anyone else," (p. 8). That is, the principle of freedom restricts the use of force to self-defense.

Self-ownership and the restriction of force to self-defense are basic principles of Dynamic II: liberty. Although they were initially developed as economic and political principles, I have applied these axioms to psychology and to personal living as well (Breggin, 1980). Personal autonomy, self-determination, and empowerment flow from self-ownership and nonaggression.

EMOTIONAL BULLYING

In the broader political and legal arena, force is defined as a *physical* intervention or the threat of it. In reality, there are many other forms of coercion, most of which are familiar from our personal lives. Sometimes authority is invoked, as "I am your father" or "I am your husband." One individual may attempt to control another by stimulating painful feelings. The victim is made to feel guilty, shameful, anxious, or numb about standing up for his or her own interests or principles. Sometimes threats of abandonment are used: "If that's the way you want it, I'll leave you."

In personal adult relationships, people have the right to reject emotional bullying and, if necessary, to leave the relationship. Emotional bullying cannot be made *illegal,* but individuals can personally refuse to subject themselves to interpersonal oppression. I will deal with this issue further in discussing coercion (in chapter 4) and family conflict (in chapter 6). Here I want to introduce the idea that all forms of bullying and threats are incompatible with voluntary *personal* relationships. They also corrupt political relationships, but they are difficult if not impossible to outlaw.

Because we are more directly in control of our intimate relationships, liberty is typically a more realizable ideal in the personal than in the political arena. It is not utopian to seek to make all of one's intimate adult relationships wholly voluntary and free of coercion; but it is utopian to expect such an outcome on a national or international scale in the foreseeable future.

Meanwhile, in the field of conflict resolution, it is generally agreed that only *voluntary participation* and *voluntary agreements* can advance parties from uncompromising conflict toward meaningful, lasting solutions (Burton, 1990a).

THE DIFFERENCES BETWEEN RESPECT AND LOVE

Respect or esteem is the emotion generated by Dynamic II activities. Respect or esteem says, in effect, "You have conducted yourself well. You are ethical. Be proud." Respect is very important in the lives of all individuals. Children need to be emotionally rewarded for their accomplishments and good attitudes. Adults want to earn similar approval for their accomplishments. In both the home and the workplace, human beings need to feel esteemed.

Respect or esteem is not the same as love. Love says, "You are valued for yourself." It is unconditional. Respect, by contrast, is a social reward or reinforcer. It is contingent on individual performance and accomplishment. Love reaches to the core or essence of the person; esteem concerns itself only with quality of performance.

Sometimes people can love without giving respect. A parent may not always approve of a son or daughter's conduct; but a parent should always strive to find love in his or her heart for a child. However, with people who are not dear to us, we may be able to respect them without loving them. This leads to an important principle in conflict resolution.

In the absence of love, respect can provide the starting point, at least, for a relationship and for the early stages of conflict resolution. If people do not show respect for each other in a negotiation or conflict-resolution setting, the relationships will further deteriorate. When beginning to work on conflict resolution as a third party or as a participant, it is important to insist upon mutual respect from the earliest stages.

The mistaken equation of esteem with love amounts to a denial of love. By confusing esteem with love we overlook the key human needs for bonding, valued relationships, or affection. Basic-needs theorist Paul Sites (1990), who has considerably influenced conflict resolution theory, has fallen into this error. Sites believes that animals and people become depressed because they lose the approval (esteem) they have been receiving:

> *In short, a feeling of depression occurs when a person's self-*
> *esteem is in some way threatened or damaged. Depression may*
> *occur, for example, when a family member or close friend dies.*
> *These are the people most likely to provide approval behavior*
> *and their death negates this.*

Sites postulates no basic human need for contact or communication with people, or to "belong to a group." People and groups provide *opportunities* for need satisfaction, but they can also thwart it; therefore people are merely *potential* satisfiers rather than beings of inherent worth to each other. Thus humans are not fundamentally drawn to be with other human beings or to love them. From such a viewpoint, society must be seen as evolving from a hodge-podge of need satisfactions without a central, comprehensive need for social life.

Even caring seems absent as a human motive in Sites's framework. For example, in Sites's view we avoid shaming other people because of an implicit agreement that people will therefore not shame us. There is no appreciation that humans tend to empathize with each other's pain even without external rewards. Nor is there any acknowledgment that human beings spontaneously desire to nurture each other, to protect each other, and to relieve each other's emotional or physical pain. Yet the existence of such social needs or values is easily explained by his evolutionary perspective. The drive toward *mutual satisfaction* and *cooperation,* as Kropotkin suggested, can be understood as a necessary outcome of evolution (see chapter 2).

Consistent with what seems like a typical male hierarchical value system (see chapter 6), Sites places enormous emphasis on *control* as central to human behavior. Altruism is seen as one more method of controlling people, i.e., getting others to think and to do what we want. That people might want something *for other people* seems beyond his system. His passing mention of altruism and his dismissal of a need for human companionship or society is the closest he comes to discussing love.

Nothing is more important in resolving conflict than to get past this erroneous equation of respect with love. As already noted, respect establishes the possibility of a meaningful relationship, but only love and empathy move people to care about each other's problems and hence to seek mutually satisfying solutions.

INDIVIDUAL LIBERTY, AUTONOMY, AND LOVE

Autonomy or self-rule is the ability to think rationally for oneself, to exercise free will, and to make independent judgments. It may be viewed as "inner freedom" and is essential to effective functioning.

In "Psychotherapy as Applied Ethics" (1971), I made autonomy the central value and working principle of psychotherapy. It certainly is an important one. Without autonomy, people are unable to pursue any set of values and goals. Without autonomy, they grow afraid and distrustful toward other people who seem more powerful. In more recent years I have increasingly sought to place liberty and autonomy within the context of love and other social values and experiences. And autonomy no longer seems to me such an easy concept to define.

In a book originally published in 1959, Dorothy Lee has analyzed how autonomy depends upon a social structure and cultural philosophy that values or loves the individual. After describing the tightly-knit structure of the Navaho family and society with its many taboos and customs, Lee goes on to focus upon the autonomy granted to all individuals:

Within this structured universe and tightly knit society, the Navaho lives in personal autonomy. Adults and children alike are valued for their sheer being, just because they **are.** *(p. 10.)*

Love is so unconditional that there is no incentive to push for personal recognition through competition and achievement. If anything, the individual is suspect for doing so. The wealthy person may even be accused of having employed malicious witchcraft.

In her book, *In a Different Voice* (1982), Carol Gilligan continues the observations begun by Lee. She finds that men have placed the values of autonomy and independence at the top of a hierarchy of values, while the lives of women more typically emphasize caring, mutuality, and interdependence. Her position might be characterized as "Autonomy is not enough."

The position taken by Gilligan, and especially by Lee in *Freedom and Culture*, raises important, difficult-to-answer problems. While autonomy in the English and American tradition has been connected to personal freedom, Lee connects autonomy to a feeling of being unconditionally valued or loved. I believe that love is required for the initial development of autonomy, and to some degree for its maintenance in adulthood; but the autonomous person as described and seemingly promoted by Lee is culturally restricted in what he or she is allowed to think about. While individual wishes are greatly respected in some of the societies that she cites, the range of these wishes and their expression is narrowly determined by the cultures. The Navaho mother can permit her child to make up his or her own mind in part because more threatening options, such as rejecting the culture, are unthinkable. By autonomy, I mean a far greater degree of inner freedom, with considerably greater cultural support for a broad range of personal choices.

Sociologist Helmut Schoeck (1966), with a much stronger libertarian bent than Lee, takes a somewhat more cynical view of similar anthropological data. It may be closer to the truth. He points out that envy plays an enormous controlling role in preindustrial societies. Envy, often expressed through the evil eye and witchcraft, tends to suppress individual initiative and to enforce group norms. For Schoeck, it is a double-edged sword. Envy enforces group coercion and prevents the domination of the group by especially powerful or competitive individuals; but it also prevents the individual from more freely developing special interests or endowments. A pragmatic theoretician, Schoeck believes that the tension created by envy is inevitable because it is an indispensable part of society's built-in checks and balances.

In an epilogue to the 1987 edition of Lee's *Freedom and Culture,* Jeffrey Ehrenreich summarizes Lee's viewpoint and brings us face to face with the dilemma of the individual and society:

Lee believed that content, fulfilled, productive, autonomous individuals—people who could value the self—needed a social environment and structure which promoted freedom, dignity, and individual diversity. She wanted to see such positive qualities structured into people's lives and not just held as principles. She wanted individuals to live in societies with social structures in which there would be ". . . absolute respect for man, for all individuals irrespective of age and sex." (p. 180.)

Ehrenreich then describes Lee's own struggle for autonomy, which brought her to reject mainstream academic life and, for many years, to refuse to write anything further. She did this by choice, but not without an identity crisis and personal suffering.

I believe that Lee's personal life, more than *Freedom and Culture* itself, expresses the sometimes inherent conflict between the individual and society. Autonomy and its corollary, personal freedom, cannot depend upon societal encouragement and reinforcement as fully as Lee had hoped. Autonomy requires facing the existential anxieties and the real life conflicts inherent in making one's own choices. Even the best of societies will paradoxically encourage autonomy while trying to discourage the individual from making unlimited choices.

Lee's work does make the all-important point that the autonomous person does not automatically spring into action with adulthood. As Lawrence Haworth has more recently elaborated in *Autonomy: An Essay in Philosophical Psychology and Ethics* (1986), autonomy must be nurtured, cultivated, and encouraged in the child. Autonomy is a natural striving within the infant who attempts, often to the consternation of its parents, to do things on his or her own without or even despite adult interference. Self-feeding by an immature infant, for example, can try any adult's patience. But, as Haworth observed, the flowering of autonomy requires the indulgence, encouragement, and support of adults. It has to be learned through its exercise in a social context. It is easily threatened and may not develop at all. Often it develops in relative degrees without necessarily becoming fully expressed.

As concentration camps and POW camps have demonstrated, even adult autonomy can be devastated by systematic undermining in controlled institutions. Erving Goffman (1961) and I (1991) have described a similar outcome in the lives of state mental hospital patients. Lenore Walker (1989) has documented how battered women can lose their autonomy and become psychologically helpless in the face of overwhelming abuse and control at the hands of men determined to rob them of their independence.

Nurturing and love in infancy and early childhood is required for the development of normal functioning in primates and humans (see chapter 2). Clinical experience shows that an unloved human being is likely to grow up lacking in basic capacities, such as autonomy (Miller, 1984; Breggin, 1991). Such an individual may become so insecure, fearful, and suspicious that he or she becomes labeled insane or incompetent.

Social and developmental psychologists have studied how children develop components of autonomy and self-determination, such as self-control, delay of gratification, mastery (the opposite of helplessness), and locus of control (the degree to which children believe that their own actions can influence the outcome of events in their lives). The research indicates that autonomy is fostered within families that warmly encourage children to be self-reliant and independent by means of nonauthoritarian, nonpunitive interventions, including praise and gentle, rational persuasion (for a review, see Seligman, 1991; Liebert, Wicks-Nelson, and Kail, 1986).

The dependence of autonomy upon normal maturation and, to some extent, on supportive conditions in adulthood is a central issue in conflict analysis and resolution. The question must always be asked, "Are all parties to the conflict in fact autonomous?" If not, then the weaker may be taken advantage of by the stronger. At the least, the nonautonomous individual will gain limited benefit from the process.

In individual psychotherapy, clients may not be able to benefit when lacking in autonomy and overcome with personal helplessness. A therapist may mistakenly encourage such clients to examine childhood trauma, only to find them becoming more overwhelmed in the face of the restimulated pain. Instead, the therapist should directly address the issue of autonomy and helplessness, helping nonautonomous persons strengthen their self-control and self-direction. In therapy, it can be futile and even damaging to emphasize other issues when clients feel relatively unable to control their inner life.

People lacking in autonomy often end up agreeing to destructive psychiatric treatments in the form of toxic drugs, electroshock, or psychosurgery (Breggin, 1991). Their psychological helplessness then becomes compounded by brain damage and dysfunction.

Whether we are talking about interpersonal or broader political conflicts, we cannot *assume* the existence of autonomous individuals without leaving relatively helpless people at the mercy of more powerful ones. A setting in which liberty is the only governing principle is advantageous to relatively competent individuals, but hazardous to relatively helpless ones. Without help from others, people lacking in autonomy cannot survive or protect themselves from exploitation. That help will only be provided where people are willing to love unconditionally and to offer gifts to others. These observations, as much as anything else, underscore the limits of liberty.

There may come a time when a person concludes that grandma or grandpa is no longer able to make decisions for herself or himself. Similarly, young children sometimes need adults to take over their lives for their own good or to prevent serious harm from befalling them. But with few exceptions, people will further their own lives and those of the people around them by standing fast for everyone's liberty. Within a context of personal liberty, individuals can far more easily develop themselves, help their loved ones, and settle their disputes and solve their conflicts through love (see chapter 6).

Mature individuals are in a position to most fully benefit from liberty. In their personal lives, they may wish to do everything they can to preserve and promote their own freedom and that of the other autonomous people in their lives. But this can never be a fully comfortable approach to life. It brings with it the anxiety of making one's own choices, often in conflict with prevailing social norms. The autonomous person may end up rebelling against society or particular social institutions when they become oppressive and when they fail to meet the basic needs of individuals.

POLITICAL LIBERTY AND LOVE

In the political arena, the problem of liberty and autonomy becomes more complex because many citizens are unable to take care of themselves or to compete adequately in the free market. Free market advocates believe that liberty is the engine of human progress—the source not only of modern technological and industrial advances, but the inspiration for human rights throughout the world (Weaver, 1947; Von Mises, 1966; Schoeck, 1966; Rothbard, 1982).

The utopian benefits of the free market have of course been challenged from many directions, including more recent fears that the "engine of progress" is in reality devouring the human community and nature alike (Galbraith, 1958, 1980; Berry, 1972, 1987; Fromm, 1976; Etzioni, 1988; Wachtel, 1989). Yet the former communist nations of Europe, as well as Asian communist nations, are beginning to experiment with the free market or capitalism as the only hope for economic survival and recovery (see chapter 9). *They* are informing *us* about the necessity of human freedom for human survival. Yet they face the most vexing problem of the free enterprise system: the degree to which it exploits less autonomous people.

The interactions between liberty and love within the larger community are complex and controversial, and will be dealt with in more depth in chapters 8–10, as well as later in this chapter. It is doubtful, for example, if liberty can be sustained without people feeling community ties with each other and without people feeling some degree of love for others beyond the immediate circle of their family and locality.

THE ORIGIN OF EQUAL RIGHTS

The principle of liberty holds that humans are equal under the law rather than equal in value. But can people have equal rights without *necessarily* having equal worth as well? If people do not have equal worth, then what is the source of equal rights? Why do we insist that strangers be respected and legally protected, even when it is not in our self-interest?

Perhaps some people do support liberty on selfish grounds, but certainly this is not true for most. Patrick Henry's rallying cry, "Give me liberty or give me death," hardly seems to reflect rational self-interest. Nor does the motto of the state of New Hampshire, "Live free or die." Whether we approve of them or not, these resounding battle cries reflect a higher ideal than personal self-interest or even survival. At the least, they reflect a *love* of liberty. To some extent, at least, they reflect a love of other people—for all human beings to be free, even at the potential cost of sacrificing one's own life.

Nor is it true that our self-interest is always best served by rejecting force and fraud. Often we can obtain a great advantage by bullying or cheating. Sometimes, as the lives of many dictators and other politicians have illustrated, force and fraud can yield enduring advantages with lifetime benefits for oneself and one's family and associates. Indeed, governments and their beneficiaries typically thrive on force and fraud. Self-interest by itself is an insufficient motive for respecting the rights of others.

Only when we care about or love people do we thoroughly and unequivocally grant them equal rights. Absent a real sense of the *inherent worth* of others, we are bound to fudge or hedge here and there about their rights. *With vast implications for conflict analysis and resolution, I believe that the lack of love among human beings is the chief cause for the rampant disrespect for rights nearly everywhere we turn. Love remains a flimsy fabric in world society, and therefore so do equal rights.*

FORCE IN LIBERTY AND LOVE

Liberty as a principle supports the use of force in self-defense, but love abhors the use of any force. Here is possibly the greatest incompatibility between love and liberty. To injure another person, even to kill someone, is considered ethical and sometimes admirable in defense of person, property, or the ideal of liberty itself. But to harm someone in a loving relationship—even in self-defense—is at best a horrible expediency. Usually it is viewed as repugnant and unacceptable.

Having stated the ideal, it must be repeated that a great deal of violence is committed in the name of love within the family and many social institutions, such as religion and psychiatry (see chapter 7). However, the experience of genuine love, which is rooted in empathy, is incompatible with violence against the loved one. This is not only an intuitive and an ethical conclusion, but an observation based on experiences with loving people. In chapter 11, the equation between love and nonviolence will be examined through the work of Gandhi, Schweitzer, and Martin Luther King, Jr. As a person develops most fully in his or her capacity to love, the use of force, even in self-defense, becomes increasingly abhorred; and nonviolent approaches to conflict resolution become increasingly valued.

SELF-INTEREST AND ALTRUISM

Advocates of liberty, such as Rothbard (1973) and Von Mises (1966), usually describe self-interest as the most natural, proper, and overriding human motive. Sometimes they view self-interest as the only *possible* human motive. Altruism then becomes a kind of hypocritical rationalization or a mere derivative of self-interest.

Most people are not motivated by self-interest all the time, not even in their economic or work relationships, let alone in their personal ones. Altruism, concern for others, the desire to maintain good will, a sense of fairness, patriotism, religious devotion, and many other constraints and ideals motivate the activities of people. Personal motives such as greed, envy, and the desire for power also affect people, sometimes causing them to act against any commonsense notion of self-interest.

Consider the actions of an art dealer who discovers that a valuable painting is being sold unwittingly for a mere ten dollars in a second-hand store. The dealer might, if he had no prior relationship with the store owner, quickly buy the underpriced art. But if he had a long-standing business relationship with the store owner that he desired to maintain, he might share some of his profit with him. This might be called "practical altruism," something still closely associated with the pursuit of self-interest. But if the dealer felt sympathy for the store owner, or if he were a close friend to him, he might announce the painting's true worth and then join his friend in celebrating his good fortune.

To argue that altruism is essentially selfish because it brings self-satisfaction is to miss the point. As the art dealer's story illustrates, acting selfishly and acting altruistically are different phenomena with frequently opposing outcomes.

The idealization of the pursuit of self-interest is, to a great extent, a male viewpoint. Women, in their nurturing or homemaking roles, cannot live by it. It is one thing for Von Mises the man to declare that most people prefer to fill their own bellies; it would be another for Mrs. Von Mises to say it. She was in all likelihood filling a number of people's bellies ahead of her own, including Mr. Von Mises's. In *Justice, Gender and the Family* (1987), Susan Moller Okin observes that theories of economic self-interest ignore or take for granted the existence of women who, at great personal cost, typically devote themselves to taking care of other people.

COMPETITION AND IMBALANCES IN POWER

In his well-known metaphor of the invisible hand, Adam Smith argued in 1759 in *The Theory of Moral Sentiments* and in 1776 in *The Wealth of Nations* that when people pursue their own self-interests (without the use of force), they unintentionally end up serving each other's needs and the needs of the society. In order to sell my product to you, I must make it conform to your expectations. Similarly, I will reject your offer, unless it meets my expectations. Thus selfish exchanges inadvertently or unintentionally cater to the needs of others and create a kind of practical altruism. This leads to a vast web of exchange, which no individual or state could artificially construct, wherein people end up satisfying each other's needs while pursuing their own.

Adam Smith's theory works smoothly as long as the ideal of voluntary exchange between equal partners is reasonably approximated; but in *most exchanges* and *most relationships,* built-in imbalances of need, competence, and power predetermine the outcome.

In the economic arena, for example, if a desperate father decides to pay his last peso, ruble, or dollar for the food or medicine necessary for the life of his wife or child, he is hardly in a bargaining position with the wealthy owner of the food market or pharmacy. Even if he has sufficient resources to strike a meaningful "voluntary" exchange with the local store owner, he is in no such bargaining position in relationship to still greater forces that determine the cost of the food and medicine, such as monopolistic industries, international banks, or global markets. If the desperate father is also relatively unsophisticated or incompetent, then he is further disadvantaged in the exchange.

In *Toxic Psychiatry* (1991) I have described how the drug companies spend millions to buy the good will of psychiatry and the endorsement of individual psychiatrists, thereby creating a psychopharmaceutical complex that dominates the drug marketplace. Individual drug experts, psychiatric organizations, the Food and Drug Administration (FDA), the National Institute of Mental Health (NIMH), and the media have contributed to the effort to promote psychiatric drugs, to the consumer's detriment.

I've come to the conclusion that the ideal of liberty—voluntary exchanges between relatively equal partners—is unattainable as a practical matter on a large scale or societal level. In a pure free market, most people would probably find themselves decidedly unfree.

Power imbalances also exist in family and male-female conflicts. As Marilyn French in *Beyond Power* (1985) has pointed out, these imbalances are built into gender relationships through the institutions, customs, and economic relations of all "civilized" societies. In the United States, for example, if a wife and mother takes a job outside the home, and then tries to bargain with her husband to get him to assume his share of the domestic chores, the outcome is predetermined. In nearly all cases, her husband is likely to refuse to help at all with the domestic chores. If the woman in turn refuses to take over *all* of the domestic duties, the children will suffer from lack of care. Motivated by love for her home and children, by a sense of obligation toward the family, and by societal imperatives placed upon her, the working mother is typically saddled with an outside job *and* an inside, domestic one at the same time.

Most relationships and exchanges do not fit the pure model of voluntary exchange in our personal lives or the free market in our economic activities. To make believe that they do is to rationalize injustice—to force the father to give up his last dollar to save his child's life or to force the mother to hold two jobs in order to maintain a home for her children is to expose the vulnerable to enslavement by those with greater power. In sum, one or another party to an exchange too often has an advantage of such proportions that the mere rejection of force by no means guarantees a "voluntary" exchange.

COMPETITION IN LIBERTY AND LOVE

Ideally, liberty or voluntary exchange leads not only to competition but to cooperation. Adam Smith pointed out how, in the making of a pin, innumerable people in the pursuit of their own profit will cooperate in the process of transforming the metal ore into a useful instrument. Despite Adam Smith, Von Mises and others who believe that competition leads to a kind of practical altruism, competition also tends to breed conflict. Cooperation may develop *within* specific business organizations or affiliations, but ferocious competition typically develops among rivals (Kohn, 1986). Unhappily, as I mentioned in regard to the psycho-pharmaceutical complex (Breggin, 1991), even the desired competition between rivals in the marketplace may be compromised when they collude to the disadvantage of the consumer.

Sports teach us a great deal about cooperation and competition. To a remarkable degree, professional sporting events are based on the uncompromising Dynamic II model that is supposed to characterize the free market. The rules are the same for all the players involved, infractions are carefully monitored and punished by objective referees or umpires, everyone participates by their own choosing and gets paid for it, and violence is usually limited to self-defense. In most sports, such as baseball and basketball, the individual competitor is not even allowed to use force in self-defense. The enforcement of self-defense remains in the hands of the umpires and referees.

What is the result of this perfect model of competitive human activity? While cooperation is greatly enhanced within each team by the common goal of winning, conflict escalates between rival teams and among their respective fans. We do not have to remind ourselves of European soccer matches to see that violence can be generated in seemingly harmless sporting competitions. High-school students in America frequently come to blows at sporting events both on and off the field.

The ideal of liberty places strict limits on the competition by excluding the use of force and fraud. But keeping the competition within these bounds, in the absence of valued relationships or loving affiliations, is hard to do. And even when the competition is contained within the ethics of liberty, it can become extremely fierce and conflicted.

The concept of liberty is an adequate prescription for how to write legal contracts. It is also workable in some bargaining situations in which no one obviously has the upper hand. It is ideal for drawing up the regulations for sporting events between relatively well-matched competitors. It is a necessary condition if people are to begin examining their conflicts with each other.

When people are embroiled in deep-seated conflicts, the principles of liberty can help define the initial framework or start-up conditions. They will not by themselves prove effective when there is marked suspicion, distrust, desperation, or hatred. They will not work where power imbalances overwhelm the seemingly voluntary exchange. Nor will they work in situations, such as "undeveloped" nations, where the principles of liberty and ethical business practices are not understood or valued. Even in a so-called developed nation, the United States, former president Ronald Reagan's inspiring rhetoric and deregulation on behalf of the "free market" helped to spawn one of the worst orgies of financial greed and fraud in the history of the country. Nonetheless, the principles of liberty are critical in establishing some of the ground rules necessary for conflict resolution.

BASIC NEEDS IN LIBERTY AND LOVE

The basic needs categorized as Dynamic II: liberty include self-esteem, autonomy, mastery, and self-determination. They are essential to effective functioning as an agent and are closely related to the principle that human beings can earn their value through accomplishments. However, we have already noted that the full expression and satisfaction of these needs are dependent upon a foundation of nurturing and love in childhood. Other Dynamic II needs overlap with love. They include security, identity, role, and meaning. It is somewhat arbitrary to place them within one or the other category. Security at an early age is dependent on love, while it later depends on liberty as well. Identity, role and meaning in life are at times generated by living according to the principle of liberty and at others by living according to the principle of love.

Most of the basic needs categorized as Dynamic I are clearly discernable from those in Dynamic II. These love needs include nurturing, empathy, bonding, oneness with people and with nature, and community. They are closely related to the principle that human beings and other expressions of life have inherent worth. They are basic to the formation and maintenance of society.

The line between liberty needs and love needs is not hard and fast, but there are very significant differences. This analysis suggests that the deepest or most complete conflict resolution involves the satisfaction of love needs.

ARE LIBERTY NEEDS INNATE?

Animals and humans alike seem to desire freedom for its own sake or for some purpose as general as maximizing opportunity for exploration, stimulation, experimentation, and choice-making. Our family pet turtle, for example, is constantly pushing the limits of her ten-gallon water tank. If she were but stronger, she would have broken through the glass barrier long ago. While she moves less vigorously after a full meal, she still shows a curiosity and interest in her environment, exploring the niches of her tank, pushing her nose into the glass walls as if to get to the places beyond, or looking about the room from her rock.

Even the patriarch of behaviorism, Ivan Pavlov (1957), postulated a "freedom reflex," in part because his dogs so vigorously resisted the confinement of his laboratory experiments. In his paper, "Lectures on the Work of the Cerebral Hemisphere," first delivered in 1924, Pavlov made clear that he meant an even more global urge for freedom:

It is obvious that the freedom reflex is one of the most important reflexes, or, to use the more general term, reactions of any living being. But this reflex is seldom referred to, as if it were not finally recognized. . . . As we know, in some animals the freedom reflex is so strong that when placed in captivity they reject food, pine away and die. (p. 184.)

Thus when modern zoos attempt to replicate natural surroundings, some animals still do not survive in captivity. One of our nearest relatives, the mountain gorilla, is among these, and therefore subject to possible extinction in the near future.

The potential for love is an innate capacity (see chapter 2). While love, as humans understand it, seems beyond her, even our turtle shows an interest in our voices and appearance, and at times seems to enjoy being handled. This reaction to humans might be a conditioned response to food, but members of her species are typically seen in the wild congregating together while sunning themselves on logs. Most likely the heaping up of bodies represents at least in part a social drive rather than competition for scarce log space. Among turtles, then, there probably is a basic need for liberty (freedom) and for love (social contact).

While it may be anthropomorphizing somewhat in regard to the turtle, it is probably correct to see these basic needs expressed in higher animals, especially primates. All the basic needs are expressed and satisfied through their social relationships. Thus both liberty and love are *psychosocial dynamics*—basic needs expressed through specific social arrangements—in animal and human society. In talking about the various characteristics of liberty or love, one is really describing their dynamics.

Is liberty a single need or several, such as freedom, autonomy, and self-esteem? Is a unitary liberty need the source of the drives to explore, to investigate, to roam about, and to seek stimulation? The same question can be asked in regard to love. Is love unitary or a combination of nurturing, caring, touching, and a variety of other needs? There is no simple answer to these questions, which are in part semantic and in part practical in nature. Whether naming a few or many basic needs, most or all of them can be classified within the liberty or love dynamics. Distinguishing when possible between liberty and love can be a great aid in understanding how our needs become expressed in society and with what consequences.

Liberty and love, as dynamics, sometimes seem to be opposed to each other, the one striving toward independence and the other toward interdependence, or the one striving toward separateness and the other toward togetherness. On the other hand, liberty and love often enhance each other. Love provides a basis for granting liberty to others and liberty provides the optimal conditions for love.

COMBINING LIBERTY AND LOVE

Before adults can love each other, they usually need to respect each other's rights, including each other's autonomy and self-determination. Before people will become vulnerable enough to love each other, they usually need guarantees that none of the involved parties will use arbitrary force. They also need to feel safe from being defrauded by lies, cheating, or misrepresentations.

Both liberty and love are basic human needs as well as social dynamics. Sometimes these dynamics seem in opposition, or at least at opposite poles, and sometimes they are complementary. In personal and group relationships there is typically an interaction between the two, with one or the other often taking central stage. Liberty is the optimal setting for the development and expression of love between adults. On the other hand, love in childhood is necessary for the development of autonomous capacities, and in all likelihood, love for other humans is the basis upon which we recognize their equal rights and liberties. Ultimately, love is the more basic human need and the necessary dynamic for the resolution of deep-seated human conflict in the personal and the political arena.

CHAPTER 4

▼ ▼

Understanding Coercion

If certain human needs are not satisfied there will be conflict. The conflict will be of such a character that no suppressive means will contain it. . . . It is mistaken not only in theory, but also pragmatically when coercive and authoritative processes of control are used in an attempt to preserve existing interest and institutions. . . . There is empirical evidence that no bargaining, negotiation, mediation, or any other such process is acceptable to authorities when they believe they have the coercive power at least to contain a situation. . . . This is the case at all social levels, in industry, in community relations, and internationally.
John Burton, Conflict: Resolution and Provention (1990)

Love lets the other be, but with affection and concern. Violence attempts to constrain the other's freedom, to force him to act in the way we desire, but with lack of concern, with indifference to the other's own existence or destiny. We are effectively destroying ourselves by violence masquerading as love.
R.D. Laing, The Politics of Experience (1967)

Civilization is a process in the service of Eros, whose purpose is to combine single human individuals, and after that families, then race, peoples and nations, into one great unity, the unity of mankind. . . . But man's natural aggressive instinct, the hostility of each against all and all against each, opposes this programme of civilization. This aggressive instinct is the derivative and the main representative of the death instinct which we have found alongside of Eros and which shares world-dominion with it. And now, I think, the meaning of the evolution of civilization is no longer obscure to us. It must present the struggle between Eros and Death, between the instinct of life and the instinct of destruction, as it works itself out in the human species.
Sigmund Freud, Civilization and Its Discontents (1930)

Coercion involves outright force or the threat of force. It also includes more subtle methods of intimidation, bullying, or manipulation. Lying, cheating, and misleading people are also coercive.

The aim of coercion is to gain power over another, to put one's own will in place of another's. In short, coercion attempts to *make* people do what they do not wish or choose to do. To refrain from coercing others, and to resist being victimized by it, we must be able to identify coercion and find better alternatives. This is true in both our personal and our political lives.

COERCION AND CONFLICT RESOLUTION

Coercion is a form of conflict resolution or, more accurately, conflict *suppression*. There is widespread agreement within the field of conflict resolution that genuine problem solving is incompatible with the utilization of coercive power (Burton, 1990a).

The use of force, except in self-defense, is the most limited and hazardous approach to relationships and to conflict resolution. It leaves little room for either party—especially the victim—to fulfill any liberty or love needs. In part because coercion encourages people to manipulate each other, to lie, and to hide their vulnerabilities and needs, coercion obstructs the resolution of deep-rooted conflict.

Oppressive actions are frequently cloaked in the language of love: "I did it because I love you" or "If I didn't love you, I wouldn't care so much." Sometimes love of God, country, or other "higher values" are invoked to justify horrible atrocities against others. In reality, both the perpetrator and the victim become impaired in their ability to love others outside the coercive dynamic. Thus coercion is the great impediment to conflict resolution.

DEFINING COERCION

According to the *American Heritage Dictionary of the English Language* (1979), to coerce means "1. To force to act or to think in a given manner; to compel by pressure or threat. 2. To dominate, restrain, or control forcibly." Most dictionaries mention compulsion and restraint, both of which attempt to thwart the individual from acting on his or her own wishes or intentions.

Based on the definition of liberty in chapter 3, *physical* coercion will be defined as the use of force for any purpose other than self-defense, as well as the use of excessive force in self-defense. *Emotional* coercion will be defined more broadly to include all forms of threats and emotional manipulation. This sweeping definition can be justified on the grounds that all forms of coercion, physical and emotional, have somewhat similar negative effects, including the subversion of autonomy and self-determination, and the compromise of self-esteem.

Physical force is not necessarily the most potent means of compelling, restraining, and demoralizing people. Battered women, for example, report that the verbal humiliation they endure is often more debilitating than the beatings (Gelles and Straus, 1988). In clinical practice, the more subtle forms of coercion often have at least as devastating an impact on children as physical brutality. Sometimes the more subtle forms, because they are difficult to identify and to resist, have an even more corrosive effect on personal development. The definition of coercion will therefore include *any* form of emotional oppression, including manipulation and emotional intimidation.

It is not easy to define the more subtle forms of coercion, such as manipulation. Manipulation can include lying or deception, using hidden agendas, providing incomplete information, or playing on someone's personal weaknesses or vulnerabilities. By stirring up fear and helplessness associated with past injuries, the oppressor can pressure the individual to alter his or her chosen course.

While the broad definition of coercion raises many unanswered questions, it can be turned to practical use with very specific applications. In particular, it reminds us that *all threatening and manipulative actions or communications, for any purpose whatsoever, have somewhat similar negative outcomes.*

THE NEGATIVE EFFECTS OF COERCION

Coercion by the most well-meaning person, for the most well-intentioned purposes, still has untoward consequences. When the outcome does seem largely beneficial, coercive methods are likely to have some negative effects, including the subversion of free will and personal freedom. As Gandhi and others have observed (see chapter 11), even force in self-defense is not free of harmful side effects, although it will not be defined as coercion.

The principle that coercion always has some negative consequences is probably not subject to proof or disproof. Rather it is an assumption or viewpoint of use in organizing experience. In testing such a hypothesis, one must rely mostly upon personal experience, including one's own inner reactions to being coerced, as well as one's perceptions of the responses of others. Beyond that, there is each person's general knowledge of human affairs. One of the aims of this book is to demonstrate the usefulness of viewing all coercion—including that which seems culturally or generally accepted, routine, and innocuous—with caution and concern. This includes the emotional bullying that routinely takes place in the family and social lives of many people, the frequently oppressive control of children in the home and schools, the similar oppression of women throughout most of the society, involuntary treatment in psychiatry, and many or most government interventions.

These two fundamental assumptions—that all forms of coercion create negative effects and that these effects are somewhat similar regardless of the form of coercion—have practical importance in how conflict resolution is approached. They encourage a close scrutiny of any and all attempts to use coercion, and they discourage its use as much as possible in human affairs. This has vast implications for many spheres of human activity in which coercion is frequently the sanctioned or most commonly accepted approach to resolving conflict, including family relationships, childrearing, most governmental activities, involuntary psychiatry, authoritarian religion, and war. This chapter will focus on interpersonal coercion, while others will focus on broader societal issues, including coercion by the state.

COERCION IN PERSONAL LIFE

It is the individual's right in his or her personal life to define coercion from a strictly personal and subjective viewpoint (Breggin, 1980). A person has the right to say "I *feel* coerced" and then to take nonviolent protective actions, such as rejecting or avoiding another adult or a situation that merely *feels* or *seems* coercive. The right to make a subjective definition of coercion, and to remove oneself from the oppressor, is central to personal freedom. Yet many people become confused and believe that they must or should submit themselves to family, friends, and other people whose attitudes and actions feel oppressive.

The principle must be modified in regard to dependent children, as well as disabled adults, especially those with whom we have contracted to help. We cannot tie a fellow mountain climber to our rope and then decide to cut it. We cannot have a child and then abandon it. We cannot agree to care for physically helpless people and then walk out on them. But in dealing with most adults in personal relationships, it is critical to retain the right to remove ourselves from situations that feel oppressive or coercive, even if love or other considerations lead us not to exercise the right at any given moment.

The subjective definition of coercion does not guarantee that an individual's perceptions will be rational. People often react with irrational fear to current situations on the basis of past negative experiences (see chapter 5). Nonetheless, any attempt to limit the right to define coercion on a subjective basis will vastly encroach upon personal freedom. A person must have the right to say, "I'm not comfortable with Harold, and I'm going to avoid him."

However, if the use of actual force is being considered, coercion must be limited to self-defense. We cannot hit people because we don't like them, their ideas, or their looks.

FORCE IN SELF-DEFENSE

Force in self-defense can become excessive and hence coercive, and therefore constraints on self-defense have been embodied in Western law. If we have disarmed an assailant, we do not then have the right to shoot him in retaliation for the harm he has done. If a relatively small child or weak adult strikes us, we do not have the right to unnecessarily injure the perpetrator in the process of defending ourselves. These issues become important in family life where adults too often find flimsy excuses for battering children and where men frequently respond to a slap in the face from a woman with a jaw-breaking counterpunch.

Within our personal lives, we can and should apply the same principle of the least possible amount of force in self-defense to emotional interchanges.

A MINIMAL STANDARD

The prohibition against the use of force except in self-defense should be seen as a minimal standard for developing loving relationships and for resolving deep-seated conflict. Often we must go beyond this standard, enduring a certain amount of aggression out of love, out of the desire to avoid doing any harm even in self-defense (see chapter 2), and out of a conviction that patience and kindness may at times encourage much better long-term results than swift or knee-jerk self-defense.

When genuine efforts are being made to end long-standing conflicts, it may be necessary for all parties to the conflict to refrain from using force even in self-defense. When conflicts have a long history, everyone involved tends to see himself or herself as a victim of aggression who is merely reacting in self-defense. This is true of married couples (see chapter 6) and nations at war alike. Restraint, even in self-defense, becomes critical to the early stages of conflict resolution. Each side is likely to continue seeing provocation as part of the now endless chain of violence, and each side will have to make every effort not to retaliate.

Love, which abhors force and rejects injuring the other person, is the most potent antidote to the use of force in self-defense. But individuals and nations who sit down at the conflict-resolution table are not initially likely to feel or to admit much affection for each other. In the beginning, restraint on the use of force can best be encouraged through a rational cost analysis. Both parties need to understand that the cost of tit-for-tat, or more massive retaliation, is too great once they have committed themselves to conflict resolution. The momentary "gratification" of striking back must be replaced with a long-range perspective on the infinitely greater rewards that will come from ending the conflict. It is the task of the therapist or conflict resolver to communicate this vision of the future.

THE PRICE OF COERCION: THE IMPACT ON THE PERPETRATOR

From the start it is important to realize that coercion has many negative effects on the perpetrator as well as the victim.

Consistent with the proposition that coercion of most kinds has certain more or less inevitable and uniform consequences, the categories of *perpetrators* and *victims* will be addressed broadly, at times referring to physical assault and at others to more subtle intimidation and manipulation. The term perpetrator will be broadly used to include anyone who coerces another. The models include more extreme forms of coercion, including violent dictators, Nazis involved in extermination programs, "madmen" who commit heinous and seemingly unprovoked violence, rapists, and wife and child abusers. Other models are drawn from family life as seen in clinical practice, including the more or less commonplace verbal and emotional abuse seen in many families. Through my psychiatric reform and forensic activities, I also have extensive experience with psychiatrists and other physicians who injure and oppress their patients.

The idea that perpetrators themselves suffer from what they do to others is foreign to many people; but in understanding why coercion should be eschewed even by the powerful, it is important to grasp the price that coercion extracts from all parties involved. Besides, most perpetrators were victims to start with. Their destructive activities are spawned in part by their own experience at the hands of oppressors. This does not mean that all abused people become abusers. Most do not. It does mean that most severe abusers were themselves victims, usually as small children.

It is also true that perpetrators often seem to benefit emotionally from their actions. Murderers and rapists, for example, often report feeling empowered and even euphoric for a time after their assaults on others. On the other hand, many brutal crimes seem perpetrated in a kind of fugue state with little overt feeling attached. Regardless of whether or not there is something akin to pleasure involved in perpetrating, there are typical negative consequences for the perpetrator as well.

PERPETRATOR DENIAL AND RATIONALIZATION

Perpetrators do not necessarily recognize, accept, or even recall their harmful actions or their consequences. Frequently, for example, they fail to acknowledge that even the most brutal violence causes suffering among its victims. Men who rape women and husbands who beat their wives almost always deny the severity of the brutality involved, including the amount of force employed, as well as the amount of physical and emotional pain that it caused. On the political scale, we recently saw the American attack on Iraq as a rather bloodless war because the United States lost so few soldiers. To wholeheartedly cheer such an outcome required denial or disregard for the hundreds of thousands of civilian and military victims on the "other side," as well as among friendly populations, such as the Kurds (see chapter 10).

Women, children, ethnic and racial minorities, slaves, mental patients, the enemy in wartime, and the poor are often the objects of systematic persecution and abuse. Perpetrators of violence against these groups frequently declare that their victims are somehow relatively immune or unresponsive to the suffering inflicted upon them. Often perpetrators and their apologists will argue that coercion and abuse is good for these victims and even that they want it. Frequently, of course, it is said that they deserve it.

Denial and rationalization of the impact of coercion is routinized in establishment theory. Women labeled witches were once systematically tortured and burned at the stake and nowadays people labeled mental patients are subjected to electroshock, lobotomies, and toxic drugs—always for their own good. Learned books have been written to say it is for their own good.

As I describe in *Toxic Psychiatry* (1991), psychiatrists commonly argue that extremely toxic drugs, such as the neuroleptics (e.g., Haldol, Thorazine, Mellaril, Prolixin), don't cause physical or emotional suffering to "mentally ill" people because their brains are different. To embellish the argument, it is said that these unfortunates suffer from biochemical imbalances that the drugs correct, thereby in fact reducing their suffering. I have heard survivors of psychiatry protest in outrage when "drug experts" make these claims. Yet the rationalizations continue, despite patient protests and mountains of research to the contrary.

Similarly, psychiatrists explain that involuntary patients often say in retrospect that they are glad they were incarcerated, drugged, or shocked against their will. These psychiatrists remain oblivious to the fact that the patients have to tell them this in order to get released or to stave off further assaults against their minds and bodies (see p. 82). Nor do they take into account that the desire to be controlled against one's will can be a sign of a self-defeating, self-hating approach to life. In my own psychiatric practice, for example, when a patient seems to want me to take over his or her life, I encourage the patient to adopt a more autonomous, self-determined outlook.

Dictators are especially fond of explaining how their efforts are directed by God for the common good. Why abject terror is required to keep their supposedly blessed citizens in submission is never fully explained, except perhaps with references to outside agitators and enemy nations.

Denial and rationalization also takes place on a more personal level. The rapist explains that women like to be forced to submit to sex. The perpetrator of incest argues that it is good for his children. There is no end to these rationalizations, both institutionalized and personal.

Truth, then, is one of the costs of coercion to the perpetrator. The perpetrator loses contact with reality. The oppressed, for example, may shock him by unexpectedly rebelling or fighting back. If the perpetrator has any genuine interest in helping or relating to the individuals he is oppressing, there will be little chance of his knowing what to offer.

SELF-DECEPTION

It is common for perpetrators to deny to themselves the very existence of their crimes. In traditional psychoanalysis, the deed is said to have become "unconscious" or split off from awareness. But when men "forget" that they have hit their wives or when mothers cannot recall that they have humiliated their children, it seems more useful and enlightening to think of these perpetrators as *lying* to themselves much as they would lie to others.

In couples and family therapy, perpetrators frequently describe their actions without "remembering" that a blow was struck or a violent epithet hurled at the victim. If the event was recent, and if the victim is present, it is usually possible to get the individual to admit to recalling what actually happened. Then rationalization replaces denial: "Oh, it wasn't so bad, was it?" or "You provoked me." When weeks, months, or years have passed, the perpetrator frequently continues to deny any recollection of the events, even when reminded of them in detail by the victim or bystanders.

Furthermore, if the victim is not available to present his or her side, the perpetrator can easily fool himself and the therapist alike. This is perhaps the gravest disadvantage of individual psychotherapy— the ease with which perpetrators neglect and cover up their harmful actions.

Has the perpetrator's "forgotten" deed become truly unconscious—locked outside his or her awareness? What does "unconscious" mean in such a context? Again, I find the concept of lying to oneself and others more useful. It can become impossible to determine who the lie is aimed at, oneself or others, and often it makes little actual difference. Nor should a deed that has become "unconscious" be treated as ethically less reprehensible. Often it simply means that the person has started lying to himself or herself as well as to others.

In summary, perpetrators often develop elaborate forms of denial, including self-deception, in dealing with their destructiveness. This can be considered one of the costs of being a perpetrator. It often prevents the perpetrator from understanding the conflict surrounding his or her activities, making the perpetrator unable to respond to the situation in a rational or effective manner.

IMPACT ON PERSONAL RELATIONSHIPS

Among the most serious effects on the perpetrator are those generated in the relationship between the perpetrator and the victim. Violence tends to break the social bonds that attach people to one another. Detachment from the victim is often accomplished by dehumanization—placing the victim in a category of lesser being, one especially deserving of manipulation, punishment, injury, or even extermination. All people outside the dominant social group are at risk for being dehumanized, including racial, religious, and cultural minorities; women; children; enemies in wartime; and various "social deviants," such as mental patients and criminals. Frequently perpetrators assign them specific negative labels, including various racial, national, or cultural epithets. Whether an enemy in wartime or a wife in domestic conflict is being abused, the tendency to dehumanize is basically the same.

Why do perpetrators dehumanize their victims? They do so in part to control or obliterate their own tendency to empathize and to love. Few people, including very oppressive ones, are wholly devoid of empathy. Perpetrators often find it hard to accept that they are treating people unjustly or inflicting pain upon them, especially if the victims are seen as "just like us" or "just like our family and friends." So perpetrators make believe their victims are different. In my own field of psychiatry, diagnosis has served this purpose for centuries. The individual labeled schizophrenic is turned into a non-person. An endless variety of brain-damaging treatments become justified, sometimes including a lifetime of incarceration under the most horrendous circumstances.

Again in order to detach themselves from what they are doing to their victims, perpetrators often convince themselves that their victims want or need to be coerced, despite evidence to the contrary. At a recent professional debate in which I participated, a psychiatrist defended involuntary treatment by citing studies that found that some patients will state in retrospect that they are glad to have been forced into treatment. I pointed out that the patients in the study were interviewed by the same doctors who had incarcerated them against their will and that the patients continued to be exposed to repeated involuntary treatment at their hands. However, the psychiatrist refused to acknowledge that the continued threat of involuntary treatment might have influenced these patients to say what the doctor wanted to hear.

We would hope that psychiatrists would have special sensitivity to the impact of coercion on their victims, yet they regularly deny that incarcerating people, or drugging and shocking them against their will, has negative effects on them. When I worked in state mental hospitals as a college student, I was told by psychiatrists that "schizophrenics" were less sensitive to changes in temperature. Thus, it was rationalized, they did not suffer from the seasonal extremes of freezing cold and suffocating heat on the poorly heated, poorly ventilated wards.

The labeling can even become microscopic. Well-known psychiatrists once argued that shock treatment works by killing sick brain cells while somehow exempting the healthy ones (Breggin, 1979, 1991).

Blaming victims is another method used by perpetrators to salve their consciences, as well as to mislead others (Ryan, 1976). Women and children are routinely blamed for the physical, sexual, and verbal abuse heaped upon them. Somehow they have elicited or evoked the violent responses against themselves. The violent madman image has been used for centuries to justify the incarceration, torture, and even death of millions of helpless mental hospital inmates (Breggin, 1991). As a psychiatrist working in mental hospitals, most of the violence I witnessed was in reality initiated by the staff. In response to involuntary incarceration and treatment, inmates do sometimes become violent, thus leading the doctors to justify further coercion.

Despite these self-protective attempts to justify coercion, many perpetrators continue to feel badly about their actions, and therefore they try to dull their feelings of empathy. They must "disconnect" from their own feelings, particularly their feelings for others. The caring place within their hearts is cauterized. This psychospiritual lobotomy is probably the most frequent psychological cost of chronic perpetration.

Perpetrators thus dehumanize their victims and themselves. This alienation from self and others is marked by a suppression of their own social feelings and their ability to love. One of the most violent offenders I have interviewed expressed more remorse than usual about what he had done, but his most marked feeling was despair for himself that he could not feel close to people.

It is of course difficult to determine whether the alienation felt by so many perpetrators is the cause of their violence or the result of it. Clinical experience indicates that violence is frequently motivated by alienation, and that violent acts then reinforce the alienation. However, it seems that even emotionally responsive people, after committing violence, suffer from alienation. This can be seen in soldiers who find themselves committing unexpected acts of violence. One reason the Nazis developed relatively aseptic murder techniques in closed gas chambers was to avoid the emotional toll that more openly brutal mass killing had taken on the soldiers carrying them out.

Although we might wish it were otherwise, *overt* or *expressed* guilt is not a common response to injuring others. Guilt, at least expressed guilt, is ironically more common in victims then in perpetrators. Former Nazis, for example, almost never displayed guilt or shame when interviewed. The same is true of men who rape and batter women. But the *victims* of Nazi brutality and the victims of male brutality frequently feel guilt and shame. Why victims feel guilt and shame will be discussed in chapter 5.

Overwhelming shame and guilt does sometimes well up within perpetrators. Many mass murderers end up turning the gun on themselves. Many Nazis committed suicide, at least after being accused or captured. However, it is unclear how much these suicides were in reaction to recognizing the monstrousness of their crimes. Some of the suicides may have resulted from shame and fear over having to face the consequences of their actions, including the humiliation of public disapproval. They would rather die than go on trial or face a death penalty. Other Nazis who killed themselves may have been trying to thwart the authorities from using them to indict others or to discredit the Nazi party.

Psychotherapists frequently conclude that the alienation found commonly in perpetrators is actually a veneer that covers unbearable guilt and shame. While this is perhaps true, the perpetrator's guilt and shame is not usually felt toward his or her victims, but toward those who have victimized the perpetrator in earlier years. For example, a man who was sexually abused as a child may feel guilt and shame about it and yet inflict the same cruelties on another generation of children without remorse. To repeat, the victim, not the perpetrator, tends to feel guilt and shame.

Most perpetrators never express any negative feelings about harming others. As Lonnie Athens dramatically documented in *The Creation of Dangerous Violent Criminals* (1989), people who commit horrendous physical assaults against innocent victims almost always have themselves been extraordinarily abused and humiliated while growing up. They feel shame about what was done to them in the past, not about what they have done more recently to others. Instead, they consider their own acts of violence to be justified in defense of their own "pride." The hapless victims of their murderous rage "deserved it" due to some real or imagined slight or insult.

Consistent with their alienation and lack of remorse, perpetrators rarely seek psychotherapeutic help. When they come to therapy, it is usually under duress from the courts or under the threat of being rejected by their spouses. In therapy, they tend to be nonreflective and "out of touch" in regard to themselves. They have little awareness of their own feelings or motives. Sometimes they can be helped by reexperiencing the humiliations they have undergone, typically in childhood; but it is much harder to help them gain sympathy for those whom they have gone on to oppress. Instead they often blame their victims for provoking them and restimulating their previous feelings of humiliation.

While some perpetrators can get in touch with their prior experiences of personal humiliation, more typically they are too emotionally cut off from their own feelings. As a result, they are also cut off intellectually from these past experiences and tend not to understand or grasp their own personal histories of being oppressed by others. Male perpetrators of sexual violence, for example, were frequently abused as children either physically or sexually by older boys and men; but often they do not recall it. If the abuse was physical, they may remember some of it, but interpret it as normal and justifiable. They "deserved" to be hit or being hit was "the way it was" in their family. If the abuse was sexual, it becomes almost impossible to get them to talk about it.

Jerome Miller, director of the Center for Institutions and Alternatives, recounted to me the stories of two men who confessed to him that they had been raped by the men they had later murdered. However, they would not let Miller tell anyone they had been raped, even though the mitigating circumstance might have saved them from the electric chair. These men were so ashamed of having been raped, they literally chose to die rather than to let a judge or state governor know about it.

As an aside, relevant to the psychospiritual approach required of healers and conflict resolvers, I asked Miller how he could maintain such profound sympathy for the extremely violent criminals with whom he often works in his rehabilitation program and in his attempts to save murderers from execution. He replied, "It comes from understanding them." He further explained that once you understand what someone has been through, it is hard to hate them for what they themselves go on to do. He didn't mean to excuse perpetrators; he meant to say that they almost always begin as victims of other perpetrators. Miller's profoundly caring viewpoint is precisely what perpetrators themselves become unable to feel or to express.

Recognizing that he himself was abused would require the perpetrator to face his own abusive ways. Conversely, to recognize his own abusive ways would require grasping what others did to him, especially in childhood. The perpetrator becomes locked into a cycle where he cannot face how he has been abused or how he has abused others.

In *Escape from Freedom*, Erich Fromm described the "authoritarian personality" produced by suppressive, rigid, and often physically abusive family life in Germany. Instead of realizing what had been done to them, and rejecting similar violence against others, the victims too often went on to become perpetrators. Later, they filled the rolls of the Nazi party.

It is commonly thought that perpetrators excuse their actions on the basis of how they grew up. To the contrary, as I've noted, they tend to deny childhood abuse. Miller, who has worked with hundreds of murderers, rapists, wife abusers, and other perpetrators states that he has never seen a case in which a perpetrator used his own childhood to excuse his conduct. I am also unaware of any such cases in my clinical experience. Oppressive authorities from childhood are often excused while the person blames himself, or more frequently, blames the people he has victimized.

EFFECTS ON PERPETRATORS OF BREAKING SOCIAL BONDS

Perpetrators often grow afraid that others will retaliate, and partly as a result of this, perpetrators tend to escalate their violence. They do so as if to deny or to defy their fear, and they do so to intimidate and control the victims from whom they fear retaliation. Perhaps their own violence convinces them that it is indeed a dog-eat-dog world as they had been taught as children. Sometimes it appears as if there is a kind of demonic potential in people, perhaps the residue of our own past hurts and our evolutionary endowment, that once allowed to express itself violently tends to grow more bold. Perhaps it is a matter of breaking the social bonds. Once the "human connection" to others has been cut by violence, all restraints are removed. Whatever the cause, violence sometimes feeds on itself, and perpetrators often tend to grow more violent with repeated acts of coercion. At the same time, they will grow more out of touch with themselves and with others.

Grandiosity is a another consequence of perpetration. Once the bond of respect and love between humans is broken, once the line is crossed in restraint toward other people—perpetrators tend to grow more grandiose. Having taken a god-like stance toward others, they begin to live the part more fully, becoming more controlling, more dominating, more self-centered. It is as if the bonds between people, and the constraints inherent in them, are necessary for our maintenance of perspective on ourselves. If we separate ourselves from others by acting violently against them, we risk becoming focused on ourselves as the center of the universe. We imagine powers that we do not have and we lose track of our vulnerability. This can lead perpetrators to do seemingly self-destructive acts, such as repeating their crimes until they get caught or until they drive their victims into violent counteractions.

This cycle of increasingly compulsive and eventually self-defeating violence can be seen in men who batter their wives until their victims rebel and even kill their tormentors (Walker, 1989). It is found in rapists and other violent persons who repeat an obvious pattern of crime until they are caught. It can be seen when political leaders initiate wars they cannot possibly win. As a medical expert in malpractice suits, I have testified in cases involving psychiatrists and other physicians who have injured their patients with drugs, electroshock, and even lobotomies, and then repeat the "treatments" again and again despite obviously worsening damage. In one case, psychiatrists nearly killed a woman with a dangerous combination of drugs and then immediately resumed it even before she was fully recovered. In another, neurosurgeons lobotomized a patient on three separate occasions. In these cases, the physicians typically refer to themselves as using "heroic treatments."

In order to control their victims, perpetrators must learn to hide from them their real intentions and agendas. A battering husband, for example, will often disguise his intent, and make promises of complete reform. So will a dictator bent on controlling or exterminating another group. By hiding themselves from their victims, perpetrators further break the social bonds between themselves and their victims. In that process, the perpetrator also begins to fool himself. Humans are such social creatures that they often prefer to lie to themselves rather than to admit that they are lying regularly to others. The perpetrator thus becomes further alienated from himself in the process of denying his own ill-intentions and malevolent actions.

As Alfred Adler (Adler, 1969; Ansbacher and Ansbacher, 1956) observed decades ago, all people want to believe they are doing the right or good thing, and that impulse, again a social one, further leads perpetrators to fool themselves about what they are doing.

Perpetrators end up tangled in a web of lies that they themselves often come to believe. Out of feelings of insecurity and inferiority, people strive for power and superiority. The power-seeking individual also loses contact with himself and with reality. He or she develops subjective "fictions"—rigid, false beliefs aimed at bolstering a flagging sense of worth.

According to Adler, the individual who strives for superiority eventually becomes "self-bounded":

The self-bounded individual always forgets that his self would be safeguarded better and automatically the more he prepares himself for the welfare of mankind, and that in this respect no limits are set for him. (Ansbacher and Ansbacher, 1956, p. 112.)

Thus individuals devoted to coercing others actually abandon their true interests, their connectedness with the human community.

Karen Horney (1950) described the fundamental "neurotic" problem as the individual's attempt to fulfill his or her idealized or glorified self-image. When this happens, according to Horney, "The energies driving toward self-realization are shifted to the aim of actualizing the idealized self," (p. 24). Instead of fulfilling the basic needs for love, creativity, and genuine human relationships, the individual pursues "the search for glory" and his or her "will to power" takes on "magical proportions." Power and control over others become the ultimate aim, with increasing alienation from self and from others.

Ultimately, perpetrators cannot genuinely love. Nor are they in turn truly loved. They cannot empathize with the individuals they seek to injure and control; and those whom they victimize must withdraw from them in self-defense. Writing in the year 1552 or 1553, Etienne de la Boetie declared:

The fact is that the tyrant is never truly loved, nor does he love. Friendship is a sacred word, a holy thing; it is never developed except between persons of character, and never takes root except through mutual respect. . . (p. 83.)

THE PERPETRATOR SYNDROME

We can now summarize the perpetrator syndrome: the constellation of attributes found in most people who persistently coerce others. Perpetrators tend to:

1. *Deny or minimize the damage they are doing to others,* for example, by failing to recognize their own coercive actions, by under-estimating the sensitivity of those they are abusing, and by imagining that the victims like what is being done to them.

2. *Rationalize the harm they are doing,* for example, by alleging that the perpetrations are ultimately in the best interest of victims, better than other alternatives, a necessary last resort, or otherwise inevitable and unavoidable.

3. *Blame the victim.* This is a derivative of denial and rationalization, but is worth mentioning in its own right. Typically, perpetrators accuse the victim of being the malicious or dangerous one, or the provocateur. By blaming others, they reject responsibility for their own actions.

4. *Suppress their own feelings of empathy,* thereby blunting their emotional responsiveness to their victims. Often they blunt their empathic responsiveness toward themselves and all other people as well, and become unable to love. They become withdrawn from themselves and others.

5. *Deny or rationalize their own prior victimization at the hands of others,* including the abuse they were subjected to as children and adults. They do not tend to excuse their perpetrations on the grounds that they themselves have been previously victimized.

6. *Persistently react with anger and blame toward others based on much earlier feelings of shame and humiliation.* Sometimes the anger is very covert and indirect in its expression. Often the feelings of shame are denied. While guilt and anxiety can also drive people to abuse others, shame seems by far the most common emotional basis for perpetration, especially in its most severe forms. Rapists and murders, for

example, are almost always driven by childhood shame. Shame will be discussed in greater depth in chapter 5.

7. *Dehumanize their victims.* The victim is defined as inferior due to his or her status or condition as a man, woman, child, criminal, mental patient, foreigner, racial minority, etc. Perpetrators try to overcome their own feelings of inferiority and to elevate themselves to a superior status by dominating others.

8. *Feel empowered through their perpetrations.* They do not feel guilt or shame about the harm that they do to others. When they do feel guilt or shame, it is in response to their own earlier victimization by others. Their perpetrations are motivated by their earlier victimization.

9. *Seek to resolve conflicts through authority, power, and domination,* sometimes directly through physical violence, sometimes indirectly through socially sanctioned authority. When they feel threatened with possible exposure or censure, they often tend to escalate their perpetrations, and may not be stopped unless confronted with overwhelming power.

10. *Become grandiose and self-centered.* They imagine that they have the power and the right to obtain their ends through force, and feel a certain degree of invulnerability, at least when they are in the act of perpetration. This can lead to the self-destructive escalation of their perpetrations to the point that they are confronted or exposed.

11. *Become alienated from their genuine basic needs,* especially those related to love.

The perpetrator syndrome is found in almost every sphere of life. It includes men and women who abuse their spouses and children, rapists and murders, bullies on the playground or in the workplace, conmen and others who prey upon the vulnerabilities of other people, most biological psychiatrists, police who resort to brutality, political tyrants, and anyone who seeks to dominate and manipulate others.

The syndrome is not always present in all its aspects, but very often it is. It can be difficult to determine which traits are derived from earlier victimization and which are the result of the actual perpetrations. The shame and humiliation tend to originate from the earlier victimization (see chapter 5) and the alienation probably results from both victimization and perpetration.

THE COST OF COERCION: THE IMPACT ON THE VICTIM

One might wish that perpetration would cause the perpetrator to feel guilt, shame, and anxiety, but more typically their victims do. While it seems easily understandable that victims might experience anxiety, and perhaps even shame, it seems at first glance more puzzling that they also experience guilt. The key, I believe, is the psychological helplessness that is engendered in the victim, making him or her vulnerable to guilt, shame, or anxiety. For example, after a young boy is beaten up in a fight, he may feel guilt for getting into a fight, shame over not performing better, or anxiety over what may happen to him in the future—all depending on his circumstances and his learned style of responding.

It is extremely important to understand the development of negative emotions as a result of victimization. It is impossible to analyze conflict without such an understanding (see chapter 5).

VICTIM DISHONESTY

While perpetrators lie to others and sometimes to themselves in order to cover up their abuses, victims learn to lie and to dissemble in order to avoid or minimize further oppression. When a victim habitually lies about his thoughts, feelings, and actions, it can become a serious impediment to conflict resolution.

Often parents ask me what to do about their child's lying to them. Their attitude generally suggests that something more should be done directly to the child. Instead, I explain that children lie out of fear and distrust. Typically, they feel unfairly coerced. Therefore, the parents need to change in order to create an environment that is relatively free of fear and distrust.

In dismay, the parents may ask me, "But what would you do if your child lied to you?" And I tell them that I would try not to punish my already intimidated child. Instead, I'd try to understand why my son or daughter was in such fear of me.

Children lie because they don't believe that telling the truth will gain them a fair hearing or a fair punishment, let alone a sympathetic, caring ear. Often lying has become a useful and even necessary defense against arbitrary authority and coercion. It can be more effective than lapsing into psychological helplessness (see chapter 5). The abused adult or child may have no other protection against arbitrary authority, capricious punishment, and hateful or insensitive authorities. As helplessness deepens in response to chronic abuse, the individual may even give up lying, throwing himself or herself on the mercy of the oppressor.

Children and other oppressed people also lie in order to manipulate the situation as much as they can. Doubting that the authority in power is genuinely interested in supporting their most basic needs for self-determination, self-esteem, or love—they seek ways around the authority through flattery, fakery, or the like. Meanwhile, they avoid at all costs becoming still more vulnerable and dependent by admitting or displaying their basic needs. "I don't need nothin' from you" is the typical response of the victim, as long as some shred of dignity remains.

No one wants to be coerced. As we have seen, humans and nonhuman alike value their liberty. In human beings, this need becomes quite elaborate. It includes the desire to think for oneself, to make choices, to exercise reason, to seek justice. As already described, the need for liberty dovetails with the need to love and to be loved. When the individual feels subject to abuse or arbitrary control, he or she tends to hide these needs in order to seem less vulnerable.

The tendency of victims to hide their basic needs is one of the great costs of oppression. A battered child or an abused woman, for example, may be the last to express his or her needs for self-respect and love. In self-defense and in defense against the pain of oppression, these needs have been buried. Often the victim no longer believes that he or she deserves to have a better life. Even when the oppressor lets up, or is gone, the compulsion to hide one's needs and feelings of unworthiness or worthlessness may persist. Thus the people most in need of great doses of self-respect and love are often the least likely to show their needs or to reach out for their fulfillment.

When the victim hides his or her needs, this can also create a cost to the oppressor. Thus abusive parents drive their children into hiding and cheat themselves of the capacity to connect to them in a loving way.

IS COERCION A BASIC NEED?

Conflict analysis and resolution theory often equates basic needs with "good" or pro-survival needs. Tendencies toward violence, greed, or envy are thus not seen as "basic needs" but as perversions or distortions, usually in reaction to frustration and helplessness.

It seems possible that built-in violent tendencies served evolutionary purposes, and became basic needs; but they now have no place in larger, more complex societies in which huge numbers of people must get along in close proximity. For example, fear and violence toward strangers could have had survival value when humans lived in smaller, more widely dispersed groups. The group that best protected itself and its territory may have most readily reproduced. It has been speculated that human beings killed off all their near-human hominid competitors. In particular, homo sapiens and Neanderthal man crossed historical paths, but only homo sapiens kept going. If we did murder our nearest of kin 100,000 years ago, it is consistent with our modern behavior as well.

Murdering strangers or upright creatures who look a little different from us did not threaten our own survival when fists, rocks, or spears were our only weapons. But violent impulses toward others is obviously self-defeating in the age of atomic weapons.

I am not wholly wedded to the biological basis of human violence. But unfortunately, it seems highly probable that human nature has not evolved in perfect harmony with the needs of a modern global community. There is every indication that it has not. This reality must be taken as a challenge rather than a cause for despair.

It is also possible that the demands of culture itself, or the inherent problems in raising human beings, inevitably create aggressive or even violent tendencies in some individuals. I see no way to come to final conclusions on these matters.

There are, of course, many dangers in the sociobiological view, as represented by E. O. Wilson (1978), that human beings are genetically aggressive. I am cautious as I suggest that the evidence favors a built-in tendency toward coercion and even violence. The socio-biological view can lead to glossing over the environmental stresses that clinical (Miller, 1984) and sociological studies (Gelles and Straus, 1988) often find at the root of extremely violent behavior. Most perpetrators were themselves victims, often in their child-hood. Genetic theories of violence can lead to an overemphasis on police control at the expense of ameliorating underlying causes in society. Often they are used to justify racism and xenophobia. Ge-netic explanations also encourage denial of the patriarchal influ-ences that cause male-dominated society to place a positive value on power, control, and aggression (French, 1985; Eisler, 1987). Within modern psychiatry, genetic and biochemical theories of violence are used to justify the diagnosing and drugging of so-called hyperactive children (Breggin, 1991). As a result, the underlying environmental causes of upset in these children, including child abuse, usually go unattended. Even obvious toxic causes, such as lead poisoning, may not be investigated. Overall, scientific arguments for genetic and constitutional causes of violence are weak (Fausto-Sterling, 1985).

Most important, *individual variations in violent behavior have no known relationship to genetic or constitutional factors* (Fasto-Sterling, 1985). There is no evidence that chromosomal aberrations, race, or other factors increase violence. The problem is not that some hu-mans are genetically more violent than others; it is that all humans have these tendencies.

Destructive behavior is sufficiently widespread and culturally universal that it seems an aspect of human nature. The desire to use excessive or unwarranted force is something most or all people seem to struggle with, and too often it is expressed in arbitrary and damaging ways. Gandhi, for example, referred to the constant struggle within himself to tame these reactions (Bondurant, 1988). Jane Goodall (1986) was disillusioned to discover that chimpanzees can become murderously violent, and she has publicly warned that human beings must also recognize and surmount this same ten-dency within themselves.

The evidence suggests that while human beings are a violent species, the manner and degree to which that violence gets ex-pressed is determined in large part by environmental experience within the family and the culture, as well as by individual self-determination (see chapter 5). A great deal of male violence, for example, is directly attributable to culture values, including patriarchy with its emphasis on domination and control (French, 1985; Eisler, 1987; Yllo and Bograd, 1988). Group support for male violence, as in wartime, mobs, and gangs, also seems to bring out the worst in men.

From my research and from my personal and clinical experience, I have come to the following conclusions: (1) All people struggle with violence within themselves, although sometimes they seem unaware of the meaning or implications of their hostile thoughts, feelings, and actions; (2) The intensity and direction of the feelings are greatly influenced by victimization in childhood and adulthood; (3) Patriarchal values of power and control encourage men to indulge in physical violence, as well as emotional abuse, often directed most viciously toward women and children; (4) Humiliation in the family and culture pushes many women to feel persistent bitterness and anger that typically becomes expressed verbally rather than physically; (5) While nearly all severe perpetrators of violence have been victims of physical abuse and/or humiliation earlier in their lives, most victimized children do not grow up to become perpetrators; (6) The human spirit can, and frequently does, overcome early environmental and later cultural pressures in order to live a more principled life.

In conclusion, coercion always has a cost for the victim. Most obviously, it creates psychological helplessness, including guilt, shame, and anxiety in the victim (see chapter 5). It encourages victims to lie and to dissemble. It also exacts a price from the perpetrator in terms of the perpetrator syndrome with unrealistic self-appraisals and an alienation from oneself and others.

Coercion, in all its many manifestations, has little or no place in conflict resolution. At best it is a stopgap measure that temporarily suppresses conflict, ultimately increasing its ferocity. Even when coercion seems a necessity, it interferes with liberty and with love, and ultimately with the resolution of conflict.

From the psychological to the interpersonal and the global, the resort to coercion remains one of the greatest obstacles to conflict resolution. Those who seek to help others resolve conflict must stand forthrightly for the values of liberty and love. Instead of pretending or attempting to take a value-free stance, they should openly seek to educate people on the hazards and costs of coercion and on the merits and benefits of liberty and love.

▼ ▼

Part II

Applying the Three Dynamics to Conflict Resolution

CHAPTER 5

▼ ▼

Resolving Psychological Conflict: Overcoming Childhood Helplessness and Vulnerability

It is easy to substitute our will for that of the child by means of suggestion or coercion; but when we have done this we have robbed him of his greatest right, the right to construct his own personality.
Maria Montessori, in E. M. Standing, **Maria Montessori** (1957)

✓ *Every defect of character is due to some wrong treatment sustained by the child during his early years.*
Maria Montessori, **The Absorbent Mind** (1969)

[C]hildhood is the key to understanding a person's entire later life. By becoming sensitive to childhood suffering, I gained emotional insight into the predicament of the totally dependent child, who must repress his trauma if there is no sympathetic and supportive person he can talk to. . . . The child in his or her helplessness awakens a feeling of power in insecure adults and, in addition, in many cases becomes their preferred sexual object.
Alice Miller, **Thou Shalt Not Be Aware** (1984)

When people are enduring stress and conflict, there comes a crucial moment when they either take control of their thoughts or lapse into helplessness. At these critical times, the central question of the individual's mental life becomes, "Will I become helpless or instead take charge of myself?"

The decision can take place out of habit and without thinking, but frequently there is an instant when the individual begins to feel overwhelmed and then consciously decides, "I give up." Often a corresponding moment can be identified when the person instead determines to "keep my head" or to "stay calm" while deciding how best to proceed. Optimally, the individual may even remain loving when confronted with hostility and rejection.

Once helplessness takes over under stress, all is lost. The person becomes a victim of overwhelming emotional reactions, other people, and circumstance. Even if circumstances turn out favorably, the victim of psychological helplessness will continue to suffer from painful feelings, and will eventually fail.

In my clinical practice, I find that psychological helplessness must be overcome before any progress can be made. When people feel helpless, learning about painful childhood experiences does more harm than good. Recalling the trauma justifies continued feelings of helplessness. If they experience good luck, such as being handed a better job or inheriting money, they will greet it with fear and dismay, and ultimately ruin the opportunity.

Nothing matters more in life than our attitude toward it. If we approach life with feelings of helplessness and doom, we'll find our prophecies coming true. If we approach life with an attitude of self-determination and hope, we will make the best of whatever situation comes along, and often we will triumph.

I use the term "overwhelm" to designate the experience of lapsing into helplessness. Overwhelm can take many forms, from the emotions of guilt, shame, anxiety, numbing, and chronic anger to the larger experiences of anxiety, depression, and even madness (Breggin, 1991).

CHILDHOOD FEELINGS OF HELPLESSNESS AND VULNERABILITY

Children begin to feel helplessness when their lives are taken out of their control or when they are abused, neglected, and abandoned. When small children are left by their parents, even for relatively brief periods, they at first protest with anger and resentment. Then they go through despair and ultimately detachment (Bowlby, 1973). They can grow up believing that detachment equals liberty, when in reality it is a form of helpless withdrawal. If we include this kind of unintentional abandonment as a form of coercion or oppression, then most helplessness can be seen as resulting from coercion and oppression.

Adults who have been conditioned to be helpless in childhood will more readily lapse into it under pressure. But all adults must struggle against helplessness when stresses or conflicts become severe enough.

The negative psychological effects of being victimized by coercion will receive the most attention in this chapter. This is relatively easy to do because coercion tends to reduce options or to limit choices. Coercion tends to breed helplessness and thus to stifle human potential. Therefore, the impact of coercion is somewhat routinized and repetitive from person to person. By contrast, liberty and love inspire individual uniqueness.

Because the individual's mental processes develop in response to interpersonal relations, an analysis of them must deal extensively with childhood. However, childhood experiences reflect values implemented by the family and other social institutions, such as religion and the state. Therefore, it is important to be aware of the family as a social institution and childhood as, to some extent, an indoctrination into society's values.

CHILDHOOD EXPERIENCES AND CONFLICT RESOLUTION IN ADULTHOOD

Coercion, liberty, and love each have their psychological or mental parallels or representations. People take attitudes toward themselves much as they do toward other people. They coerce and hate themselves, have esteem and grant liberty to themselves, and love or treasure themselves.

How people relate to themselves vastly affects how they treat others as well. It is difficult, if not impossible, to hate oneself and to love others. It is equally difficult to love others and to hate oneself.

Whenever people enter conflict situations, childhood experiences of helplessness become restimulated. To understand conflict resolution among adults, we must see how their childhood experiences rear up under stress.

CHILDREN AND COERCION

Childhood often smacks of coercion. It is an involuntary relationship. No one, as far as we know, chooses to be born or hand picks his or her parents. Despite the best-intentioned parents, children will at times feel like prisoners, if not of their parents, then of childhood itself.

The power imbalance between parents and children—in size, authority, experience, economic resources, etc.—is so great in the early years that children are bound at times to feel intimidated and overwhelmed. Since parenting inevitably requires a certain amount of enforced control, even in an ideal family, all children will be acutely aware that they are at times being coerced. It is virtually impossible to get through childhood without a legacy of feeling helpless.

Even within the most harmonious families, children will *typically* feel that they cannot entirely trust their parents. Under the best of circumstances, people will often disagree on issues important to their lives. Conflict is commonplace between husbands and wives, for example, on issues of money, sex, communication, domestic chores, and childrearing. It is also frequent between bosses and employees. But the likelihood of substantial disagreement is increased when one party to the conflict is a child and the other is an adult. Their viewpoints, for innumerable reasons, including maturity and generational differences, are likely to differ. Yet the parents have the resources with which to win any conflict. The result is that almost any child will monitor what he or she tells to a parent. Conflict is not "resolved" but submerged, sometimes to break out at a later date. Often it merely adds to the unspoken gulf between parent and child.

In many if not most families, the situation is much worse. Many children grow up under extremely unfavorable circumstances. Children are frequently hit by their parents, and often sexually abused, neglected, or abandoned (see chapter 4). They also suffer dreadfully from watching their parents abusing each other (Jaffe, Wolfe and Wilson, 1990; Yllo and Bograd, 1988). Most children feel, to one degree or another, threatened and unloved. Often they witness severe conflict and even violence directed at other members of their family by one or both parents. While children are no longer legally considered to be property, often they are treated by adults as if they were.

The emotional, physical, and sexual abuse of children, and its aftermath, has now been documented from many directions. Sources include early psychoanalytic studies of children (e.g.,

Bowlby, 1973; see also chapter 2); decades of clinical literature (e.g., Miller, 1984; reviewed in chapter 4); and a recently burgeoning research literature (Wyatt and Powell, 1988; Wolfe, 1987; Green, 1989; Athens, 1989; Jaffe, Wolfe, and Wilson, 1990; Gelles and Straus, 1988; see also chapter 4). What once was commonsense observation and clinical hypothesis—that childhood abandonment and abuse scars the individual, sometimes for life—is now a demonstrable fact.

Not only families, but schools and religious institutions often neglect and abuse children. The schools in particular have recently come under increasing criticism (Carnegie Council on Adolescent Development, 1989). Children often feel like unwilling inmates of their homes, schools, and churches.

Nowadays children are also exposed to an enormous amount of violence outside the home. In many inner cities, the violent death of young people has become commonplace. Gunshots can frequently be heard down the block. Everywhere children are watching violence on TV news and especially in TV features and movies. Beyond violence, there is a variety of other expressions of coercion routinely accepted in the "real life" dramas presented on TV and in the movies.

The amount of coercion experienced or witnessed by children has many negative consequences. In their intimate lives, they often internalize the problem, turning aggression on themselves, or they attack others who have not offended them. As they grow up in society, they come to accept coercion as an inevitable part of life. Oppressive governments, for example, often pale in their violence against adult citizens compared to what children experience within their families. The child then brings to adulthood the viewpoint that conflicts large and small can and should be handled by coercion. Rarely does the child grow into adulthood believing that voluntary agreements can be trusted and that love can ameliorate extreme or hard-to-resolve conflict.

THE BASIC STRESS PARADIGM: HURT, FEAR, AND HELPLESSNESS

When people undergo prolonged or severe emotional pain, they develop what I call the Basic Stress Paradigm. Three words summarize the essence of this negative experience: *hurt, fear,* and *helplessness.* This analysis parallels Bowlby's description of the child's response to abandonment: protest (against the hurt), despair (extreme fear), and detachment (helpless withdrawal).

The Basic Stress Paradigm can be summarized:

1. *Hurt:* Any negative experience and the painful emotions associated with it.

2. *Fear:* The *inevitable* response to severe or prolonged feelings of hurt.

3. *Helplessness:* In children, the *inevitable* outcome of severe or prolonged fear.

By hurt, I mean any feelings of discomfort, from physical pain through all the variations of emotional distress. The word *pain* will at times be used instead of hurt; but hurt has the value of suggesting both the painful cause of the discomfort and the subjective response of feeling injured. The response to intense hurt is fear; and the response to severe or chronic fear is helplessness, including feelings of overwhelm, incompetence, inability to think straight or to cope, and withdrawal. Fundamentally, the individual "gives up trying" and accepts the role of victim.

The Basic Stress Paradigm can be linked to basic-needs theory. Individuals feel hurt or injured when their basic needs are thwarted. These include *all* the basic needs, such as the needs to be loved, to be self-determining, to have security, and so on.

THE NEED TO AVOID PHYSICAL PAIN AND DEATH

Survival needs are often mentioned in conflict resolution analyses, but typically they are given little attention. The specific need to avoid physical pain is not usually addressed at all. Nonetheless, the need is among the most urgent. It provides the basis for the commonplace use of corporal punishment to control children, as well as for the male abuse of women. It is also the basis for torture in the political arena.

The need to avoid pain is closely associated with another basic need that is rarely examined in the field of conflict resolution—the need to avoid death. It too is sometimes subsumed under survival needs, but the specific threat of death plays an important role in human psychological, interpersonal, and political life.

Unlike some other basic human needs, the need to avoid pain and to avoid death are obviously shared with most if not all forms of animal life. The two needs are so primary that they find expression in all three dynamics. For example, they motivate the Dynamic II right to self-defense. They also motivate Dynamic I values. The fear of death has long been recognized as a major contributor to the search for spiritual values, such as the importance of lasting and loving relationships and the belief in God and an afterlife. But in Dynamic III: coercion, the needs to avoid pain and death play the most obvious role. In every aspect of life, coercion gains its strength by threatening individuals with pain and death. Even in their domestic lives, women and children, and more rarely men, learn to conform their behavior before these two grave threats.

THE BASIC STRESS PARADIGM AND LEARNED HELPLESSNESS

Helplessness is the debilitating end product of a Basic Stress Paradigm. In the *Psychology of Freedom,* I spoke of psychological or emotional helplessness. Martin Seligman's term, learned helplessness, is more familiar and probably better. In his latest book, *Learned Optimism* (1991), Seligman describes learned helplessness as "the giving-up reaction, the quitting response that follows from the belief that whatever you do doesn't matter," (p. 15). The following analysis, while using his term, is based on my own observations.

Learned helplessness is the opposite of autonomy and self-determination. Helplessness is usually learned after severe, chronic coercion. That is, the Basic Stress Paradigm is frequently the result of coercion.

The key to defining learned or psychological helplessness is the limitation it imposes on the individual's use of his or her full faculties. Learned helplessness is self-defeating in any situation other than that of propitiating hostile authorities. Sometimes an individual can learn to feign helplessness when faced with hostile authorities. The person remains self-determined and autonomous, but fakes a helpless role. That is not what is meant by learned helplessness, which is a role that the individual actually accepts for himself or herself.

Learned helplessness is a mental state or emotional reaction, rather than a realistic response. An individual may in reality be more or less *physically* helpless if partially paralyzed, tied up with ropes, or imprisoned in a small room. But the most physically helpless person, if conscious, need not be overcome with psychological helplessness. He or she can still do everything possible to remain self-determining—to control his or her own mind or spiritual state. This individual realizes his or her realistic limitations, but refuses to adopt an attitude of helplessness.

People who suffer from developmental retardation often act helplessly, mostly because they have been so frequently humiliated and victimized. But even these impaired persons will not display learned helplessness if they have been encouraged to use their existing capacities to the fullest. Psychological helplessness is an attitude about ourselves rather than a reality.

In my experience, learned helplessness is frequently a more active process than simply quitting. The individual, having been rewarded for helplessness, displays it in the hope of pleasing authorities, gaining their sympathy, or avoiding their antipathy. Young women, for example, are taught by the culture that helplessness in regard to physical danger is appealing to men. Young men, perhaps to justify future demands upon their wives and to emulate their fathers, become helpless about household chores, such as cooking or doing the laundry. Too often parents find helplessness in their children endearing. Or parents find it easier to deal with their children when they lack self-determination or spunk. People who want to substitute their own will for the will of others will encourage learned helplessness in their victims.

ORIGINS OF LEARNED HELPLESSNESS

Small children easily respond with helplessness when faced with what seems to them to be overwhelmingly difficult challenges. Most parents and teachers know the importance of helping children not to give up in frustration or panic when faced with learning something new. When children are not given this support by their parents or other authorities—or worse, if their parents or authorities actively undermine them—children easily adopt an attitude of helplessness toward specific challenges or toward life in general.

Helplessness can be learned as an adult and also as a child. The strongest people can lapse into helplessness immediately after a severe physical or emotional trauma. An otherwise self-empowered individual abruptly becomes frightened, irrational, confused, overwhelmed, unable to make decisions, and simply unable to cope. I have worked with male rape victims who have been diagnosed "schizophrenic" as a result of one assault. The growing literature on post-traumatic stress disorder shows that a single trauma, such as rape, or more prolonged stress, such as chronic wife abuse or warfare, can leave a legacy of lingering helplessness, sometimes to a seriously debilitating degree. In general, the reaction is most severe where another human being, rather than nature or chance, is a perpetrator. Being intentionally victimized by another person disrupts our Dynamic I connectedness to other people.

Authoritarian religions, cults, schools, and other institutions also encourage helplessness in order to enforce their control. In a total institution (Goffman, 1961), such as a prison or a mental hospital, or in the home of a severe wife and child abuser (Walker, 1989), victims learn to be helpless in order to avoid further abuse and even death. In Nazi concentration camps, almost everyone learned to be helpless, including captured military officers and political leaders.

It is difficult to "act" helpless without ultimately becoming helpless. Individuals who develop a particular role in order to placate their oppressors will tend to adopt the role as their viewpoint.

The role or identity of helplessness will often be strongly defended by individuals. They will argue that their helplessness is inevitable. For example, they will insist that they cannot learn to think straight under pressure, and will resist attempts to help them learn to do so. This resistance indicates that they feel that being helpless has some (usually unidentified) advantage, such as staying out of trouble or gaining sympathy. Or they may feel that their condition or the situation is so utterly hopeless that it is not worth risking further defeats and failures. Simply ignoring their problems and conflicts may seem the best alternative when all hope is gone.

GUILT, SHAME, 'ANXIETY, AND NUMBING

Guilt, shame, and anxiety, as well as emotional numbing and compulsive anger, can be understood as derivatives of learned helplessness (Breggin, 1980). They can usually be traced back to Basic Stress Paradigms in childhood, or to overwhelming adult experiences, such as rape, torture, and solitary confinement.

The human mind is complex and tends to seek explanations or reasons for the hurt, fear, and helplessness that it experiences. The Basic Stress Paradigm tends to become integrated into a broader understanding of life. Guilt, shame, and anxiety are, to some extent, attempts by the victim to label, explain, or channel his or her hurt, fear, and helplessness.

The literature on guilt, shame, and anxiety is too enormous to review here (e.g., Kaufman, 1989, and Morrison, 1989, on shame; Freud, 1936, Sullivan, 1953, May, Angel, and Ellenberger, 1958, and McCullough and Mann, 1985, on anxiety). Instead I will summarize my own understanding of these three emotional reactions (also see Breggin 1980, 1991).

Whenever we trace the roots of these emotions into childhood, we shall find a Basic Stress Paradigm. Occasionally the hurt will be a circumscribed event or series of closely related events, such as a death in the family or identifiable episodes of abuse; but more frequently there would be a pattern of estrangement, abandonment, neglect, or oppressive interactions, sometimes lasting an entire childhood, involving one or more family members and other significant children or adults.

NUMBING AND ALIENATION FROM SELF

When emotions become unendurable, they will sometimes be blocked, wholly or in part, from consciousness. The individual can become emotionally numbed. Often, but not always, guilt, shame, and anxiety will be found not far beneath the surface. Even deeper down, of course, is the original hurt, fear, and helplessness. As already discussed in chapter 4, perpetrators of severe abuse tend to experience a numbing or an alienation from their own feelings.

THE ESSENTIAL CHARACTERISTICS OF GUILT, SHAME, AND ANXIETY

There are a number of different ways to distinguish among guilt, shame, and anxiety. The following is a sketchy psychological shorthand intended for practical use, rather than as thoroughgoing analysis.

1. *Blame:* The direction of blame helps identify the emotion being felt.

   In guilt, blame tends to be directed inward. The individual sees himself or herself as the source of the problem. The essence of guilt is "I am bad, evil, harmful. I do this to myself. I deserve what I get." Instead of feeling accused by others, the individual feels deserving of blame.

   In shame, blame is almost always directed outward. Other people are humiliating, controlling, or rejecting the victim. The essence of shame is "People make me feel like I am worthless, a defective, a nobody, an outsider." Where no specific outside source is named, the individual feels inferior in comparison to other people or by societal standards. Shame almost always encourages a person to hide or withdraw from others, unless the individual overcompensates with a defiant public display.

   In anxiety, blame is assigned nowhere. The individual experiences something closer to the original basic stress triad—hurt, fear, and helplessness—but without identifying any source. Anxiety is experienced as a kind of emotional know-nothingness. The essence of anxiety is "I don't know what is happening to me; I'm unable to cope; I can't make decisions; I'm overwhelmed and helpless."

   In summary, guilt directs blame inward, shame directs blame outward, and anxiety directs it nowhere.

2. *Anger:* Anger follows blame.

   In guilt, anger is directed inward, and suicide is its most extreme result.

In shame, it is directed outward, and causing harm to others is its most extreme expression. Because one feels humiliated and impotent in relation to others, one tries to triumph over others. Most people who commit murder do so in the midst of a shame or humiliation reaction: "You can't do this to me. I'll show you." As described in chapter 4, shame tends to fuel the perpetrator syndrome.

Anxiety leaves the individual unable to direct anger toward anyone or anything. The person feels hopelessly confused and frustrated by the onset of emotion which seems to come not from a source but from "out of the blue."

3. *Potency:* The sense of power or powerlessness differs in each emotion.

People who feel guilty often believe that they do have an impact on others, albeit a negative one. Typically they have been taught by their parents, "You have made me miserable," or by their religion, "You are evil."

People who feel shame tend to see themselves as impotent, as if they cannot affect others; and in outrage over this, they will do extreme things to others. They have been taught by their families, "You don't count, you are ridiculous, you don't fit in."

People who become overcome with anxiety tend to feel something close to impotent, but it has a different coloration. It feels more like incompetence or helplessness. They have been taught, "You can't do it; you can't handle it; you might as well give up."

THE FUNCTIONS OF ANGER

Anger, as already noted, can be generated as reaction to guilt or shame, and ultimately, as a reaction to any injury. In chapter 4, I discussed the probability that there is a built-in tendency toward violence in human beings; but whatever the ultimate roots of anger and violence in human life, it is clear that pain and hurt, and especially humiliation, usually acts as the trigger for violence against others.

Most psychotherapists will confirm that persistent or seemingly unprovoked rage is usually traceable to chronic victimization in childhood. The defensive reaction becomes fixed in place, especially if the individual identifies with his or her anger, feeling that "It's all I've got." To stop being angry seems tantamount to "giving in" and to becoming vulnerable to further injury. Often pride leads the angry person to declare, "I'm not hurt at all, I'm outraged." Being angry rather than being hurt becomes a matter of pride.

Because it usually occurs as a defensive response to emotional pain, anger should be viewed as a superficial emotion. The "deeper" emotion is the original hurt. When the person then decides to stop expressing anger, he or she becomes more able to feel and to deal with the underlying painful emotions and frustrated basic needs for liberty and love.

In resolving conflict, people need to accept that their anger is driven by feelings of injury. When two embattled individuals acknowledge to each other that they feel hurt, they can feel both more potent and more vulnerable at the same time, and both feelings facilitate the resolution of conflict.

People feel more potent when they learn that they do have the power to inflict pain on each other. Often this comes as a shock to both parties because each has been feeling unable to impact on the other. "You mean, I'm really getting through?" is a typical response. Nothing fuels violence more than feelings of frustration and impotence; and so when people feel more able to affect the other person, they usually feel less driven to attack.

When people learn they are hurting each other, they also become vulnerable to each other. This allows a husband and wife, a parent and child, or even political antagonists, to work on the underlying pain, hurt, and frustrated needs. It can come as a relief to have it out in the open: "Yeah, all this fighting hurts me." It allows people to begin to address their overall pain in the relationship.

Venting anger is of little help in relieving it. If anything, the chronic expression of anger tends to become a compulsive pattern. Having demeaned and injured other people, we want to rationalize what we have done. We fan the fire of our own anger as a means of justifying our past offenses. This leads to a cycle of violence. To achieve self-insight and to resolve conflict, it is usually necessary to inhibit anger and to feel the underlying pain.

Does anger serve any useful function? It can be important in self-defense to discourage an aggressor who won't respond to reason or to appeals for more peaceful conflict resolution. It can signal to ourselves and others that we are hurt and need to be treated more gently. People who are *unable* to feel their anger will need to get in touch with it. But in general, anger generates far more conflict than it ever resolves.

The person who gives up anger as a method of conflict resolution loses very little, and opens the way to more ethical and loving approaches.

PATTERNS OR LIFESTYLES OF REACTIVITY

Typically a person's life will be colored by a tendency toward one or other of these responses, or a particular combination of them. Thus, the same stress may provoke entirely different reactions in individual people, depending upon the person's pattern. If, for example, a pet gets loose from the house and is run over, each will respond differently. Guilt-ridden persons will find themselves at fault, blame themselves harshly, and declare that they do not deserve to have a pet. Shame-ridden people will feel that others will blame them, that they will be seen as "dumb" or "stupid" for allowing it to happen. Anxiety-ridden persons may feel that life is fragile, that there is danger everywhere, that they are not competent to take care of themselves or a pet. The numbed person will, of course, not experience his or her feelings, but rather an increase in remoteness from them.

IDENTITY AND EMOTIONAL REACTIVITY

People often identify themselves with their patterns of emotional reactivity. They believe that feeling humiliated, guilty, anxious, angry, or numb is "a part of them" or basic to their personality.

A great deal has been said about shame as the most basic threat to identity. Kaufman states:

Shame is the affect of inferiority. No other affect is more central to the development of identity. None is closer to the experienced self, nor more disturbing. Shame is felt as an inner torment. (p. 17.)

In a similar vein, Morrison connects shame to narcissism—the core feeling of self-worth. The shamed person feels fundamentally defective.

However, identity is a stake in any of the emotional reactions. I have already noted that people often make anger central to their identity. People also become identified with their feelings of guilt, shame, anxiety, and even numbness, especially when these emotions are overwhelming. The guilty person's identity is that of "bad person" or "source of trouble"; the anxious person's is that of "incompetent, unable to cope"; and the ashamed person's is that of "worthless" or "defective." Meanwhile, the numbed person is likely to feel "out of touch" with his or her identity.

Surprisingly, people sometimes struggle to hold onto these negative identities, perhaps because they seem so integral to their personalities and their life experiences; perhaps because they are afraid that there is nothing else for them to feel. I find it useful to suggest to people that love can become a more solid and far more satisfying identity.

GUILT AND REMORSE

Can guilt be deserved? Doesn't it ever result from wrong-doing? In my experience (Breggin, 1980), guilt is rarely if ever a direct response to actual bad deeds. As I described in some detail in the previous chapter, perpetrators typically do not react with guilt to their crimes. Guilt is an emotional reaction, derived from helplessness, and usually based on childhood experiences of hurt and fear. Indeed, the origins of guilt are usually no longer within the individual's consciousness.

When adults do feel guilty in relation to something bad they have done, it is usually due to restimulation of childhood guilt. There is an emotional association between the bad deed and a guilt-provoking childhood experience. In short, guilt is an irrational reaction rooted in childhood helplessness rather than in adult remorse. In my practice, I have seen murderers who show no guilt and innocent people who are overwhelmed with it.

But does guilt serve a useful purpose in inhibiting destructive behavior? Sometimes, perhaps. But more often it tends to make people irrational and resentful, and thus it motivates destructive actions.

Remorse is another matter. It lacks the self-hate and self-loathing characteristic of guilt. It does not mire the person down in helplessness. The person who is genuinely remorseful feels autonomous and self-determining, and eager to take new and better actions. Often the remorseful person experiences an increase in self-esteem through recognizing the wrong deeds and correcting them. Remorse is usually very easy to distinguish from guilt, which instead overwhelms and demoralizes people, makes them feel badly about themselves, and frequently leads to helpless inaction or further destructiveness.

Even genuine remorse is probably not a significant motivator for benevolent human conduct. Instead, the motivator comes from a much more positive source. Oliner and Oliner's study of *The Altruistic Personality: Rescuers of Jews in Nazi Germany* (1988) provides evidence that the most seemingly sacrificial behavior, risking one's life for Jews during the holocaust, was *not* the result of guilt or even lofty ideals. It was motivated by empathic bonding—love.

According to Oliner and Oliner, children who became rescuers as adults were treated tenderly and leniently while they were growing up. Their eventual "moral heroism" was the result of extensive social ties and empathy, rather than guilt or even a sense of duty or obligation. Oliner and Oliner described the development of empathic social connectedness in the future rescuers:

It begins in close family relationships in which parents model caring behavior and communicate caring values. Parental discipline tends toward leniency; children frequently experience it as imperceptible. It includes a heavy dose of reasoning. . . . Punishment is rare. (p. 249.)

To repeat, guilt and other painful or burdensome feelings are not a reliable source of benevolent behavior. Empathic love *is* that reliable source.

DYNAMIC III: COERCION AS THE ROOT OF THE BASIC STRESS TRIAD

Basic Stress Paradigms and their derivative negative emotions usually result from experiencing the effects of the coercion dynamic.

Often these reactions result from obvious oppression in the form of emotional, physical, or sexual abuse. Often they are caused by emotional neglect which, in the case of the dependent child, is itself a form of abuse. This neglect need not be intentional—it can be the product of an emotionally damaged and withdrawn parent—but the impact on the young child can be overwhelming. If we categorize neglect as coercion, then Dynamic III includes nearly all of the worst things that happen to children.

Sometimes, however, the Basic Stress Paradigm is caused by misfortunes, such as illness, death, natural catastrophes, or war, that are beyond the control of anyone in the child's life. However, as already noted, clinical experience and recent studies of posttraumatic stress disorder confirm that the most debilitating emotional responses result from direct actions by people. For example, the British found during the London blitz of World War II that being in terrifying bombardments was not nearly so stressful for a child as being sent away from one's parents to the safety of a countryside nursery (Bowlby, 1973). Furthermore, even when a child is seemingly injured by a severe trauma, such as the death of a family member, the most stressful part of the experience is frequently associated with neglect or abuse by other adults. For example, the child may have been ignored while the family member was dying in the hospital or the child may have been made to feel guilty about the death.

SELF-DEFEATING REACTIONS

Guilt, shame, anxiety, numbing, and chronic anger are ultimately self-defeating reactions. In childhood, they may have served some limited purpose. If the sexually abused six year old blamed herself rather than her father, this may have kept her from being further injured by him. Or it may have maintained her much needed faith in her parent's ultimate good intentions. If the "mamma's boy" acts helpless, it may endear him to his mother and postpone her rejecting him because of his "manliness." If the shy girl learns to shrink away in the presence of parents or authoritarian teachers, it may keep her out of trouble and earn her approval as a "nice child." Similarly, if emotions are overwhelming, temporary numbing may enable the person to continue a semblance of normal activity. Chronic anger may be useful to a child in fending off oppression or in bolstering his or her pride.

But in the long run—and especially as the child grows into an adult—guilt, shame, anxiety, numbing, and persistent anger become self-defeating. The individual's emotional signal system will arbitrarily push the person one way or another—toward feeling guilty, ashamed, anxious, numb, or angry—without regard for the individual's basic needs, interests, or rational values. Actions required for successful living, or even for survival, may be stifled by overwhelmingly painful feelings. A woman, for example, may feel too guilty to leave an abusive husband. A man, out of shame over his "cowardice," may die in battle or in a bar fight, rather than retreat or get out of trouble. Overcome by anxiety, an individual may fail to deal with a life-threatening emergency involving himself or herself, or a loved one. People may become numb or angry in situations in which other emotional responses, such as love, are needed.

The emotions that grow from the Basic Stress Paradigm suppress the fulfillment of our basic needs. They interfere with rationality and with love; they are the source of low self-esteem and even self-hate; they prevent the individual from pursuing his or her self-interest, as well as the interests of loved ones. Indeed, any one of the negative emotions is likely to rear up at times when the individual has the opportunity to improve his or her life, for example, by choosing a new career, going to school, making a relationship, or even pursuing a healthy lifestyle. The negative reactions tell the individual, "No, you cannot do or get what you want." They do so by overwhelming the individual with guilt, shame, anxiety, numbness, or anger when faced with opportunities. Many people have little or no idea about what they want out of life or how they would like to live their lives, because the mere thought of these issues brings up their typical helpless responses.

OVERCOMING BASIC STRESS PARADIGMS AND LEARNED HELPLESSNESS

Overcoming Basic Stress Paradigms and their effects is an aspect of psychotherapy and conflict resolution in general, and hundreds of volumes have been written about it. Indeed, the Basic Stress

Paradigm is itself a simplified way of looking at psychological causation, a somewhat crude model that I hope will be helpful in conflict resolution. The overall problem of the origin and amelioration of irrational, self-defeating conduct is of course too large for this book. For practical purposes I want to focus on some of the basic steps in handling the Basic Stress Paradigm, learned helplessness, and the associated emotional reactions of guilt, shame, anxiety, and numbing, as well as compulsive anger.

IDENTIFYING THE NEGATIVE EMOTION AND REJECTING ITS IMPACT

As a start, the individual suffering from self-defeating emotions should learn to identify each of them by name. The descriptions I have provided of guilt, shame, anxiety, numbing, and anger can be helpful. People can feel considerably liberated simply by knowing that they suffer from a specific kind of irrational emotion. Consciously recognizing, "I'm being driven by shame," can help to subdue and control the emotion. The individual can now reject the emotion as a foreign intruder, an alien response from earlier hurtful experiences.

People are surprised and encouraged by the idea that they can both identify and refuse to respond to an emotion. I often compare these emotions to wild beasts and explain, "If you refuse to listen to them or to do their bidding, they lose their power over you. But if you respond to them and act according to their dictates, they grow stronger and more demanding." After such an explanation, a motto like "I won't feed my anger," can be very helpful.

Of course, simply deciding not to act in response to an emotion is easier said than done; but it is an important beginning, one that people often do not think about.

SUBSTITUTING BETTER PRINCIPLES OF LIVING

Once self-defeating emotions are identified, it is possible to consciously practice replacing them with more rational and loving principles. Understanding Dynamic I: love and Dynamic II: liberty can provide people with better ways of looking at their internal and external conflicts. The individual can learn to replace their coercive internal messages with attitudes consistent with liberty and love, including self-respect and self-love, as well as respect and love for others.

Helping people understand how to satisfy their basic needs is another important step. They can learn that emotional reactivity is not the answer, and that implementing liberty and love in one's life and in the lives of others is the best approach.

REEXPERIENCING BASIC STRESS PARADIGMS

If the participants in a conflict are willing, more intensive therapeutic approaches can be taken to relieve the underlying Basic Stress Paradigms. This is an accepted and essential part of couples or family therapy (see chapter 6), but it can sometimes be done as well in workshops dealing with racial, cultural, and other societal and even international conflicts (see chapters 9 and 10).

Early in his career, Freud experimented with relieving childhood stresses by encouraging the patient to reexperience or "abreact" them. Nowadays a variety of cathartic methods are used. The individual recalls and reenacts the original hurts, sometimes by using role-playing, mild suggestion, guided fantasies, or other methods to encourage childhood recollections. The adult may end up reexperiencing not only the childhood feelings, such as guilt or shame, but the original more painful Basic Stress Paradigms of hurt, fear, and learned helplessness. This same uncovering process is possible when the original trauma is of more recent origin, such as a severe accident or the death of a loved one. It is useful for focusing on isolated trauma or on lifelong patterns of hurt in the form of rejection, abandonment, and other stresses.

If a person can discover and relive the original childhood trauma or stress, the exaggerated adult reactions can often be reduced. Awareness of the raw feelings of childhood hurt can defuse their impact. The adult can learn that there is no longer any reason to feel so much hurt, fear, and helplessness. The source of the compulsive emotional reaction—the earlier Basic Stress Paradigm—becomes placed correctly in an earlier time, and no longer seems so appropriate. When the source is identified, the individual can declare, "This isn't reality today; it's something out of my past," this makes it easier to reject the negative emotion.

To defuse the original hurts, they must be reexperienced *from the viewpoint of an autonomous adult.* The cathartic experience must not become overwhelming. This last point is critical. Individuals should not be encouraged to reexperience earlier feelings of hurt, fear and helplessness unless they can do so as self-determining adults. It is the therapist's task to support the individual's sense of mastery and to approach the original trauma or stress only when the individual feels ready to handle it in a confident and competent fashion. Reexperiencing old hurts in a helpless fashion can reinforce them.

Sometimes it is helpful to explain that different people respond very differently to the same stress, depending on their own particular style of reactivity. That is, the reactions are not inevitable. A person doesn't have to react with guilt to a particular experience. Someone else might respond with anxiety or shame. And still another person might manage the stress in a rational and loving manner. It is the person's style, not the stress, that determines the undivided response. And a style can be changed.

It is, however, important not to ridicule the person in making comparisons to others. The point, instead, is that all people have these reactions, but they are particular to each person, and that no one is required by the stressors to respond in one way or another.

EXTERNALIZING THE INTERNAL CONFLICT

Guilt, shame, anxiety, numbing, and compulsive anger can be viewed as internal conflicts. They are analogous to conflicts between separate persons. Often they are experienced by the individual as if "two personalities" are contending, the one with the positive desires to fulfill basic needs, the other with negative responses to any such suggestion. When Freud developed his ideas of the Id, Ego, and Superego, he was adhering to that tendency to separate our inner conflicts into seemingly separate parts of ourselves, a metaphor for internalized persons.

Role-playing and psychodrama methods can be helpful in externalizing internal conflicts by having the individual or other persons play the internal parts. In this manner the individual gets a chance to reexperience and defuse the underlying hurts, and also to see them in greater clarity as events external to himself. Indeed, that is much of their origin—in social events external to the individual.

Again, the principles do not differ substantially from those involved in resolving and preventing conflicts between separate individuals and groups. The ultimate answer is a cleansing love for self and others that declares one's mind a guilt-, shame-, and anxiety-free zone, an arena in which painful emotional reactions from childhood are replaced by more independent and loving attitudes. Instead of self-hate, the individual learns to accept his or her individual rights and inherent worth as a human being.

EMOTIONAL REACTIVITY IN INTERPERSONAL CONFLICT

External conflict tends to stir up our earlier conflicts and hurts. We end up not only in conflict with another person in present time but with people from our past, and hence with ourselves. People who wish to manipulate and control others often capitalize on the victim's negative emotions. If clever about it, they may zero in on the victim's chronic style of guilt, shame, anxiety, numbing, or anger. A car salesman, for example, might play on any number of themes: (guilt) "You're not going to buy after all the time you have taken and the trouble you've caused?"; (shame) "You mean you can't even afford that much?"; or (anxiety) "Do you think this car or any other like it will be around forever?"

When Freud spoke of transference, he was identifying the tendency of adults to reexperience emotional reactions from childhood when in stressful adult situations. In the classical psychoanalytic situation, few of the client's basic needs were met. The "blank screen" analyst did little, for example, to show respect or love for the client. Faced with this real-life rejection, the client often "projected" onto the analyst feelings from earlier relationships in childhood. Clients would love or hate their analysts much as they loved or hated their parents. In fact, the so-called transference was complicated by the fact that the therapist was being abusive by withholding basic need satisfaction in an intimate relationship. Under such frustrating conditions, the individual is indeed likely to be overwhelmed with reactions originally generated during childhood experiences of hurt, fear, and helplessness. These early childhood reactions are likely to be stirred up in any new situation, including therapy; but they are not as likely to become overwhelming if the therapist is warm and caring rather than hostile, remote, or "objective" (see chapter 6).

Interactions between people, compounded by their own inner conflicts, can become complex. In couples or family therapy, however, they often become readily apparent (see chapter 6). Both members of a couple, for example, may feel so much shame about themselves that they will not "give in" for fear of risking further humiliation. The man who dominates his wife may fear looking like a "wimp" if he gives up his macho attitudes. His wife, in turn, may be afraid to stop tongue-lashing him, for fear she will lose her only defense against humiliation. While each may be aggravating the other's negative emotions, each is also reacting to experiences buried in the past.

A man feels so guilty about hurting his girlfriend that he repeatedly tells her that he has done "everything possible" to be good to her. She in turn reads this to mean that he is telling her that "no one will ever be able to relate to you," which inspires in her feelings of both anxiety and shame. Meanwhile, since he hardly ever feels anything but guilt, he cannot understand her anxiety and shame reactions; and similarly, she cannot figure out his intentions, because she has little inner experience with guilt. Thus these emotional reactions, if not identified and controlled, can disrupt an otherwise loving relationship.

EMOTIONAL REACTIVITY IN POLITICAL CONFLICT

Earlier Basic Stress Paradigms are frequently reactivated when people confront political coercion and conflict. Guilt and shame over the Holocaust, for example, has been identified as a force that keeps Israelis from reaching a compromise with the Palestinians. Similarly, shame over being overpowered and defeated by the Israelis can keep many Palestinians from resolving their conflicts with the Israelis (see chapter 10). Often these emotional reactions have still deeper roots in the family life of the respective cultures and their tendencies to foment guilt, shame, or anxiety. All this vastly complicates the problem of conflict resolution on any level, but it cannot be overlooked.

The examples in the discussion of interpersonal conflict could easily be translated into examples of political leaders in a conflict resolution setting. When two leaders who have opposed each other for years finally sit down to try to resolve their conflicts, they may react as irrationally to each other as any other feuding couple.

A leader's childhood reactions of guilt or shame can make it nearly impossible for him to hear correctly what someone else is saying. Or they may prevent him from making an otherwise reasonable compromise. Perhaps he is so prideful (a shame reaction) that he is more interested in his public appearance than in solving the actual problems. Perhaps he cannot make any concessions for fear of feeling shamed. Perhaps he feels so guilty that he is afraid to do anything that will cause his own constituents to be angry at him.

AN OVERVIEW OF PSYCHOLOGICAL CONFLICT AND CONFLICT RESOLUTION

The interaction between personal emotional reactivity and conflict resolution is addressed throughout this book. Here I want to summarize some of the salient points.

First, Basic Stress Paradigms, including learned helplessness and the associated negative emotions, usually result from experiences along Dynamic III: coercion. They can also motivate people to perpetrate against others. They play a major role in the generation of conflict and in disrupting conflict resolution.

Second, in any conflict situation, people will bring in their personal style of reactivity, whether it is guilt, shame, anxiety, numbness, chronic anger, or, most frequently, various combinations of them. When the reactions seem to impinge on the individual's identity, they may utterly disrupt progress in conflict resolution. Most people will defend their identity at almost any cost, including death. This can lead to an absolute unwillingness to show "weakness" by compromising or changing one's position.

Third, conflict of any kind tends to restimulate and exaggerate earlier Basic Stress Paradigms, vastly complicating conflict resolution. This is true whether the people at the conference table are husband and wife or opposing political leaders. Being in a leadership role does not make one immune to the effects of childhood trauma and stress.

Fourth, the prospect of attempting to resolve a conflict can so restimulate Basic Stress Paradigms that an individual will reject entering into the conflict resolution process. Or having entered in, the individual may disrupt it. The therapist or conflict resolver may have to work with all parties to help them control their reactivity before they come together.

Fifth, it can help the participants in the conflict if deeper therapeutic techniques can be introduced. However, this should only be done voluntarily and without shaming anyone. Often it may be necessary to apply them before or separately from the conflict resolution process (see chapter 6). Unfortunately, a deeper therapeutic approach is not something that a national political leader is likely to consent to. Therapeutic techniques aimed at handling emotional reactivity are being applied in conflict seminars for potential leaders and for others somewhat below the level of president or dictator (see chapter 10).

Sixth, not only individuals but institutions (e.g., churches, schools, military organizations) and entire cultures implement their own styles of emotional reactivity. America had prided itself in never having lost a war, and this undoubtedly reinforced President Nixon's and President Johnson's reluctance to withdraw from Vietnam under the humiliating shadow of defeat. Their need for "peace with honor" may have long delayed the resolution of the conflict. Similarly, as we shall discuss further, the shame of losing in Vietnam may have in part motivated America's massive attack on Iraq in the Gulf War. President Bush was clearly able to manipulate these feelings to further his policy.

Obviously, the personal reactions of leaders are not nearly sufficient to explain political events like war; but they are contributing factors. They can become especially important during the conflict resolution process.

Lastly, the presence of emotional reactivity should never be used to undermine or deny the reality of other issues in a conflict. A battered woman, for example, will frequently react with seeming "paranoia" and debilitating anxiety when in the presence of her abusive husband. After prolonged brutalization, she may even react this way in his absence. A child may indeed seem "hyperactive" as a result of abuse. American psychiatrists diagnosed Saddam Hussein as a madman, but this was rhetoric to rationalize our own ferocious attack on the Iraqi people (see chapter 10). It will be suggested that Arabs and Israelis are burdened by their own characteristic emotional reactivity; but there are *real reasons* for this, rooted in their political and personal history.

Although an individual style of emotional reactivity contributes to the conflict, it may not be the cause of it. It may even result from it. Furthermore, other more contemporary issues are often of overriding importance. Psychological analysis should never be used to discredit an individual or group's viewpoint or claims during a conflict.

Psychology should enable people to liberate themselves from all coercive influences, both internal and external, so that they can more fully live by the principles of liberty and love.

▼ ▼

CHAPTER 6

Resolving Interpersonal Conflict within the Family

[M]ature **love is union under the condition of preserving one's integrity,** *one's individuality.* **Love is an active power in man;** *a power which breaks through the walls which separate man from his fellow men, which unites him with others; love makes him overcome the sense of isolation and separateness, yet permits him to be himself, to retain his integrity. In love the paradox occurs that two beings become one and yet remain two.*
Erich Fromm, The Art of Loving (1956)

For one human being to love another: that is perhaps the most difficult of all our tasks, the ultimate, the last test and proof, the work for which all other work is but preparation.
Rainer Maria Rilke, Letters to a Young Poet (May 14, 1904)

There are situations, moments in life, in which unawares, the human being confesses great portions of his ultimate personality, of his true nature. One of these situations is love. In their choice of lovers both the male and the female reveal their essential nature. The type of human being which we prefer reveals the contours of our heart.
José Ortega y Gasset, On Love (1957)

Members of a couple are in an extraordinary position to grow in their ability to love, and to help each other to live ethical and happy lives. The focus in this chapter is on professional couples therapy or conflict resolution; but any person can apply these same principles to resolving his or her own problems or disputes with family, friends, and coworkers. Conflict resolution is an essential part of personal growth and the development of more fulfilling relationships.

COERCION IN COUPLES CONFLICT RESOLUTION

Much of what has already been said about coercion may be summed up in one principle: coercive reactions always produce negative reactions, whether immediate or delayed, and have little or no place in conflict resolution (see chapter 4). This applies to couples as well as countries. In *Getting Together* (1988), Roger Fisher and Scott Brown make the same point in their summary of "An Unconditionally Constructive Strategy." Under the rubric of "noncoercive modes of influence," they write "Even if they are trying to coerce us, neither yield to that coercion nor try to coerce them," (p. 38). They devote a chapter to practical alternatives to coercion, including "attack the problem" (and not the person), "treat negotiation as joint problem-solving," "remain open to persuasion," "explore interests," "invent multiple options," and "try to persuade them of what's fair," (p. 139). They also encourage finding a beneficial way to leave a conflict rather than to resort to coercion.

From the start, coercion must be "left at the door"—outside the office or conflict resolution setting. For a fully successful resolution, both partners must eventually forsake all such tactics in their everyday lives. In personal relationships, this means giving up not only threats of force and abandonment, but subtle manipulations through deception, or through stimulating guilt, shame, anxiety, and numbness.

Often people learn each other's "emotional buttons" and then press them. Jane knows that Jim can't stand it when she cries (guilt) or when she suggests he is an inadequate wage earner (shame). Jim knows that Jane can't stand it when he hints that he might start drinking again or leave (anxiety).

By the time most couples seek help, they typically are deeply enmeshed in Dynamic III: coercion. Often they are bullying each other with threats of leaving, having an affair, or getting family and friends to choose sides. Often the children are being manipulated into the conflict. Sometimes men are openly using or threatening force. Almost always, both parties are trying to inflict a spectrum of guilt, shame, and anxiety on each other. Abusive language and attitudes are commonplace.

The therapist can and usually should quickly intervene to point out the nature of coercion and its various manifestations. The therapist's initial role, it can be explained, is to help the partners stop abusing each other. Generally, agreement can be relatively easily reached on the benefit and even *necessity* of stopping hostile communications. It can take much longer for the couple to believe that the aggression can in fact be stopped. It may take still longer for them to trust each other's intentions and convictions.

While each person will have to struggle through the process of personally rejecting force, threats, and emotional manipulation—some progress can often be made in this regard after one or two sessions. One week later, Jim may be able to boast that he has not once threatened to leave or to start drinking again, and hopefully Jane will acknowledge that it is true. One or two such steps in the right direction can begin to instill mutual confidence. Giving up coercion is often much easier than learning new, positive ways of relating. It is usually a prerequisite as well.

If one of the partners resists personally giving up oppressive tactics—such as abusive, accusatory language—then conflict resolution is greatly slowed down. This individual is probably so stuck in childhood Basic Stress Paradigms—so driven by hurt, fear, and helplessness—that giving up hostility now seems too dangerous. In his or her mind, being "tough" (meaning angry and hurtful) is the only way to "get anywhere."

The person who is compulsively destructive usually feels deeply humiliated, nearly worthless, and unable to forgo revenge and retaliation. Sometimes he or she has experienced too much abuse from the partner to easily set it aside. Often these reactions require individual work outside the couple's therapy. The hurt individual feels too vulnerable and humiliated in front of the partner, and therefore cannot explore patterns of emotional reactivity that predate the relationship.

The feeling and expression of anger, in Adler's words, can become a lifestyle (Ansbacher and Ansbacher, 1956). The person identifies with anger as an essential aspect of his or her personality and fears becoming too vulnerable to attack without its regular exercise. In childhood, this chronic rage may have given the injured youngster a sense of pride and security against attack; in adulthood, it injures other people and drives them away, and makes every encounter a source of fear and anxiety. The adult must learn that the defensive and aggressive strategies developed to cope with an abusive childhood are no longer appropriate or effective. The very trait the individual most prizes, his or her capacity to fight back, may have become the cause of unending failure in social relationships.

Compulsive withdrawal or numbing presents an equally if not at times more difficult problem. The person who is numbed often presents a veneer of rationality that can be difficult to penetrate. Because this person is literally unaware of his or her own basic love needs, progress is again slowed down. In withdrawing behind a façade of rationality and objectivity, the individual feels superior and secure, but loses out on connectedness to others. Again, the individual's most-prized trait, the defensive capacity to remove himself or herself from seeming danger, becomes the cause of chronic failure. The lifestyle learned in childhood must be abandoned for effective adult living.

When abuse has reached severe proportions within a relationship, especially if it has escalated to violence, then a cessation of the abuse should be an absolute requirement. An immediate end to abuse is most urgent when a man is battering his wife, but it can also be important when a man or woman is verbally abusing his or her spouse. Especially in regard to physical violence or threats, the therapist should immediately intervene and explain that battery is not only unethical and antithetical to the principles of conflict resolution, it is illegal and criminal.

The victim should be informed that any assault on her is a criminal act and that if she feels threatened, she should take appropriate defensive actions such as moving out, calling the police, or obtaining a restraining order. The batterer should also be instructed that physical assault is criminal and that any hint of a physical threat is wholly unacceptable. Recent research on family violence confirms that a firm policy against male violence, including involvement of the criminal justice system, is a powerful deterrent to battering (Gelles and Straus, 1988). While assuming this "tough" stance on abuse, the therapist should show concern for *both* parties to the conflict.

Withdrawal or numbing, especially when masquerading as rationality, is also very destructive. It is important from the start to try to define numbing as a "problem" rather than as a strength. This can be difficult for men to accept, but little progress can be made as long as a man identifies strength with being emotionally unresponsive. Similarly, if a woman equates strength with being able to get viciously angry, she must overcome this obstacle as well. Since anger is a natural response to feeling chronically humiliated it may be hard for her to experiment with more gentle approaches to expressing her hurt and resentment.

The therapist should acknowledge to the abuser the difficulty of abruptly and completely abandoning his or her habitual tactics. Especially with the man, it is important to explain that he will become much more effective in satisfying his basic needs through a more respectful, loving attitude. It should be explained that the ability to create a loving relationship is the most powerful way to create a happy life for oneself.

Of course, if a person is unwilling to acknowledge any underlying Dynamic I needs, there is little or no hope for a loving conflict resolution. But at least in the private practice of voluntary psychiatry, few participants are totally out of touch with these shared human desires and values. At any rate, teaching a couple to control and reject coercion is inseparable from teaching them about voluntary exchange and eventually about love.

LIBERTY IN COUPLES CONFLICT RESOLUTION

Liberty permits the use of force in self-defense. While retaliation and legally defined self-defense continues to play a role in societal relationships, in personal relationships even force in self-defense has too many adverse consequences. Both parties usually feel so injured that they view all of their coercive actions as defensive or retaliatory. In insisting upon the right and even a need to verbally degrade a partner, an individual may repeat a litany of offenses by the partner extending years and even decades into the past. Typically both the husband and wife believe the other to be ultimately responsible for the hostile and destructive quality of the relationship. At some point, they must become willing to surrender their resentments in the interest of making a new beginning based on the principles of love and even forgiveness. Short of this, conflict resolution will remain limited.

An attempt should be made to discourage the use of force, even in self-defense—except of course where physical safety or important property are at stake. This helps people give up being aggressive even when they feel it is justified on the grounds of self-defense.

It helps to point out that both parties are inextricably enmeshed in emotional preemptive strikes and in retaliation, and that the couple take a brief holiday from it during the sessions. It is also helpful to remind them that if they love each other, they also feel pain when they inflict pain. Often there is quick mutual agreement about this, and each may be pleasantly surprised to discover that the other feels badly about causing hurt. Despite the various gratifications involved in "fighting back" (e.g., retaliation, getting even, pride in standing up for oneself), each partner usually does find it distressing to hurt the other.

My general experience in couples work indicates that most people can and will control their more violent tendencies when they realize that forgoing coercion will better enable them to fulfill their basic Dynamic I and II needs. As a therapist or conflict resolver, I am willing to appeal to a whole array of principles, from self-interest to morality and empathy, depending on what helps the individual forgo emotional or physical bullying.

The principles of liberty focus on the contractual part of relationships—voluntary exchange with each other. Often this dynamic is in disarray when couples are in serious conflict. Agreements about sharing responsibility, for example, are usually confused by feelings of guilt and resentment. Often the individuals in conflict have no idea about distinguishing between exchanges and gifting. Indeed, they may feel they are doing favors for each other simply by carrying out routine responsibilities.

Almost any loving relationship also has an aspect of voluntary exchange. Friends do favors for each other not only out of love, but often out of an awareness that kindnesses will be returned. Friends also spend time together because they need partners for special activities, such as playing tennis or cards. In romantic relationships and especially in marriage, exchanges are important, but too often they are arranged without any real discussion of each person's desires. In the traditional family, the husband earns the money to support the family and the wife takes care of the household and probably the children as well. As already noted, this model tends to persist even when both partners are working outside the home. In most of these families, the exchange is unfairly tipped toward the husband. Many feminist theorists, with good reason, doubt if truly voluntary exchanges can take place between men and women in patriarchal society (French, 1985).

There are many subtle exchange issues between couples. Few

people have exactly the same sexual desires or experience the same sexual rhythms. Few people prefer exactly the same restaurants, movies, TV shows, or vacations. Again, bargaining and compromise may take place. But even in these instances, a genuine mutual concern with each other's preferences may lead individuals to work toward solutions in which each feels satisfied. It may become difficult to differentiate which they end up enjoying more: their own need satisfaction or that of their loved one. In the process, the couple will grow in their trust and their love for each other.

Often basic needs find differing expressions. One person wants to be held and another wants to be listened to. One likes continual companionship, another more alone time. One person needs financial security, another likes to take risks. Meeting these needs within the marriage may require negotiation, at least in the beginning, before love leads to mutual satisfaction.

Respect and self-esteem are generated in the voluntary exchange process. People feel good about themselves and about each other when they can successfully negotiate their way through a conflict toward mutual basic need satisfaction. Love is generated when people reach beyond negotiation and seek to help each other.

Recognizing the distinctions between esteem and love, between exchange and gifting, can help people begin to make sense out of their conflicts. A woman realizes that her husband's offers of affection always have "strings attached." They are really attempts at exchange. Both develop a better idea about love as unconditional. Both realize they have never given or received it, but determine to try to learn.

A man realizes that he loves his wife but doesn't respect her. A woman realizes she respects her husband but doesn't love him. Both partners realize that they once loved each other very much, but that the love has become lost in the bitter fighting. A woman realizes she is tired of being told "I love you" when she isn't being given a modicum of respect.

Mediation in itself is not the ultimate role of the therapist or conflict resolver. The aim is to teach principles of conflict resolution that the individuals can use for themselves. Often this can be done through example by helping them resolve problems during the session; but the ultimate goal is to give people the tools for resolving disputes without outside help. Relating through love is the single most important principle.

LOVE IN COUPLES CONFLICT RESOLUTION

Practical guides to conflict resolution often suggest the importance of love without explicitly or fully dealing with it. In *Getting Together*, Fisher and Scott discuss unconditional acceptance as a basic concept. They refer to the Bible as teaching "Love thine enemy," (p. 153), but do not fully explore the implications. Similarly, in *No-Fault Negotiating* (1987), Len Leritz declares "The degree of our success in negotiating is usually determined by the quality of relationship we have with the other person," (p. 7) and "Negotiating is a process of creating mutual understanding," (p. 10). Again, the implications are not fully explored. The concept of negotiation may itself be the stumbling block. Thoroughgoing conflict resolution reaches beyond bargaining or reconciling competing interests. It reaches toward a loving affiliation that recognizes the equal importance of each other's basic needs. In love, people treat each other's needs as if they were their own.

It will usually become apparent rather early on that there are limits to bargaining, compromising, and otherwise achieving voluntary exchanges in the absence of love. Helping people experience love requires patience. This is not surprising. Since love tends to resolve conflicts, loving couples do not as often end up in a therapy or conflict-resolution setting. On the other hand, love can also motivate people to save or to improve their relationship. Furthermore, the three dynamics do not exist in a rigid hierarchy of progression: love and hate, tenderness and violence, often coexist.

People may love each other very much, while nonetheless behaving very badly toward each other. Due to the ravages of their own Basic Stress Paradigms, or due to misunderstandings or serious practical problems, people who already love each other may nonetheless find their relationship failing.

Sometimes the couple may be aware of loving each other despite their conflicts; more often they can recall a time years earlier when they were "in love," a feeling that now seems tragically remote. If they never loved each other and are starting from scratch, the eventual flowering of romance is less promising, but not altogether out of the question. If the therapist can help them recapture feelings of love from earlier years, conflict resolution can be expedited.

THE FEAR OF LOVE

Love can be frightening, and when people "fall in love," they usually fall into fear as well (see chapter 2). Because romantic love can become the most intense expression of our adult social needs, it can amplify all of our social fears as well. Love not only heals the vast reservoirs of hurt within us, it can also hurl us into them (Breggin, 1980).

Love, especially romantic love, usually reactivates early childhood experiences of rejection, betrayal, and loss. It confronts us with how our parents and other relatives related to each other. It also recharges any previous adult hurts associated with love. Often an individual made one attempt at romantic love, perhaps in his or her teens or early twenties, and then, feeling badly hurt, "gave up on love." Now that protective barrier is threatened and fear sets in again.

Because of its intensity, romantic love brings out the worst—as well as the best—in us. On falling in love, it is commonplace for previously independent men and women to turn into helpless dependents. After they have committed themselves to a new love relationship, partners are likely to be shocked by the abrupt display of irrational conduct by their loved ones, as well as by themselves.

It is no wonder that people find it so hard to begin and to maintain passionate love relationships. It can be helpful for a therapist or conflict resolver to acknowledge the inevitability of fears and irrationality, and to teach people to break through them in order to get in touch with their loving feelings again.

ENCOURAGING LOVE

How does one "teach" or encourage love?

There are many different approaches to this, including explaining and discussing the nature of love, identifying it as an important aspect of life, and asking people about their personal experiences. A variety of popular books can also be useful. Didactic presentations should be limited to a brief few minutes and specifically addressed to the clients' thoughts, feelings, and experiences. Hopefully these brief presentations stimulate greater hope for the possibility of love in their lives.

When face to face with each other in a session, people can be encouraged to make eye contact or even physical contact, such as holding hands, and to risk feeling their more tender feelings toward each other. If people are feeling shy or defensive, they can experiment with feeling these emotions without expressing them. Guided activities such as these are only useful, however, if both partners feel ready to experiment with feeling or displaying more love and if both freely wish to enter into these potentially embarrassing interpersonal experiments. No pressure should be applied to get anyone to participate.

People often feel more hopeful about feeling love when they recall and consider less threatening experiences of love, such as their affection for a childhood friend, a pet, a work of art, a plant, or a place. They realize that they have the capacity for unconditional love and that they have experienced it in other circumstances. Very frequently the individual will then respond, "Oh, but it's so much safer to love my cat or my plants . . ." That revelation provides the opportunity for exploring the fears surrounding love for other human beings.

In helping people understand love, the aura, beingness, or personal attitudes of the therapist is probably the single most important factor. Does the therapist love, cherish, or treasure his or her clients? Does the therapist radiate pleasure or even joy on seeing them? Does the therapist really care about their well-being? Does the therapist take pleasure in learning more about each one of them? Does the therapist take delight in seeing them happy, both as individuals and with each other? Does the therapist love his or her work as a therapist or conflict resolver? Does the therapist display a zesty enjoyment of others and of life in general?

Ever since Carl Rogers (1961) first began to study the beneficial effect of the therapist's positive regard for the client, studies have continued to confirm his findings. In his review, James McConnell (1989) summarized:

Psychological change almost always occurs in a supportive, warm, rewarding environment. People usually "open up" and talk about things—and try new approaches to life—when they trust, admire, or want to please the therapist. (p. 509.)

In *Toxic Psychiatry* (1991), I described studies confirming that a warm, supportive, empathic approach is the most effective therapeutic approach regardless of how disturbed or incapacitated the patient may be.

Consciously or not, the client will evaluate the therapist as a person, and will be inspired or disillusioned by what he or she perceives. In chapter 10, in regard to Jimmy Carter's work as a peacemaker, it will be observed that the conflict resolver can play the same inspiring role in larger political conflicts.

Love, as it is defined in this book, is a joyful awareness characterized by treasuring, caring, mutuality, a desire for closeness, and empathy. If the therapist expresses these attitudes toward his or her clients, other people, and life in general, then the therapist is creating a healing environment.

I am not suggesting that the therapist or conflict resolver should fake a loving viewpoint. The therapist should actually develop these attitudes, for his or her own personal sake and for benefit of everyone involved in his or her life, including clients. Furthermore, if the therapist has a special difficulty feeling love for a particular client, it is up to the therapist, as a paid professional, to search out why his or her natural caring response to people is being withheld. The therapist should seek to open his or her own heart to the client or diplomatically suggest that the client seek another therapist. Every effort must be made not to communicate any rejection of the client.

No one is likely to meet an ideal standard of loving all or most of the time. What *is* required is a basically loving attitude and a profound conviction that love is the best way of life and the ultimate method of conflict resolution.

THE THERAPEUTIC OR CONFLICT-RESOLUTION SETTING

A well-constructed and maintained therapy setting greatly facilitates the possibility of people loving each other. Earlier in my career (Breggin, 1975), I described psychotherapy as a mini-utopia in which the client has the opportunity to experience a more protected and loving relationship than might otherwise be possible.

In general, people put in close proximity for periods of time will tend to feel affinity for each other. If the encounters include emotional sharing, love gains still more encouragement. In short, people who get to know each other tend to get to love each other. This principle has proven itself true in a variety of professional settings from psychotherapy to politically oriented conflict resolution workshops involving avowed enemies. It is obviously at work as well in other social and occupational settings.

Of course, people sometimes learn to dislike each other when they are thrown together. The therapist's or conflict-resolver's task is to minimize that possibility, while maximizing the more positive outcome.

The therapist's capacity to love in the therapy setting is enhanced by the rules that protect the integrity and separateness of the setting. The therapist limits social contact to the sessions themselves, avoiding the complexities and pitfalls of trying to extend it outside the office. The client deserves a quality of relating that is often beyond the ability of both the therapist and client outside the safety of the sessions.

Even if therapist and clients alike seem potentially capable of intimacy outside of the office, they are not likely to manage it while dealing with the most intense and painful issues in the clients' lives. Few, if any, experienced therapists would try to be a therapist or conflict resolver with friends on any regular on-going basis. A therapist might use his or her skills on occasion to help a friend, but a routinized therapy relationship is a whole other matter.

Within the therapy setting, sexual intimacy is unacceptable. Because of the inherent power imbalance between the therapist and client, romance too easily becomes exploitation. Therapy is disrupted and becomes potentially abusive when passion intervenes.

The therapist also places time and energy limits on the relationship so that it will not become overtaxing. Finally, the therapist is committed to being completely ethical in the treatment of all clients, and in demanding the same in return.

The therapist does not allow himself or herself to be abused physically or emotionally. This is an important point: therapy or conflict resolution is not the place where the client gets to "unload" on the therapist. Verbal attack, or any other form of coercion, is not good for the perpetrator and certainly not good for the victim, even if the victim is an experienced professional.

Unfortunately, the same warning must be given to therapists.

"Treatment" must never become an excuse for verbally or physically abusing the client. All people, regardless of their emotional problems, deserve the same respect for their dignity. In regard to biological psychiatry, physical treatments such as medication, electroshock, and lobotomy can easily become thinly veiled expressions of violence on the doctor's part (see chapter 7).

These built-in protections make the therapy a kind of mini-utopia of interpersonal relations in which the therapist is protected from stress, enabling him or her to be as rational and loving as possible. Meanwhile, the same protections encourage the clients to more easily and freely communicate with each other and with the therapist. However, the therapist is paid with money and with the satisfactions inherent in the work, but not specifically with love. Some clients may reciprocate with love, but the therapist must be prepared to help people who remain unwilling or unable to do so.

The therapist must be sure that he or she is not using "love" to manipulate the client. Furthermore, the therapist must be careful not to overwhelm the client. Most people are limited in how much love they can accept at any given time. The therapist's task is to remain sensitive to client responses so that the expressed caring or affection is not experienced as threatening or faked by the client.

Maintaining sufficient restraint is not very difficult, as long as the therapist does not try to satisfy his or her own basic love needs through the therapy. If the therapist remains oriented to the clients's feelings, he or she will not reach out in a frightening manner. Nor is it artificial or "fake" for the therapist to consciously control personal expressions of love. People restrain expressions of positive and negative feelings throughout daily living in response to multiple factors, including social convention, etiquette, the needs of others, and their own inclinations.

While therapists with specific religious convictions might differ from me, the aim of couples therapy or conflict analysis and resolution is *not* to assure the survival of the relationship or marriage. The aim is to help resolve deep-seated conflicts. The relationship or marriage may or may not prosper, depending on the wishes and abilities of the partners.

The conflict-resolution process also offers other benefits to the individuals, including self-realization through a better understanding of themselves and others, and a greater awareness of the principles of liberty and love in everyday life.

BASIC STRESS PARADIGMS

It is worth repeating that any current conflict will restimulate the negative results of past conflicts and their related Basic Stress Paradigms. Hurt, fear, and helplessness—expressed as guilt, shame, anxiety, numbing, and anger—rear up from the past to affect our current conflicts. The individual's childhood reactions become part of the current problem. A man who was often abandoned as a child, perhaps by being left alone at night when very small, may overreact to any hint of abandonment in adulthood. A woman who was screamed at or who heard a lot of screaming as a child may become frightened and irrational the moment a voice is raised.

People in conflict also undergo new Basic Stress Paradigms. After frequent episodes of abuse, betrayal, or abandonment, the hurt turns to fear and eventually to helplessness. I have seen men driven to suicidal despair by relentless guilt-provoking verbal assaults from their wives, and, more frequently, I have seen women driven into helpless outrage by the humiliating attitudes and actions of their husbands.

Some psychoanalysts would say that the *real* roots of each person's problem predate marriage and adulthood; but in my experience, a destructive relationship can, in and of itself, wholly demoralize an otherwise sound human being. Often a person needs, more than anything, to find the courage and confidence to leave an oppressive relationship.

SOCIAL INSTITUTIONS AND INDIVIDUAL PSYCHOLOGY

Individuals are of course enormously influenced by social institutions and the values they implement, including how these institutions cause, worsen, or prolong conflicts. The family, through its child rearing function, usually leaves the most indelible marks on the individual. Educational, religious, fraternal, military, and other institutions also play a role. TV, Hollywood, and the news media are major contributors to individual value systems.

Nearly all of society's institutions have one set of values in common—male patriarchy. The influence of patriarchy must be taken into account on every level of conflict resolution, from spousal to international disputes (French, 1985; Lerner, 1986; see chapter 11).

Patriarchy promotes and implements the values of "power over" and domination. It views human relationships in terms of hierarchies: who is superior and who is inferior.

In personal relationships, in both obvious and subtle ways, men tend to subordinate, ridicule, and control women. While either a man or a woman may be the chief abuser in any particular relationship, most men in most marriages are imbued with a sense of superiority over their wives and seek to impose controls upon them. Often men express their superiority by claiming to be more rational and sane (see Breggin, 1991). By withdrawing and inhibiting their feelings, they create a façade of autonomy and competence. By the time most couples seek help, the woman feels deeply humiliated by her husband's attitudes, which have reinforced her earlier humiliating experiences as a woman and girl.

In couples therapy, it is difficult to imagine an in-depth understanding or resolution of serious conflicts without dealing with issues of patriarchy and male domination. Most couples in therapy are enacting or resisting typical male-female stereotypes (described in detail in Breggin, 1991). Very often, the husband assumes a viewpoint similar to that of a biologically oriented psychiatrist. He is aloof, "objective," seemingly rational, and believes that his wife is emotionally unstable and mentally ill. He feels she makes demands on him emotionally that make no sense. He yearns to be "let alone." In turn, the wife feels humiliated, deeply emotionally deprived, and overtly angry. She feels controlled and rejected by him, and longs for deeper communication.

Typically the husband injures her by withdrawing emotionally and by looking down upon her; she injures him by verbally attacking and ridiculing him. He gives her no help with the domestic chores, even if she is working full time; and she undermines his sense of worth and potency, often by rejecting him sexually.

Both the husband and wife feel victimized by the other and justify their aggressive tactics as retaliation for injuries perpetrated by the other. But beneath these gender stereotypes both are feeling thwarted in their basic needs for respect, love, companionship, and security.

In international politics, the male dominator viewpoint prevails in nearly every conflict through the exercise of economic power and the threat of war. Patriarchal politics exerts an influence on all of society, from the TV and the media to the little boys playing guns or bullying each other in the school yard. Violence is treated as a rational solution to conflict. As in the attack on Iraq, war is reported by the media as if it were a computer game. The destruction or suppression of other people is rationalized on the grounds that they are "different" and "inferior" (see chapter 10).

CHANGING VALUES IN THERAPY AND CONFLICT RESOLUTION

In several of my earliest publications, I stressed that the principles of the free-enterprise system are essential to the conduct of psychotherapy. Not only does the client pay the therapist or clinic, the client is encouraged to develop Dynamic II ethics of autonomy and independence. I urged therapists to recognize that therapy is a form of applied ethics and politics, and suggested that they make free enterprise values central to their practice.

Experience has continued to confirm the essentially ethical and political nature of psychotherapeutic processes, but also the need for a more subtle awareness and a more complex analysis of the values involved. First, I have come to place increasing emphasis on the negative influence of patriarchal values, especially the use of power to suppress conflict. Power and coercion as values impinge on people in their everyday lives, including outright sexism and more subtle forms of authoritarianism. Second, I now see more pitfalls in rigidly free-enterprise values. Third, and closely related, I more openly embrace the role of love in therapy and in life. And finally, it now seems inescapable that there are inherent and sometimes unresolvable contradictions in trying to live by the principles of both liberty and love, even though we must strive to reconcile these two ideals.

ILLUSTRATING THE CONFLICT BETWEEN LIBERTY AND LOVE

I recently had a session with one of my patients, Jeb, that underscored the potential conflict between liberty and love in professional relationships, such as therapy and conflict resolution. The issue was fees.

When Jeb first came to see me six months earlier, he was hard pressed to pay my usual fee, and so I reduced it by about ten percent. Now he unexpectedly sold the rights to a project he had been working on for years, and overnight he had become wealthy.

It rather quickly occurred to me that he could now easily afford to pay my original fee and that it would be fair to ask him to do so. However, as far as I could recall, I had originally neglected to raise the possibility of readjusting his fee at a later date, and so I wanted to ask his permission to do so. I also didn't want to seem greedy or insensitive, and therefore hesitated to follow up on his good fortune by immediately asking for more money. So I waited a couple of months before bringing it up.

Jeb is a very quiet but extremely intelligent young man who has trouble knowing and expressing his feelings; but when I said that I would like to increase my fee to its original level, he flushed with color, became silent, grinned uncomfortably, and generally looked uneasy. After a few minutes, he explained that my request seemed entirely reasonable and ethical. He agreed that he could and would pay the increase, but . . . but that he felt somehow . . .—the words were hard for him to find—"confused, upset, disappointed, hurt."

Our conversation went on to traverse territory I've frequently covered around the issue of fees, but with more mutual openness than usual. There were moments when I too flushed, became silent, grinned uncomfortably, and generally looked uneasy. The following summary of our conversation highlights some fundamental issues of liberty and love, of capitalism and caring.

Although Jeb kept reassuring me that my request was reasonable and that he planned to comply, he wished in his heart that our relationship was more like a friendship, that I cared about him more as a person than as a paying client, and that therefore it wouldn't have occurred to me to think about money. My asking him for the few dollars more, he said, reminded him of his childhood feelings that no one cared about him—that he as a person simply wasn't important. Indeed, expressing these feelings brought up some important new insights into his childhood.

Perhaps some therapists would have played up Jeb's own references to his childlike feelings. They might have felt and even said that Jeb was being childlike by "wanting something for nothing," and so on. But it did not strike me that way at all.

Among other things, I was noticing my own "childlike" feelings, and sharing them with Jeb as well. While he had wished that I cared enough not to even think about money, I had wished that he cared enough to realize, as a newly wealthy man, that it was only fair to pay the original fee.

While I was expressing this part of myself to Jeb, I was also reassuring him that in no way were my feelings rational. That is, I did not in reality want him or expect him, as my client, to be focusing his attention on my needs. But I did think it might be helpful for him to know that he was not alone—that his therapist was also struggling over the contradictions between free-market principles and love in a therapeutic relationship.

I had also hesitated to bring up raising my fee because I didn't want to hurt Jeb's feelings. I did genuinely care about him. Indeed, as I told him, I would have reduced my fee further had it been necessary to allow him to come to therapy while working on his long-term project. I didn't want him to have to give up either his therapy or his much-loved work. And to compound my ambivalence, I felt that *not* bringing up the fee would deny an important issue. After all, the fee had been reduced because he was financially in need of it, and that was no longer the case. I wanted to address his feelings about it, and if helpful to him, to share mine as well.

Perhaps some mental health professionals would conceptualize my session with Jeb in psychoanalytic terms. They would say that Jeb was suffering from "transference" (his childhood emotional reactivity directed at me) and that I was suffering from "counter-transference" (my childhood emotional reactivity directed in turn at his transference). I did not view it in that manner, and the session turned out to be very productive. Jeb expressed his tender feelings more openly than ever before in therapy. I also shared my own feelings with him. He was able to affirm that all of his reactions, including the conflicted ones, were acceptable and understandable; and that we two men could share ourselves at an awkward moment and come out the better for it.

I now believe that all people, deep down, want to be loved for themselves. The nuances will differ from person to person; but all persons want to be loved and cared about. These desires make it almost inevitable that conflicts will come up in therapy about paying fees.

It also seems apparent that on a larger societal scale, capitalism and caring are bound to conflict. There is nothing in the profit motive that necessitates caring about anything but money. Other values must contain and ameliorate the drive to maximize profits (see chapter 8).

Put in more abstract terms, there are inherent contradictions between liberty and love. While liberty can be the staging ground for love, it can also get in the way of it. It *is* difficult at times to have both a capitalistic and a caring relationship, and this is true in both the personal and the societal arena.

PROFESSIONALISM AS A SOLUTION

In professional relationships, in part to ameliorate these contradictions, restraints are usually placed on the profit motive. Although I know at least one psychiatrist who has acted differently, the vast majority of mental health professionals do not believe that they are supposed to charge each individual person as much as he or she can be pushed to pay. Yet that is a basic free-market principle: to charge what the traffic will bear; to maximize profits.

In Jeb's case, for example, I did not try to raise his fee beyond my usual one, even though he could have easily afforded it. In my experience, few professionals, including lawyers, try to charge each client as much as possible. The usual terse explanation is "I'm a professional" or perhaps "I'm in a service profession."

But there's a deeper, if unsaid, reason why professionals don't usually try to squeeze every penny they can from their clients. There is an element of *caring* in being a professional. There is an imperative to orient to the client's needs as well as toward one's own. Gilligan (1982) has pointed out that women often make mutual satisfaction one of their highest values; professionals often do the same, without necessarily acknowledging it.

It is not merely a matter of "good business practices" or "wanting to keep my customers." In professionalism, there's a *higher standard* than mere profit. That standard includes regard for the client's interests. When regard becomes unconditional—separated from the profit motive—it moves from Dynamic II: liberty toward Dynamic I: love. Unhappily, there has been an increasing tendency among some professionals to become "mere businessmen," but most people lament this as a breach in ethical standards.

When people know each other, affection or personal regard more easily modifies the unbridled pursuit of self-interest. The conflicts become more difficult to resolve on a societal level where members of the community have little or no personal contact, no obviously shared tasks, and few cultural ties (see chapter 9).

INVOLUNTARY CONFLICT RESOLUTION WITH COUPLES

Involuntary conflict resolution is probably a misnomer. When one or another participant has been compelled to participate—for example, by court order, civil commitment, or threats of harm from another person—conflict resolution becomes badly distorted. As discussed in chapter 4, threats and force make honest, open communication almost impossible, and instead encourage lying and deception. Basic needs cannot safely be disclosed in situations of such great vulnerability and so their satisfaction is prevented. When coerced into anything, most people focus their attention on doing whatever is necessary to escape from the coercion or to limit its impact. The agenda of "staying out of trouble with the authorities" is not conducive to conflict resolution.

Even in seemingly voluntary situations, power imbalances obstruct the resolution of conflict. If one side has vastly greater resources or authority, a situation tends to become coercive. Dynamic III, with its untoward consequences, slips into place.

Every effort should be made to make any conflict-resolution effort as voluntary as possible. When this cannot be done, the therapist or conflict resolver should weigh the possibility of ending the process or refusing to participate. Other avenues may then prove more useful. For example, if a man has been battering his wife it may be necessary to institute criminal proceedings before attempting therapy or conflict resolution. Once the criminal matter is resolved, the perpetrator can more freely decide whether or not to enter into a therapeutic or conflict-resolution program.

IMPLICATIONS FOR PSYCHOTHERAPY

Psychotherapy is best understood as a form of conflict resolution. The therapist helps clients resolve internal conflicts, as well as conflicts with family members and society. As the vignette about Jeb and myself illustrates, the therapist's conflicts with his or her clients are also grist for the therapeutic mill. Some conflict is unavoidable over one or more routine issues, such as fees, scheduling, therapeutic approaches, and the length and content of sessions.

In these conflicts with clients, the therapist's ethics and caring are most sorely tested, and yet this aspect of therapy has great potential benefit for the client. If the client discovers that the therapist relates, at times of conflict, in a respectful and loving manner, then the client will probably develop an increased sense of personal worth, and improved skills in dealing with people.

As I discuss in *Toxic Psychiatry* (1991), adherence to the highest principles of conflict resolution becomes even more important with severely disturbed individuals. These severely hurt people are often more easily overwhelmed by coercive, uncaring tactics or attitudes. Unfortunately, these emotionally injured people are most likely to find themselves victimized by destructive psychiatric interventions, such as involuntary "treatment," massive drug doses, and electroshock.

OVERVIEW

Any thoroughgoing interpersonal conflict resolution process must address all three dynamics: coercion, liberty, and love. The parties to the conflict must learn to forsake the use of force, except in self-defense, and to negotiate agreements according to the principles of liberty. But that is not the end of it, and at some point in the relationship, the parties to the conflict ideally will begin to care about each other in new and more loving ways.

They will see themselves in each other, and mutually address each other's needs and values. Where they perceive differences, they will be pleased and delighted by them. They will look out for each other as they do for themselves. They will at times find themselves so deeply concerned about the fulfillment of each other's needs that distinctions between self and other, selfishness and altruism, will be rendered meaningless. They will take care of each other's needs on a level that neither one could possibly do alone.

The above description of a loving relationship is not farfetched.

It is, in fact, a commonly held ideal of family life, marriage, and friendship. While it is rarely fulfilled in all aspects, it is often approximated.

As described in chapter 2, empathy and the desire to help begin within the first year or two of life, and they can be cultivated throughout life. Parents, spouses, lovers, and friends frequently put the needs of loved ones above their own. Ethical professionals, as well as people in general, often find themselves "not taking advantage." Sometimes at great personal cost, they promote the interests of others in their family, social, and occupational lives.

In all spheres of life, people often take better care of each other than they could take care of themselves on their own. Often people freely sacrifice for each other without even considering it a sacrifice. While the therapeutic and conflict-resolution fields have not paid sufficient attention to the love dynamic, it remains the foundation of individual well-being, the critical ingredient of social life, and the ultimate source of both individual happiness and harmony among people.

CHAPTER 7

▼ ▼

The Role of Psychiatry in Conflict Resolution

Some paradox of our nature leads us, when once we have made our fellow men the objects of our enlightened interests, to go on to make them the object of our pity, then of our wisdom, ultimately of our coercion.

Lionel Trilling, **The Liberal Imagination** *(1979)*

Psychiatry is a method of social control. It gives the power to confer exemptions and excuses; it gives the power to lock people up and throw away the key.

Jonas Robitscher, **The Powers of Psychiatry** *(1980)*

By its very nature, psychotherapy must pretend to supply an objective, kindly, and human atmosphere to those who wish to express their deepest feelings of pain and sorrow. The tragedy is that this legitimate need is exploited, even if with the best of intentions, by "experts" who claim to offer what has never been theirs to give.

Jeffrey Masson, **Against Therapy** *(1988)*

The most severe personal conflicts have been relegated to the mental health profession. If a person becomes despairing, suicidal, or seemingly mad, almost everyone agrees that psychiatry has the best answers. Many societal conflicts, like crime and homelessness, also lie within the province of psychiatry. Yet modern principles of conflict resolution, including the concepts of liberty and love, have had almost no impact on the mental health profession.

As a psychiatrist, I have been dismayed to watch modern psychiatry reduce psychological problems and conflicts between people to biochemical defects within one specific individual. While there is little or no scientific basis for the new biological psychiatry (Breggin, 1991; Cohen, 1990; Coleman, 1984), the ideology has gained widespread support. Ironically, psychiatry's growing reliance on genetic and biological theories comes at precisely the moment that clinical and empirical research is confirming the childhood origins of adult problems and emotional pain (reviewed in chapters 4 and 5).

A child who rebels in a dysfunctional home or fights the burdensome routine of school is labeled hyperactive and given Ritalin. An elderly woman who becomes depressed over being ostracized and abandoned is labeled major depression and given shock treatment. A man who cannot find work or housing is labeled schizophrenic and forced into a state mental hospital.

Too often, little or no effort is made by psychiatry to identify and satisfy the individual's basic needs. While the patient is seen as incompetent, no attempt is made to support his or her autonomy and independence. No attention is given to the conflicts between the individual and other people, such as his or her family, school, or community. Instead, psychiatry takes a short cut: It diagnoses the person as mentally ill, explains away the problem as genetic and biochemical in origin, and subdues the patient with drugs, electroshock, and hospitalization (Breggin, 1991).

To say that psychiatry rejects Dynamic II values, such as liberty and self-determination, is no exaggeration. Psychiatrists intervene as outside authorities to diagnose people and to prescribe for them, often against their will. As I describe in "Iatrogenic Helplessness in Authoritarian Psychiatry," (1983), physical treatments, such as drugs and electroshock, tend to make the patient more helpless and dependent—more suggestible and amenable to psychiatric control.

To say that psychiatry is a loveless approach is also no exaggeration. Psychiatric training encourages the doctor to relate in an aloof, controlling and authoritarian manner, rather than with a warm and caring approach (Breggin, 1991). Contemporary psychiatric principles and practices are at odds with those of conflict analysis and resolution that seek to empower the individual and to encourage collaborative decision-making.

PSYCHIATRY AND INTERPERSONAL CONFLICT RESOLUTION

When psychiatrists treat a patient, they usually single out one member of an interpersonal conflict for their attention. Others involved in the conflict escape diagnosis and treatment but may in reality be more the source of the problem. The conflict is then suppressed by locking up, drugging, or shocking one of the members into a more submissive state.

When psychiatrists intervene in family conflict, they will single out one or another member of the family as "mentally ill." A child, for example, is restless or rebellious at home and is labeled hyperactive. A wife is despairing about her marriage, stops doing the housework, won't get out of bed. She is diagnosed depressed. A husband is filled with rage, much of it stemming from childhood Basic Stress Paradigms, and tries to stifle his pain by drinking. He is labeled alcoholic.

Many individuals who become diagnosed by psychiatrists are in reality suffering from oppression. This is especially apparent in children because they are more obviously subjected to events outside their control. The psychiatrically labeled child is, in most cases, a victim of obvious family conflict, often including emotional, physical, or sexual abuse (Breggin, 1980, 1991; Miller, 1984; Green, 1989). Sometimes the child is directly reacting to marital discord. At other times, the child simply has too much energy and creativity to be contained within stultifying homes or classrooms.

Whether the problem lies in the child's family or the school, the child is further injured by being diagnosed and treated. The family or the school should be helped to respond better to the child's basic needs for love, security, and stimulating education.

Childhood stresses eventually become internalized as Basic Stress Paradigms and psychological conflict, and many adults suffer from the result of experiences they can no longer recall. The adult who hallucinates voices talking to him through the walls of his house may be reexperiencing the dread of overhearing his parents speaking in a threatening manner through his bedroom wall when he was a small child. The grown woman who thinks her insides are rotting may be driven by the horror of incestuous abuse as a child (for further discussions, see Breggin, 1991).

Basic Stress Paradigms or internalized conflicts from childhood often impinge on adult conflicts in a marriage (see chapter 6) and other areas of adult life. A woman becomes immobilized by fear whenever her husband looks at all aggressive; a man collapses in guilt whenever his wife complains about anything.

However, not all adult emotional problems result from childhood experiences. More often than generally realized, women are driven to despair by physical, sexual, and emotional abuse in their ongoing marriages (Walker, 1989). Sometimes, men are pushed into severe depression when they cannot cope with continuous verbal abuse from their wives.

In summary, when psychiatrists "treat mental illness," they are manipulating and controlling people who instead need someone to address their basic needs and conflicts. The psychiatric interventions tend to suppress conflict, often at great cost to the person labeled "patient." The conflict model is far more appropriate and effective than its psychiatric counterpart.

PSYCHIATRY AND THE HOMELESS

Psychiatrists also enter the arena of conflict resolution on a social and political scale. The profession originated during the industrial revolution as a method of bypassing legal restraints on the incarceration of homeless street people (Foucault, 1965). Civil commitment proceedings were instituted throughout the Western world permitting the indefinite incarceration of homeless, unemployed, and sometimes mad people. State mental hospitals, within which the profession originated, were lockups for the poor. Some became self-sustaining feudal systems in which the once homeless inmates now became completely self-supporting with their own dairies, farms, mechanics, tailors, and so on.

By the 1930s these giant lockups, which shoved the problem of poverty under the institutional rug, had become too large and unmanageable. Lobotomy and various shock "therapies" were developed for subduing the inmates (Breggin, 1979, 1983a). In the 1950s, drugs were developed that induce chemical lobotomies (Breggin, 1991). These drugs—called neuroleptics, antipsychotics, or major tranquilizers—remain in widespread use in institutions of all kinds, and in clinics and private practice as well.

Despite the new drugs, the hospitals remained overflowing. Then in 1963 the federal government's disability payment programs began to cover psychiatric diagnoses, and, for the first time, patients declared psychiatrically disabled could receive a meager sum to help them live at home, in nursing homes, board-and-care homes, and sometimes on the streets. Thus began so-called deinstitutionalization, which was mostly a transfer of patients to private facilities, with the cost shifted from the state to the federal government. This series of events is better described by the term transinstitutionalization than by deinstitutionalization (Brown, 1988; Mosher and Burti, 1989).

The economic policies of the Reagan and Bush administrations resulted in a vast increase in the numbers of homeless. The real wages of the poor dropped, low-cost housing subsidies decreased, housing costs went up. The result was a massive escalation in people who could not afford housing.

Now psychiatry is attempting to reinstitute its old policies in what might be called reinstitutionalization. Here psychiatry moves into an area of societal conflict—what to do about the poor and homeless—and offers an easy political solution: lock them up against their will. That many of these people may show psychiatric "symptoms" is beside the point. First, being homeless can make a person seem crazy. Second, people who are more helpless or less competent (including people who seem mad) are the first to suffer from adverse economic conditions. What these unfortunates need is not involuntary incarceration and drugs, but improved economic circumstances, including, if necessary, nonmedical forms of support from society.

Many of those who are now unable to cope with society, including thousands of street people, have been brain damaged by previous psychiatric treatments. Even those who are neurologically impaired and relatively helpless don't need state mental hospitals. They don't need to be declared "biochemically imbalanced," only to have genuine biochemical imbalances inflicted on them by means of highly toxic drugs. What they do need is a safe haven in which they can be free from these abuses (Breggin, 1991; Breggin and Stern, in press; Mosher and Burti, 1989).

A few years ago I interviewed several dozen homeless people at two California drop-in centers. Some were interviewed alone and some in groups. With one exception, all agreed that no matter how hungry or cold they became, they would never voluntarily enter a mental hospital. They preferred the streets to psychiatric incarceration and "treatment." The one exception was an older woman who said that she would go to a hospital before she'd starve, but survivors of psychiatry in the group arose to warn her never to take the risk.

Some of these homeless people had undergone brief counseling, which they recalled as positive, and none were hostile to "talking doctors." All of these people rejected biopsychiatric interventions, often preferring the hazards of the street to those of the mental hospital. They remind us that involuntary hospitalization and treatment are aimed at serving the convenience of a society that does not wish to confront its conflicts with the poor and the disabled.

PSYCHIATRY AND VIOLENCE: THE LATEST INITIATIVE

For a few hundred years, psychiatrists have claimed to be specialists in predicting violence, thereby justifying the involuntary treatment of presumably violent individuals. Thus they intervened in both family disputes and criminal proceedings to suppress conflict by incarcerating one of the members "for his (her) own good."

Then in the 1974 Tarasoff decision in California, a psychiatrist was held responsible for the violent acts of one of his patients on the grounds that he could have warned the patient's potential victim. Psychiatry did an abrupt turnabout and began to claim that it could *not* predict violence.

I became heavily involved in psychiatric reform activities in the early 1970s in a successful effort to stem the resurgence of lobotomy and other forms of psychiatric surgery. A group consisting of two Harvard neurosurgeons and a Harvard psychiatrist had obtained government funds on the grounds that they were developing a form of psychiatric brain surgery that could treat violent ghetto rioters. Thus they exploited the public's fear of racial violence to obtain publicity and federal funds for a psychiatric solution to the most frightening of our national problems during that period. A critical political problem was to be solved by oppressive medical means (see Breggin, 1991, pp. 418, 426, 427).

The suggested use of psychosurgery for the control of violence was one aspect of larger federal strategy aimed at establishing a series of violence centers in association with well-known urban psychiatric centers. The thrust was biological and genetic with reliance on involuntary treatment, behavior modification, and physical interventions. Psychosurgery for the control of violence was stopped largely as a result of efforts organized through the Center for the Study of Psychiatry and the funding of the violence centers was prevented by a larger coalition.

Twenty years later—at the moment this book is being completed—the federal mental health establishment is again planning a national biomedical program for violence control, and with a decidedly racist thrust. Frederick Goodwin, a biological psychiatrist and the highest ranking federal mental health official, had stepped into a controversy when he compared the inner city to a "jungle" and further compared inner city young men to Rhesus monkeys who are preoccupied with killing each other, having sex, and reproducing. As a result of the furor, I wrote a letter to the *New York Times* and consulted with an aide to U.S. Congressman John Conyers. I received the transcript of Goodwin's remarks as he delivered them to a meeting of the National Mental Health Council. It discloses the "violence initiative," the hitherto unpublicized *top priority* for federal mental health funding starting in 1994. The aim of the violence initiative is the early identification of genetically and biochemically defective young inner city men who will be studied and subjected to involuntary incarceration, behavior modification, and/or drug treatment.

The violence initiative specifically rejects any attempt to identify or remedy social, economic, or cultural causes of violence, such as racism, unemployment, and poverty. As a biomedical strategy, it will locate the problem within supposedly defective individuals who presumably suffer from genetic and biochemical disorders.

Not only will the violence initiative distract society from the true causes of inner city violence, it poses a monstrous threat to civil liberties and to the well-being of those at whom the program is aimed. Goodwin initially estimates that 100,000 children and young people will be targeted. Inevitably, most will be black and inevitably the numbers will grow.

On March 19, 1992, I sent out "An Urgent Message from the Center for the Study of Psychiatry," accompanied by a review of A Dangerous New Biomedical Program for Social Control: The Federal "Violence Initiative." It is the opening round of an educational campaign to alert the nation to this latest biomedical attempt at social control. By the time this book comes out, that educational effort will hopefully be in full swing.

PSYCHIATRY AND THE PSYCHOTIC PERSON

Psychiatry derives much of its power from the claim that it offers special understanding and indispensable medical approaches to people labeled psychotic, such as so-called "schizophrenics." In fact, it offers patients little more than chemical lobotomy and involuntary confinement.

On the other hand, there is ample evidence for the efficacy of more humane, nonmedical approaches. These caring, psychosocial alternatives have been described in a number of places (Karon, 1989; Mosher and Burti, 1988; Breggin, 1991; Breggin and Stern, in production). The superiority of the psychosocial approach for very disturbed people labeled "schizophrenic" has been demonstrated in controlled studies (Mosher and Burti, 1989; Karon, 1989).

My career in mental health began as a college student when I worked in a student-run treatment program for state mental hospital inmates. As untrained college sophomores and juniors working with individual inmates of the institutions, we were able to get the vast majority out of the hospital in less than a year (Breggin, 1991).

People who are so fragile that they distort or withdraw from reality are in special need of tender, caring approaches. These injured persons are less able than stronger people to survive the assault of authoritarian, coercive, and toxic treatments. Anyone who feels sufficiently worthless and humiliated to imagine being Jesus Christ will be especially demoralized by being told that he or she is in reality "a schizophrenic" who is biologically and genetically defective.

People who are drastically impaired in their capacity for social relationships need supportive social relationships from friends, family, rehabilitation workers, or psychotherapists. Often they need help with supervised housing or employment. It would be more helpful, more humane, and in the long run less expensive if society offered them what they need—safe havens staffed by nonprofessional, caring people. Because nonprofessional, nonpsychiatric interventions are less expensive, the overall cost to society would be reduced.

PSYCHIATRY REINFORCES THINGNESS

Modern biobehavioral psychiatry falls almost wholly into Dynamic III: coercion (see the Three Dynamic Table, p. 261). Dynamic III: coercion describes the conditions created by any authoritarian and totalitarian institution, such as a mental hospital or prison. In *Asylums* (1961), Erving Goffman showed how state mental hospitals turn patients into docile inmates devoid of self-respect or self-determination. The same dismal results were achieved in the USSR and Eastern Bloc countries through decades of political totalitarianism (see chapter 10). Thus, the values imposed on patients in almost any Western mental hospital parallel those inflicted on the citizens of the Russia, Poland, Hungary, and many other European nations a few years ago. Carrying our comparison still further, the problem of "deinstitutionalizing" a long-term psychiatric inmate is not different in kind from the problem of bringing a middle-aged Soviet citizen into the era of *perestroika* and *glasnost.*

The philosophies of European communism and American biobehavioral and institutional psychiatry have much in common both in principle and outcome. Both are authoritarian, materialistic, and reductionist; both demean their victims and render them more helpless. Thus, it is no coincidence that nearly all of the descriptive phrases listed as Dynamic III: coercion in the table can be applied equally to both totalitarianism and to biological, institutional psychiatry.

When humans are most irrational and oppressed, they tend to view themselves as "things," as summarized in the Three Dynamics of Human Progress table in the column entitled "Thingness." For example, patients labeled psychotic often believe they are being controlled by outside forces, from extraterrestrials or people who don't really know them, to farfetched energy waves and remote control devices.

As I describe in an article in *The Journal of Existential Psychology and Psychiatry* (in production), psychiatry is likely to view irrational and oppressed human beings in the way they view themselves—as defective, disabled devices, rather than as struggling human beings. When the patient says, "I am controlled by radio waves," the psychiatrist answers, "In fact, you are controlled by genetic defects and biochemical imbalances." When the patient says, "People want to control me," the psychiatrist responds, "If you really believe that then you should be controlled." The psychiatrist then fulfills the patient's worst fears by locking her up "for her own good." Psychiatry reinforces the mental patient's worst self-image as lacking in autonomy and self-determination, unworthy of human love, and deserving of coercion.

Too often, the psychiatrist actually pushes the patient further into mental helplessness by giving suppressive drugs and electroshock. Already feeling like a defective objective, the patient is made neurologically dysfunctional by the treatment. I suggested the term *iatrogenic helplessness* to describe the biopsychiatric principle of maintaining authority and control by damaging the patient's brain (Breggin, 1983). The production of brain dysfunction encourages the patient and doctor alike to view the patient as a defective mechanism lacking in free will, autonomy, or higher spiritual aspirations.

THE OVERALL FAILURE OF THE MENTAL HEALTH PROFESSIONS

As a profession born of involuntary treatment and state mental hospitals, psychiatry is historically rooted in coercion. Its original mandate, still in force, was to suppress conflicts between the homeless poor and the remainder of society by locking up the homeless (Foucault, 1965).

Often psychiatry uses outright force in the form of incarceration and involuntary drugging, and sometimes even involuntary electroshock. More often it uses the *threat* of force, plus moral authority, to control and manipulate people (Breggin, 1964). Seemingly voluntary psychiatric patients frequently remain in treatment out of fear of being coerced if they attempted to quit.

When patients are legally voluntary, psychiatry's approach too often remains Dynamic III: coercion—the dehumanizing of the individual into a defective object or thing by means of biochemical and genetic theories, psychiatric diagnoses, and brain-disabling treatments.

Even more psychologically oriented mental health interventions frequently end up dehumanizing the recipient of the services by diagnosing and manipulating them (Masson, 1988; Cohen, 1990). Since biobehavioral psychiatry tends to set the official standard for mental health practices—for example, through its textbooks and diagnostic manuals—much of what passes for mental health treatment does more harm than good.

Despite its vast opportunity to do so, the mental health profession has not spearheaded our understanding of the damaging effects of childhood abuse. Despite the public's view of psychoanalysis as focusing on the harm done to children by their parents, Freud actually helped delay recognition of the widespread extent of childhood abuse. As a result, his life's work encouraged the oppression of children and the discrediting of adult clients who had been abused as children (Miller, 1984; Masson, 1984).

As Jeffrey Masson has documented in *The Assault on Truth* (1982), Freud used his theory of the Oedipus complex to cover up the sexual abuse of young women and children. When he was rejected by his colleagues for making known that his female patients had been sexually abused as children, he instead made up the Oedipal theory, which claims that patients imagine, desire, and invent the abuse.

Most of the advances in understanding child abuse have come from renegades within the mental health profession, such as Alice Miller (1984), or from those wholly outside the profession, often in the field of social psychology or sociology (see chapter 5). The profession has been especially remiss in its failure to raise issues about patriarchy and the male abuse of women and children. Many psychiatric textbooks, for example, fail to mention these critical issues and also continue to use blatantly sexist diagnoses.

BRINGING TOGETHER PSYCHOTHERAPY AND CONFLICT RESOLUTION

Chapter 6 outlined some of the basic principles of psychotherapy from a conflict resolution viewpoint. Psychotherapy or "talking therapy" can be provided by a variety of professionals, including psychiatrists, psychologists, social workers, and counselers, and also by volunteers and noncredentialed individuals (Breggin, 1991). Attitude is more than any technique. A loving, empathic, enthusiastic approach on the part of the therapist will influence the outcome positively for the client (see chapter 6).

When psychotherapists help people, often they do so despite their training. The best psychotherapists, without necessarily realizing it, utilize a conflict analysis and resolution model rather than a medical model. They help people overcome both intrapsychic and extrapsychic conflict in order to find more personally free and loving approaches to life. These therapists reject the psychiatrically oriented diagnostic and treatment methods they were taught in school.

Experienced psychotherapists often agree with the thrust of this book, that therapeutic help should not prescribe or direct the individual toward particular outcomes. Rather, psychotherapy provides a healthy relationship that encourages personal growth and it implements principles that facilitate self-realization and human community.

Meanwhile, little or nothing about liberty and love is taught to mental health professionals or discussed in the literature. Because traditional psychiatry so offends the principles of liberty, it simply ignores the issue in its books and teaching programs. Psychologists have proven somewhat more willing to examine questions of personal freedom. Love, the ultimate method of healing the wounded heart and resolving human conflict, is rarely addressed anywhere in the mental health community.

Many psychotherapists do learn about loving approaches through their own experiences in therapy and through sharing their feelings with trusted colleagues. Unfortunately, this is left to chance and personal initiative, and is too often discouraged by formal education or training.

As psychiatry has become increasingly authoritarian and biological, fewer and fewer psychiatrists have even an inkling of these more human approaches. The mantle for offering good psychotherapy has fallen to nonmedical specialists, such as psychologists, social workers, and counselors. But the biopsychiatric hegemony tends to corrupt the entire field.

Individual well-being and the good of society is far better served by a conflict-resolution model that emphasizes liberty and love than by the psychiatric model. While there may be little hope in the near future for reforming psychiatry, there is much hope for conflict analysis and resolution, and for psychotherapy; but only if they divorce themselves from traditional psychiatric theory and practice. In the ideal scenario, psychotherapy would eventually become a part of the overall field of conflict analysis and resolution.

▼ ▼ ▼ ▼ ▼ ▼ ▼ ▼ ▼ ▼ ▼ ▼ ▼ ▼ ▼ ▼. ▼ ▼ ▼ ▼ ▼ ▼ ▼ ▼ ▼ ▼ ▼ ▼ ▼ ▼

CHAPTER 8

Resolving Conflict within Business Corporations

There is an epidemic of disaffection subverting the organizations of America, whether they be public or private. Increasingly more people view their jobs as sentences to be served rather than as opportunities for the realization of their personal dreams. The disaffected are losing any significant belief in their unique worth to their organizations. . . . Too many believe that happiness— however it is defined—is to be found only outside of the job.
David K. Hart, in The Revitalization of the Public Service by Robert Denhardt and Edward Jennings, Jr. (1987)

Most people still believe that every kind of large-scale adminis- tration must necessarily be "bureaucratic," i.e., an alienated form of administration. And most people are unaware of how deaden- ing the bureaucratic spirit is and how it pervades all spheres of life. . . . Bureaucrats fear personal responsibility and seek refuge behind their rules; their security and pride lie in their loyalty to the rules, not in their loyalty to the laws of the human heart.
Erich Fromm, To Have or To Be (1976)

Large corporations, as well as Mom-and-Pop corner stores, are supposed to represent the principles of liberty, the free market, and the pursuit of self-interest. Given the potential conflict be- tween liberty and love, capitalism and caring, it is important to explore whether or not corporations can implement the principles of love within the workplace.

CORPORATIONS AND THE FREE MARKET

In reality, of course, corporations rarely if ever compete in any- thing approximating a free market; nor are they run purely for the benefit of profit-hungry shareholders. Large corporations thrive amid innumerable government benefits, from the transportation infrastructure paid for by taxpayers to the innumerable contracts and services provided by government agencies. Tariffs, labor laws, and myriad federal regulations control competition to the advantage of existing corporations. Often corporations engage in monopolistic practices, fixing prices, setting interest rates, and so on. Furthermore, they often fail to pursue the profit of their shareholders. One "golden parachute" scandal after another has testified to how executives place their own self-interest above that of the actual owners of the businesses. Often corporations become rigid bureaucracies with nearly as much automatic tenure as the oldest federal agencies.

Even smaller companies do not function within a free market. Typically they are subjected to government regulation in the form of taxation, building, and health codes, and the regulation of their specific activities, such as home and office construction, food supplies, or health services. Many of these regulations serve more to limit competition than to protect the public.

This chapter cannot provide a thoroughgoing analysis of the complex topic of corporate structure and function, or the limits of free enterprise. Rather, it can illustrate the usefulness of the Three Dynamic Theory in evaluating an important societal institution, the large corporation. In particular, it examines the actual and potential role of love in corporate life.

DYNAMIC I IN MODERN CORPORATE LIFE

In a 1986 conference at Rice University organized by Konstantin Kolenda entitled *Organizations and Ethical Individualism* (1988), psychologists, philosophers, and political scientists addressed the issue of the moral basis of American institutions, especially corporations. Several contributors addressed Dynamic I issues, and there was a remarkable consensus around the need for more caring and loving values throughout society, including the business world.

After proposing a theory of psychological individualism, which closely parallels my own viewpoint, Alan Waterman suggested that corporations provide one avenue for self-realization or self-actualization—the fulfillment of a variety of liberty and love needs, including autonomy, identity, and meaningful relationships. Many theories about enhancing corporate function, he pointed out, support the individual employee's striving for self-fulfillment. As examples that confirm his observations, he cited William Scott and David K. Hart's *Organizational America* (1979), William Ouchi's *Theory Z* (1981), Thomas Peters and Robert H. Waterman, Jr.'s *In Search of Excellence* (1982), and John Naisbitt and Patricia Aburdene's *Reinventing the Corporation* (1985).

Ouchi's book applies Japanese business techniques to America through what he calls the Theory Z approach to management. The aim is to increase productivity. The management style requires Dynamic I qualities, such as trust and intimacy, a "close familiarity" among employees (p. 8). He also emphasizes "subtlety," which in part means sensitivity to individual capabilities. Clearly he believes that the effective corporation provides for many of the basic needs of its employees through what he calls an "industrial clan."

Naisbitt and Aburdene in *Re-inventing the Corporation* emphasize that the economic necessities of the 1970s were responsible for the changing climate of American corporations. These stresses include the "demise of industrial America and stiff competition from global rivals such as Japan," (p. 2). The authors believe that the burgeoning information society will require new values and approaches. Yet these new values themselves are in many ways traditional. Naisbitt and Aburdene observe:

We are entering a dynamic period when the economic imperative for a more competitive, more productive work force is leading us back to the kind of humanistic values expressed in the philosophy of Kollmorgen Corp., "trust, freedom, and respect for the individual." Douglas McGregor's Theory Y, which states, in effect, that people will be more productive if they are treated with respect, was not wrong; it was simply twenty-five years ahead of its time. (p. 2.)

In passing, they acknowledge the potential impact of women in the new corporate world. Women sometimes need to learn from men how to be more "comfortable with power and conflict"; but men in turn have things to learn from women:

*We are re-inventing the corporation into a place where intuition
is respected and where the leader's role is that of a facilitator,
teacher, and nurturer of human potential. This means that
women can transform the workplace by expressing, not by giving
up their personal values. (p. 242.)*

The successful corporation of the future, according to Naisbitt
and Aburdene, will not ignore social problems, such as education
and women's issues. It will respond directly to themes of social
and personal responsibility.

Employees, according to the same authors, will want to "make a
commitment" to their corporations; but to do this, corporations
will have to provide an inspiring vision. They conclude, "The word
will get around which companies have nourishing environments
for personal growth, and those will attract our best and brightest,
thus assuring their survival into the next century," (p. 300).

Peters and Waterman's *In Search of Excellence* provides similar
lessons. The authors focus on the need to stand out, and quote
existential sociologist Ernest Becker: "Society . . . is a vehicle for
earthly heroism. . . . It is the burning desire for the creature to
count. . . . What man really fears is not so much extinction, but
extinction with *insignificance.*" On the other hand, they realize, the
desire for distinction can conflict with the desire to belong.

Successful companies inspire a belief in the individual, Peters
and Waterman observe; but their book lacks any inspiring set of
values of its own. We have a call for inspiration without any in-
spirational content.

Scott and Hart, the authors of *Organizational America*, were themselves at the 1986 Rice conference with which this discussion began. Scott presented a paper he wrote with Terence Mitchell,
entitled "The Problem or Mystery of Evil and Virtue in Organizations." It describes the usually unspoken aim of management to
"exist in a mutually satisfying, harmonious condition of virtue,"
(p. 48).

Scott and Mitchell assert that individuals have the potential for
evil and for virtue, and cite contemporary corporate acts to support
both conclusions. Their thrust is to "reduce the venom in organizations" and to "cultivate in organizations, like the woman in the
garden, a certain tenderness and compassion toward others without which we cannot flourish as individuals," (p. 69).

Another of the Rice presentations even more directly addressed what I call Dynamic I: love. David Hart discussed "Management and Benevolence: The Fatal Flaw in Theory Y." Hart believes that caricatures of corporate organizations as inducing either good or evil are too shallow. Life in corporate America "might be mundane, but it is scarcely hideous," (p. 74). The main problem is to help corporations become more conscious of "the complete person," and his or her needs. This requires a shift away from viewing the worker strictly as a producer.

Hart too cites Douglas McGregor's Theory Y management as an attempt to introduce humanistic psychology into business, but concludes that the results have not been encouraging. Criticizing many of the authors who promote humanistic values, Hart concludes that they have a "fatal flaw: the failure to take seriously, and to incorporate, the concept of *benevolence* into Theory Y theory and practice," (p. 75).

Hart sets the problem in its historical context—the Seventeenth and Eighteenth centuries, with Thomas Hobbes on the one hand denigrating the human being's potential for benevolence, and Adam Smith defending it (see chapter 2).

According to Hart, it is a fundamental mistake for corporations to aim at *control* over employees in the interest of productivity. He rejects as immoral the notion that "leaders should use the self-esteem needs of followers to better control them, and thus, to more effectively achieve organizational goals," (p. 83). But even humanistic approaches to management, he observes, act as if self-interest rather than self-actualization primarily motivates human activity. As a result, the corporation does not value individual employees for their intrinsic worth as human beings, but merely for their productivity.

Hart cites benevolence as the missing factor in the equation. By benevolence, he means "the noninstrumental love of others; a love that is complete in and of itself," (p. 87). Here Hart seems in full accord with the Dynamic I concept of unconditional or noncontingent love. In my own words, love is not an exchange but a gift. Hart agrees that, consistent with human nature, organizations and society must raise love for others onto a par with self-love, that love and self-love are in fact inseparable.

Hart says, "To be fully benevolent, the principle of love for others must be clearly understood as fundamental to human nature and its entailments clearly understood," (p. 95). Among the entailments, Hart believes, "The key aspect must be the intention to be benevolent because one loves others" not because one wishes to gain something from them in exchange. Thus he clearly distinguished between Dynamic II: voluntary exchange and Dynamic I: gifting.

In concluding, Hart believes that "until we return benevolence to its right place, our organizational reforms will be both incomplete and insubstantial," (p. 96).

All management theory and practice must be derived from the dual aspects of human nature: the love of self and the love of others. In the workplace or in all society, according to Hart (1988), love leads us to respect the needs and the rights of others:

I must call every man "brother" and every woman "sister"—and be called "brother" by them. . . . It means that any unjustice done to another is intolerable, because one cannot endure the thought of hurt coming to the loved brother or sister. The assumption of moral obligations of brotherhood and sisterhood is the ultimate guarantee that the rights of all will be preserved. (p. 90.)

Hart's viewpoint closely approximates the basic theme of this book: that love is the source of human rights and conflict resolution (see chapter 1). Again consistent with my viewpoint, Hart finds that the persistent denial of love and the reliance on coercion leads to psychological numbing. In another paper (1987), Hart describes "the feelingless functionary" who submerges himself or herself in the larger institution without concern for moral principles or human outcomes.

Corporate management is obviously not alone in its numbing attempt at moral neutrality. It is a problem for society and "moral philosophy must be made accessible to scholars, practitioners, and ordinary citizens alike," (p. 96). Consistent with the growing movement away from the use of technical and academic language (see chapter 11), Hart calls for the reform of philosophy to make it comprehensible and relevant to the ordinary person. He believes, much as I do, that moral philosophy, including specifically benevolent ideals, should be a part of public discussion—just as

Emerson, James, and Dewey, among others, made much of their idealistic writing available to the public.

At the same Rice conference on ethical individualism, in a presentation entitled "Social Organization and Individual Initiative: A Eudaimonistic Model," David Norton sought to unite the concepts of individualism with the good and happy (eudaimic) life. In his initial paper, he did not directly address issues of benevolence and love for others; but in response to criticism on this point from Hart, he appended an enlightening "Afterword," discussing the connection between egoism and altruism, self-love, and love for others. He declares that self-love matures into love for others, and that "a life that does not include unselfish love for others is significantly incomplete. Indeed, love by definition *is*, I think, unselfish," (p. 125).

Norton supports the Dynamic I principle that love transcends distinctions between self and other, making individual interests into mutual ones. He seems to conclude that self-love is the primary or ultimate motivation behind self-actualization, of which love for others is a part. However, I am not inclined to spend too much time making distinctions between Norton's view on the one hand or Hart's or mine on the other. In each case, love is acknowledged as playing a central role in human life.

My own presentation at the Rice conference was entitled "Evaluating Human Progress: A Unified Approach to Psychology, Economics, and Politics." It was gratifying to see that most of the participants, including those with the greatest experience in the field of business management (Scott and Hart), were converging on the same values and themes. My presentation concluded:

Liberty and love generate each other. Love, a joyful awareness of others, encourages us to value the freedom of others as we value our own. Liberty, the absence of arbitrary force, gives us the best opportunity to become aware of others and hence to love them. (p. 157.)

WOMEN'S VALUES

More recently there has been a growing awareness of the values that women can and do bring into the workplace. Sally Helgesen has made them the subject of her book, *The Female Advantage* (1990). Helgesen notes the same Dynamic I trends as I have summarized in this chapter and calls them "feminine principles":

We feel, many of us, that women are more caring and intuitive, better at seeing the human side, quicker to cut through competitive distinctions of hierarchy and ranking, impatient with cumbersome protocols. Our belief in these notions is intuitive rather than articulated; we back it up with anecdotes instead of argument. Some women feel ashamed of their belief in feminine principles; some are scoffing, others proud, even defiant. (pp. 4–5.)

Helgesen's book is written in a readable, popular style, and perhaps of necessity lacks some of the depth of a more thorough feminist analysis, such as Marilyn French's *Beyond Power*. But she draws upon relevant background literature and observes "female values of responsibility, connection, and inclusion have been devaluated in our culture, which tends to celebrate the lone hero, the rugged individual," (p. 233). (See also Gilligan, 1982.)

Helgesen believes times are changing: "the female view that one strengthens oneself by strengthening others is finding greater acceptance, and female values of inclusion and connection are emerging as valuable leadership qualities," (p. 233). Her hope is:

As women's leadership qualities come to play a more dominant role in the public sphere, their particular aptitudes for long-term negotiating, analytic listening, and creating an ambience in which people work with zest and spirit will help reconcile the split between the ideas of being efficient and being humane. (p. 249.)

FROM KARL MARX TO SMILEY BLANTON

The idea that human beings need to approach labor in a loving manner is not new. It can be extracted from the concept of "estranged labor" as presented in Karl Marx's early work, *The Economic and Philosophic Manuscripts of 1844.*

Marx's writing can be difficult to decipher, and I fear that his supporters may be overly generous in describing his attitude toward humanity as basically loving. At times, however, he does say that when labor becomes an involuntary necessity under the control of others, the individual loses his or her personal connection to the experience. Laboring thus loses its intrinsically joyful quality, as well as its direct connection with the individual's personal life. As a result, the individual becomes alienated from his or her labor. Since the process of work is central to one's personal and social experience, the individual becomes self-alienated and alienated from society.

From Karl Marx to Smiley Blanton is a great leap, but one worth taking. Chapter 2 introduced psychiatrist Blanton, the author of *Love or Perish*. Approaching the problem of work from a hybrid of psychoanalytic and Christian values, Blanton believes that the duality of human nature—love and hate—is especially apparent in work. Work often requires aggressive activity, and yet it must be loving in order to be ultimately satisfying. Like Marx, he laments that work has become coerced and soulless in modern times:

We are no longer personal slaves, but work has increasingly become a kind of soulless tyranny in itself. Under modern industrial conditions, more and more people find that they have little genuine interest in what they do. They are but tiny cogs, as a rule, in a huge machine directed by remote corporate management. (p. 133.)

According to Blanton, people must feel that their work is meaningful, creative, and loving, and they must be rewarded with love as well as money. Despite his sermonizing tone, Blanton's conclusions are similar to those of many social scientists:

No man can win true happiness unless he learns to work with loving hands. No society can endure unless it permits its members to work the miracle of love in their daily tasks, on however small a scale. (p. 148.)

JOY IN THE WORKPLACE?

Interesting observations have been generated by research based on Mihaly Csikszentmihalyi's concept of flow and reported in *Optimal Experience* (Csikszentmilhalyi and Csikszentmilhalyi, 1988). Flow is the positive experience of work or play when people are fully involved in doing what they intrinsically value doing, "something that is worth doing for its own sake," (p. 29).

Csikszentmilhalyi compares the concept of flow to Maslow's self-actualization and "peak experiences"; but he has tried to analyze it into components suitable for scientific research. The concept of flow has many philosophical antecedents, and in a general way, can be viewed as the opposite of what Marx called "alienation."

The person in flow feels confronted with a meaningful challenge that he or she is capable of meeting. Thus, there is a sense of mastery. The tasks are freely chosen, and there is a sense of autonomy and personal freedom. Consciousness becomes wholly focused, there is "total absorption" with a diminished awareness of the passage of time. Awareness and action become one. The individual finds the process intrinsically enjoyable and worthwhile, and is satisfied with the result.

Models for the flow experience have come from athletes, artists, scientists, professionals, and others who become deeply involved in their work or play. Those who study flow believe that it is a cross-cultural, universal experience.

Flow is a combination of Dynamics I and II. It designates the experience summed up in "I love what I'm doing." Consistent with Dynamic I, the sense of self and other is diminished, there is no sense of sacrifice in exerting energy and spending time, and the process is enjoyed for itself. Research in *Optimal Experience* also confirms that flow tends to require a Dynamic II context of freedom and autonomy. Conversely, when people are subjected to Dynamic III: coercion, flow is disrupted.

Is flow possible on the typical job? Studies reported in *Optimal Experience* show that it is possible, but only under relatively ideal conditions. Even in professional roles that seem to offer many creative opportunities, people frequently feel frustrated and unfulfilled, and must seek flow elsewhere in their lives. Meanwhile, working class people often give up the hope for anything better and succumb to a life with little flow (e.g., see pp. 47–49).

Not surprisingly, flow advocates believe that it not only enhances enjoyment but also work productivity. In *Optimal Flow,* Judith LeFevre concludes:

Since flow enhances activation, concentration, and creativity, it is likely that performance would improve by increasing the amount of time spent in flow. In addition, increases in flow may improve morale and prevent burnout, since motivation and satisfaction are also enhanced. (p. 318.)

COUNTER-CURRENTS

Not everyone agrees that employees can or should get "in the flow." Indeed, values associated with self-actualization may be losing out in the workplace. In *The New Individualists* (1991), Paul Leinberger and Bruce Tucker forecast the eminent demise of individualism. The search for the "authentic self" is becoming outmoded. It will be replaced by "the artificial person," an identity that is a nonidentity, a self that is embedded in and a reflection of the complex network of relationships characteristic of the modern corporation. The authors suggest, with seeming ambivalence, that the "artificial person" may be necessary in America's postindustrial era.

There are other signs that self-actualization and other higher values have a diminishing place in the modern business world. None of us can help but be shocked by the flood of corporate greed unleashed by the Reagan-Bush era. We can only hope that the seemingly endless disclosures of scandals are having a salutary effect. Nor are we unaware of the materialistic values summed up in the word Yuppie.

AN INHERENT CONTRADICTION?

There is a built-in obstacle to the humanizing of corporate life that few of its advocates seem to take into consideration. It is the same problem we found in psychotherapy (see chapter 6) as the conflict between capitalism and caring.

The purpose of the corporation is profit-making and its function is to compete in the supposedly free market. The values inherent in profit-making and competition must be modified or ameliorated in order to facilitate a more loving, open, and trusting environment.

Consider, for example, Paul H. Weaver's analysis of *The Suicidal Corporation* (1988). As a free-market advocate, Weaver envisions corporations moving toward a more honest affirmation of self-interest, the profit motive, and a competitive free market. While Weaver acknowledges that the Reagan years fell short of promoting a consistent set of free-market standards, he believes that Reaganomics did to a limited extent create an environment more conducive to the free market. He also believes that the younger generation of corporate executives is much more free-market oriented than the previous one.

When Weaver describes the ideal free-market corporation, he says nothing about the "self-actualization" or "self-realization" of individual employees. He does favor a strong code of ethics and believes that "A scrupulously honorable, customer-oriented, product-honoring ethos should prevail," (p. 241). Consistent with the highest free-market standards, he presses corporations "to strengthen the shareholder and customer interests in the corporation, and to subordinate the management interest in them," (p. 244). Corporations, according to Weaver's free-market philosophy, should have a "mission that transcends the career interests of the executives."

Weaver's ideal employee pursues neither self-actualization nor self-aggrandizing careerism; he or she is dedicated to the interests of the shareholders, which includes the needs of the customer and the principles of the free market. Consistent with Dynamic II: liberty, Weaver believes that working within a genuinely capitalistic corporation will give employees a sense of pride or self-esteem.

Weaver's analysis is totally consistent with Dynamic II: liberty, and probably represents the best we can expect from the promotion of free-market values. Unless the views of free-market advocates are drastically modified along the lines suggested by David Hart and myself, there is little hope that the coming years will see a substantially more loving workplace for many or most Americans.

THE FUTURE

As big business encounters increasing difficulties competing in a global marketplace and adjusting to the nation's persistently sluggish economy, what direction will it take in regard to caring values in the workplace? Will it become more efficient and streamlined at the expense of individual self-development and even individual jobs? Or will it find a way to implement more caring and joyful values among its employees? Will the influx of women help to humanize the corporation, or will women ultimately be swept along by the competitive values that are seemingly inherent in corporate functioning?

I doubt that loving values can be thoroughly integrated into an institution whose *mandate* is profit-making, and whose *survival* and *prosperity* depend on outdoing the competition. Without a drastic change in the fabric of American values and social institutions, the corporation will reject those employees who fail to perform competitively. As long as productivity in the interest of profit is the measure of an employee's value, it seems unlikely that many corporations will be able to transform themselves into more caring communities. Indeed, since management must hire and fire on the basis of productivity and profit, management would be hypocritical to speak too loudly of unconditional love or benevolence toward its employees.

Are these conclusions an indictment of capitalism? They do reflect a realistic appraisal of the more or less inevitable results of relating through Dynamic II. Liberty can become the optimal context for love; but when liberty is the be-all and end-all of institutional values, progress toward a more loving environment seems gravely limited and to some extent futile.

While corporations can make a greater effort to take the edge off internal competition and to otherwise "tenderize" the workplace, there may be inherent limits to the process. Different corporations in a variety of Western countries continue to experiment with these limits. It will be interesting to see how the Soviet Union and the Eastern Bloc nations try to solve these conflicts (see chapter 9).

Some unethical business practices are in fact due to a lack of free-market principles. Multimillion-dollar golden parachutes for executives of failing companies result from the personal greed of those executives at the expense of the shareholders. Corporations should function more honestly, and hence efficiently and more honorably, by devoting themselves to shareholder profits and other free-market ideals, and by rejecting government subsidies and special privileges. People will generate self-esteem and respect for others in a more ideal free market environment; but it is hard to see how they will gain in self-love and love for others, and genuinely experience "flow."

Modern society desperately needs a multiplicity of institutional opportunities for people to find loving relationships and community, but large corporations will probably at best make a small contribution in that direction. Society will have to provide a variety of alternative institutions offering better opportunities for joyful activity, self-development, and community.

Meanwhile, corporations can try to provide community and personal opportunities for self-development consistent with the overall aim of profit-making. If a corporation can create a more satisfying community experience, its employees will function with less stress and with more genuine enthusiasm. Good morale will help almost any organization perform better; and while good morale is not nearly so profound as love, it is a step in the right direction.

There is little or no danger that corporations will be injured by introducing more loving and community-oriented values. The competitiveness inherent in the free-enterprise system will prevent a corporation from going overboard. "Bankrupted by love" seems an unlikely epitaph. Without fear of ruining American capitalism, we can urge corporations to try harder to meet their employees' needs for love and community.

LIBERTY VERSUS LOVE IN SOCIETY

In the meantime, even more radical questions will continue to be asked about the free-enterprise system. As both Marxist and antistate critiques have documented, the so-called free-enterprise system quickly learned to provide security for itself through a broad web of state support. Since the beginning of the industrial revolution, as John Kenneth Galbraith has described (1958, 1980), capitalists have used government to build their own safety net to protect them from competition, economic downturns, and failure. Big business has sought much more than a safety net from government; it thrives on government largess of all kinds, from public support of the transportation infrastructure to defense spending, subsidies, research funding, monetary policy, and protectionist tariffs. Capitalism, as it now exists, is dependent upon and is inseparable from the state.

Whether we will ever see a genuine free market implemented on a large scale remains speculative. Whether we would *want* to see such a radical experiment remains controversial. It would be almost impossible to predict its overall effects, but it might quickly degenerate into monopolistic coercion.

The size and power of the state requires limits in order to reduce coercion within society. But in reducing government intervention, it would be cruel and unjust to take away the safety net from the poor before seeing if the rich can do without theirs. Chapter 10 will focus on the plight of the poor in modern society, as well as the overall balance between coercion, liberty, and love in society.

CHAPTER 9

▼ ▼

Resolving Societal Conflict: Eastern Europe in Transition; Poverty, Hunger, Redistributive Justice, and the Environment

Free individuals, able to render relatively rational decision-making, are found only within communities, because only in such communities do people find the psychic and social support that is required to sustain decisions free of pressures from the authorities, demagogues, or the mass media. Individuality does exist, but only within these social contexts.
> *Amitai Etzioni,* **The Moral Dimension: Toward a New Economics** *(1988)*

Our economic system and our relation with nature have gone haywire because we have lost track of what we really need. . . . So long as we persist in defining well-being predominantly in economic terms and in relying on economic considerations to provide us with our primary frame of reference for personal and social policy decisions, we will remain unsatisfied. . . . To the degree that we measure our lives in terms of social ties, openness to experience, and personal growth instead of in terms of production and accumulation, we are likely to be able to avoid a collision course with our environment without experiencing a sense of deprivation.
> *Paul Wachtel,* **The Poverty of Affluence** *(1989)*

All the members of human society stand in need of each other's assistance. . . . Where the necessary assistance is reciprocally afforded from love, from gratitude, from friendship, from esteem, the society flourishes and is happy. All the different members are bound together by the agreeable bands of love and affection. . . .
> *Adam Smith,* **The Theory of Moral Sentiments** *(1759)*

The activities of individuals easily become obscured when the focus is on society; but individual persons are the only source of human activity. There are no "social forces" except those that are generated by persons, and no collective will separate from the impact of the many individual wills expressed within society. There is no great collective ghost or spiritual cloud that emanates from individuals and then looms over them with a life and power of its own. Social conflict is the product of multiple individual conflicts. Even when the conflicts become embodied in institutions, such as political parties or governments, individual persons are the source of everything that is done in the name of the institutions.

Of necessity, needs and values such as patriotism and religion may lead us to speak as if society is a being with a life of its own separate from and acting upon its members. In part this also reflects the reality that institutions and ideologies, although created by people, end up influencing how people think, feel, and act. And so we speak of how schools, religions, songs, movies, and political doctrines stir up patriotic feelings; but the actual feelings exist and are processed in individual people.

Leaders of society, for better or worse, may influence many individuals at once, reinforcing the mistaken perception that "social forces" rather than individual human actions are at work. Indeed, oppressive leaders want their subjects to believe that they are being carried along by something greater than their own willingness to submit. Writing in the Sixteenth century, la Boetie eloquently described how the dictator and the oppressive state depend ultimately on the submission of individuals. Speaking of tyrants, he declares:

But if not one thing is yielded to them, if without any violence they are simply not obeyed, they become naked and undone and as nothing, just as, when the root receives no nourishment, the branch withers and dies. . . . Resolve to serve no more, and you are at once freed. I do not ask that you place hands upon the tyrant to topple him over, but simply that you support him no longer; then you will behold him, like a great Colossus whose pedestal has been pulled away, fall of his own weight and break into pieces. (pp. 51–53.)

That individuals create society is a potentially radical concept. In la Boetie's hands, it became a clarion call for nonviolent civil disobedience (see chapter 11).

While individuals remain the source of all action, we can examine the ideologies, philosophies, and religions that they have created, and how these in turn affect the basic needs, thoughts, and feelings of members of the society.

BASIC PREMISES

Two basic premises are worth recalling:

First, conflict resolution does not prescribe specific outcomes. It enables people to seek out the best possible solutions for themselves as individuals and a group, consistent with the principles of liberty and love.

Second, the conflict-tree metaphor reminds us that conflict resolution requires the recognition of our shared humanity. Even within families and among friends, viewing the other person as a different and lesser human being raises an impenetrable barrier to conflict resolution. In racial, religious, and class conflicts, the antagonists may never become intimate with any of the people seen as our adversaries; and so they find it especially easy to declare others alien to themselves and to humanity.

While it seems more difficult to love people from different races, religions, or socioeconomic classes, to resolve conflict, we must bring down the psychospiritual barriers that divide us. We must "climb back down" the conflict tree to our common root of shared human needs and aspirations (see chapter 1). Ultimately, we must make peace with the "tree" itself—with nature.

The reader might wish to review the table in chapter 1 that summarizes the principles of love, liberty, and coercion, as well as the simplified Three Dynamics Table (see p. 261).

THE STATE AND COERCION

As we begin to look more broadly at society, we immediately come face to face with the state. The state or national government is not the same as society or community, which may be viewed as an affiliation or bonding of people through shared resources and land, common interests and values, or culture and history. The state, as a political entity, holds people together through coercion. Risking a certain amount of oversimplifying, the state is based on coercion, the community on love.

State and local governments do not necessarily represent the values of the various groups or individuals within their boundaries. The recent collapse of the Soviet Union has made that abundantly clear. Government is a central organization with a monopoly over the use of force, backed up by armed forces and police (Hayek, 1944; Nozick, 1974; Oppenheimer, 1975; Nock, 1973). The degree of coercion it exerts varies from nation to nation, but the basic principle remains. The state is founded on coercion. If this were not so, government, and functions such as taxation, would be replaced by voluntary community association and charity.

The state can, of course, roughly coincide with community. Unlike the citizens of the former Soviet Union, most Americans identify themselves with the federal government. Society and state are often viewed more or less as one. Nonetheless, the state, unlike the actual community, ultimately depends on force, and must frequently resort to coercion to enforce its laws. Imagine, for example, if the U.S. government stopped using the threat of force to collect taxes. How many citizens would freely pay the full amount demanded each year by Congress and the Internal Revenue Service? Even with its monopoly on coercion, and with general agreement among citizens on the need for some taxation, the federal government is unable to collect all the taxes it imposes. Most other nations have even more difficulty getting their citizens to pay up.

To illustrate the importance of state coercion, imagine if couples in conflict with each other could routinely resort to government intervention, including the police, to solve their problems. Instead of working out their differences, they would resort to lobbying the state legislature to get their interests enforced. Nowadays, married couples can seek state intervention only on rare occasion, such as contested divorces or physical abuse.

In general, when people or institutions can resort to force, they will not develop more creative methods of conflict resolution. Chapter 8 described how psychiatry relies upon state power to accomplish many of its aims, with the result that psychiatry offers few genuinely valuable alternatives. Similarly, in the former USSR, coercion was the overriding method of dealing with conflict, with disastrous results. Conflict, long suppressed, finally erupted and brought about the destruction of the system. Since nearly all conflicts had been subject to Communist party and state intervention, methods of voluntary conflict resolution did not develop or atrophied. With the collapse of the totalitarian state, people had no institutional mechanisms for dealing with their ethnic, economic, and other societal conflicts.

Under a more democratic and constitutional government, force tends to be less obtrusive. Most U.S. citizens do not become preoccupied with the jails and guns that back up the law, until they come into conflict it. Only a rare social critic challenges submission to democratic state authority (Rothbard, 1973, 1982; Von Mises, 1966, 1969; and others cited earlier in this section).

That coercion is such an accepted part of each citizen's life should not blunt our awareness of its consequences. The lack of awareness makes the effects of coercion more insidious and potentially injurious.

THE STATE AND CONFLICT RESOLUTION

Because coercion is so central to government activities, it vastly encumbers the state's attempts to resolve conflict. Coercion, as emphasized throughout this book, is largely incompatible with conflict resolution. When the state attempts to resolve conflict, it enters into the dispute as both a source of power and money, and as a source of outright coercion; and in these capacities, the state tends to generate increasing conflict.

In modern society, interest groups vie for control of the state apparatus in order to coerce others into meeting their needs. First one lobby and then another wants more of whatever it seeks through government intervention. Since one group's claim is inevitably at the expense of at least one other's—or there would be no need for coercive state intervention—other interest groups feel compelled to escalate their own demands merely to keep up. A cycle of competition and conflict over the control of state power is inevitable.

Interest groups seek to fulfill myriad needs through the state. Some of the motivation is at least partly altruistic, as in promoting health care and welfare for the poor, public education, and civil liberties. Other aims are more obviously selfish. Meanwhile, everyone in the society ends up competing for government largess and government power: individuals, religious and cultural groups, labor, business, various professions, different age groups, towns, cities, states, and so on. Any one citizen may be benefitting from and suffering from the effects of a multitude of competing lobbies.

What if, instead, the state became an institution devoted to conflict resolution—a place to turn for help in resolving conflicts without resort to force? Suppose the state helped groups to assess the cost of coercion and unrelenting conflict, and worked to bring them together in more mutually satisfying ways?

The concept of the state as an institution of conflict resolution is at present visionary; but the fulfillment of that vision might become possible as the principles of conflict resolution become better understood and as people gain faith in the possibility of less coercive, less conflicted community. As the state evolved into an instrument of conflict resolution, it would eventually cease to be a state. It would become a true community—a place where people solve their problems through collaboration and without resort to force.

THE FORMAT OF THE CHAPTER

Because of the variety of issues, this chapter is divided into four parts. Each deals with the potential conflict between state and community, between coercion and love.

PART I: Liberty and Love in the Former USSR

PART II: The Cost of Coercing Good Deeds

PART III: Hunger, Poverty, and Redistributive Justice

PART IV: Liberty, Love, and the Environment

To provide continuity, many examples will be drawn from two regions of the world, the former USSR and the United States.

Part I: *Liberty and Love in the Former USSR*

The transformations taking place in the former communist societies make it easier to examine the interaction between psychological and political factors, as well as the effects of coercion, liberty, and love.

BASIC STRESS PARADIGMS BEHIND THE IRON CURTAIN

Nearly everyone who visits or reports from the former USSR and former Eastern Bloc nations describes learned helplessness as an endemic impediment to growth in these societies. In many ways, life in these closed, totalitarian societies was one neverending Basic Stress Paradigm of hurt, fear, and debilitating helplessness.

The imprinting of fear and helplessness was not complete, however, especially within the younger generation. A Czechoslovakian professor explained to me that the teaching of communist ideology in the schools was so bumbling that it failed to crush the spirit of young people. On the other hand, after a lifetime of indoctrination, most older people have been unable to adjust to a more self-determined way of life.

Conflicts between people both restimulate and draw upon the painful emotions associated with Basic Stress Paradigms. The same is true in regard to race, gender, ethnic, class, and other societal conflicts. While racism and sexism, for example, exist in their own right, they are also fueled by Basic Stress Paradigms of hurt, fear, and helplessness. And they initially bring them about as well.

In *Escape From Freedom* (1941) Erich Fromm showed how the suppressive nature of German parenting contributed to the development of Nazism. Alice Miller has more recently made similar observations. It is now generally accepted that personal frustration feeds racism, sexism, and other forms of prejudice. It also feeds submission to totalitarian regimes. Totalitarian regimes in turn create the conditions under which especially severe Basic Stress Paradigms are caused or reinforced.

A DOSE OF LIBERTY IN UNEXPECTED PLACES

To nations floundering economically, liberty—meaning individualism and capitalism—now seems like the only road to progress. Even the acme of hatred for Western ideals, Iran, sees the practical necessity of creating a capitalist enclave to lead the nation out of its economic quagmire. The government has created an "Islamic glasnost," an offshore island, Qeshm, based on a market economy. Vietnam as well has been encouraging capitalism and seeking an infusion of U.S. investments.

In China, where totalitarianism has once again suppressed much of the overt spirit of political liberty, the economy is continuing to improve. In a recent analysis in the August 25, 1991 *Washington Post*, Daniel Southerland points out that the Chinese have found ways to continue to encourage the spirit of capitalism despite their politically oppressive regime. Large foreign investors find it increasingly easy to prosper in China, and many small businesses have moved in. Decentralization of the economy is progressing and the nongovernmental sector is growing, including both private businesses and collectives. Even the collectives increasingly pursue self-interested, capitalistic policies, while continuing to call themselves socialistic. Individual Chinese have found a way to "pursue their own self-interest in a practical way" and an "entrepreneurial class" is prospering.

That all this is happening in China serves to remind us that liberty is everywhere connected to what most people consider economic progress. Too many well-intentioned social critics and idealists try to envision a world devoid of self-interest, competition, and free-market economics—without realizing that liberty is rooted in our basic needs and inspires much of what human beings accomplish. What is needed is not the abolition of freedom, but the development of a stronger context of love.

THE NEW INDIVIDUALISM IN THE
EASTERN BLOC AND RUSSIA

In Russia and the former Eastern Bloc nations, anarchistic extremes of capitalism are coming alive, although as of yet in a relatively stumbling and ineffective manner. Ayn Rand fled the Soviet Union as a young woman and went on to write *The Fountainhead* (1943) and *Atlas Shrugged* (1957), two fiercely individualistic, pro-capitalist novels. Now the often heartless and rapacious heroes of her novels are coming alive in her rejected homeland. This is not surprising. The totalitarian outrages that inspired Rand's extreme individualism are also motivating the newly liberated generation.

In a July 7, 1991 *Washington Post* article entitled "Brash New Breed 'Building Empires, Not Evil Ones,' " David Remnick describes what may be called the "Russian Randians." In an interview, twenty-four-year-old entrepreneur German Sterligov declares:

Why should I pity the poor and the lazy. Pity the sick and the weak, okay, but if the rest want to live in poverty—God help them. If they want to be slaves—well, then every slave has dignity before God. But history is made by the individual, not the crowd. It is only when the ignorant crowd takes part in the historical process that it turns into a mess.

My generation despises the system. It killed everyone and everything it touched. This was the richest state in the world and they destroyed it all down to the bone! But older people don't understand us. Their psychology is all screwed up. They are used to being equal in poverty and they assume if you have any money, you are a crook. (p. A 22.)

With the exception of the references to God, which are probably ironic, and with the exception of pity for the "sick and the weak," these statements rival those of the most ideological Randian. This new breed of extreme individualists, generally considered anachronistic in the United States, is playing an increasing role in Russia and elsewhere.

Further on in Remnick's article we hear contrasting views from the father of one of these fledgling capitalists. He laments:

Social ideals of equality, social security and a simple love for
other people *play a much greater role for me than for [my son].
Maybe he is right. Maybe to talk about social justice, you have
to make society rich first. . . . But still, I can't be indifferent if I
see the rise of millionaires who live on other people's labor. I
can't bear that. (p. A 22,* emphasis added.)

Of course, neither side is without fault or flaw. The young entrepreneur is callous to the plight of the older generation that was
victimized by the communist regime. The new capitalism that the
younger generation reveres is already spawning widespread fraud
and degrading the lives of many people less able to compete in the
new system. Nor is the father's lament for lost love wholly con-
vincing. He longs for a "simple love for other people," which in
reality was used to justify one of the most oppressive systems in
the history of the world.

A NEW ENTHUSIASM FOR LIBERTY

At psychology and conflict-resolution conferences I attended in the
United States in the early 1990s, the group that most consistently
spoke enthusiastically about the values of freedom were visitors
from Eastern Europe. Some of the professors talked specifically
about overcoming the "learned helplessness" developed over years
of communist indoctrination and about how to stimulate "human
agency" and "individualistic democratic" political processes.

During my lecture on the Three Dynamic Theory at one of the
conflict-resolution conferences, I suggested, "Communism at its
best is an attempt to implement love through coercion. There's a
built-in contradiction." It seemed to me that the newly liberated
Eastern Bloc members of the audience most fully appreciated my
remarks.

One East European professor described the innovations she and
her colleagues had made on T-Groups, one of the original sensitivity
training methods popular in America in the late 1960s. With information on newer group techniques unavailable behind the Iron Curtain, they had developed their own innovations to encourage
communication and negotiation, as well as personal assertiveness

and autonomy. Thus they tried to help people overcome the effects of a state that had thwarted all such aspirations.

Polish social scientists described how Polish youth have, in a mere few years, progressed from attitudes of apathy and indifference to those of initiative and competition. Recently, I spent time with two sisters from a former Eastern Bloc nation. One had bravely fled many years ago, the other was now on vacation from her homeland, urging her sister to return to the new "land of opportunity" for daring entrepreneurs.

Some older social scientists from Poland and Czechoslovakia are wary of too strong an "individualistic" and "anarchistic" influence among some of their youth. The nearly overnight blossoming of these sentiments among the young suggests that the spirit of liberty is embedded in human nature. Ironically, the newly liberated youth sometimes fail to appreciate that America's much admired capitalism is modified by a complex safety net funded by government.

Rarely do Americans so consciously examine the values of individualism, autonomy, and freedom that are implicit in our legal, economic, and political system. Among academicians and intellectuals, these values are frequently denigrated in favor of social justice. But Eastern Bloc leaders are now keenly aware of the importance of liberty in their personal lives and they hold out the hope that American-inspired capitalism will rescue their collapsing economies as well. Yet they, along with most citizens, also display skepticism, fear, and confusion in dealing with these new ideals. They now favor everything from private property to freedom of speech, while nonetheless feeling frightened over the potential havoc wreaked upon older cultural values and a caring community. In their inner conflicts and in their real life dilemmas, these people embody the contrasting and sometimes incompatible values of liberty and love.

THE FAILURE OF SOME AMERICAN INTELLECTUALS AND SCHOLARS

On August 19, 1991, like many other Americans, I awoke to the dismaying and depressing news that a hard-line communist coup had taken place the night before in the USSR. I was attending the annual convention of the American Psychological Association in San Francisco at the time, and had the opportunity to attend a workshop quickly convened in response to these events. It was led by peace activists, including psychologists, social psychologists, and related professionals.

I expected an outpouring of loving support for the brave Russian souls who were risking their lives by opposing the coup, even by lying down in front of tanks. I also anticipated many expressions of sadness over the looming danger that the bravest and most freedom-loving Russians might soon be slaughtered in the coming days. Since the Russian resistance fighters were risking their lives for values we had helped inspire in them, the least we could do was to empathize with them.

I heard no such empathic, freedom-loving themes from the professionals who had hastily gathered in response to the coup. Instead, I heard the following:

1. *We shouldn't judge Russians by American standards; they are "different" because they are starving to death and might need a more authoritarian leadership, such as that provided by the coup.* The shocking "they are different" theme was repeated without a voice being raised in protest.

2. *Americans must do nothing to upset the coup leaders, such as showing solidarity with the freedom fighters or with the rebellious national groups in the Balkans and Eastern Europe.* In effect, the group identified with the aggressors and sought to placate them, while immediately giving up hope for the victims.

3. *We must find ways to help people like the coup leaders overcome their fear of reform, so they can realize that progress will improve their lives as well as everyone else's.* This hope seemed incredibly naive. The coup leaders, their associates, and their families of course had an enormous personal stake in resisting change and in maintaining the old order.

4. *America had its own civil war, and we would have resented interference, and so we should mind our own business during the coup.* The Russian coup and U.S. Civil War hardly seem comparable. It would have been more appropriate to compare the coup to a potential military takeover in the United States.

5. *The Russian reformers want to implement an American-style free market, and that is one reason not to support them against the coup.* This statement was greeted with widespread approval.

6. *America's leadership tries to create enemies to distract us from our own domestic problems, such as racism and poverty, and we must therefore discourage the American people from hating the coup leaders.* All governments, including ours, tend to create enemies in order to distract their citizens from domestic problems. On the other hand, on the day of the coup there seemed many good reasons for strongly favoring the reformers over the coup leaders.

7. *Avoiding nuclear holocaust is more important than who happens to lead the USSR at any given time, so we must not do anything to antagonize the coup leaders.* This seemed a widely held feeling in the workshop, even though the coup had been in power for less than twenty-four hours. Peace at any price became temporary peace at the cost of possible future war, since the coup leaders were known to be far more militaristic than the reformers.

8. *It is sad to witness the decline of a "great nation" like the Soviet Union.* This nationalistic sentiment, perhaps appropriate toward a country like Canada or the United States, seemed inappropriate to an empire made up of so many captive states, cultures, and citizens.

No one at the meeting protested these pronouncements, yet rightly or wrongly, they would have struck the average American as outrageous. They would probably enrage the average Russian as well, and most certainly the average Hungarian, Pole, Czech, or Balkan citizen. While some of the concerns being shown did have a kernel of truth to them, the overall thrust was devoid of empathy for or identification with the Russian victims of oppression. Instead, sympathy and some overt support went toward the coup leaders.

What motivated these highly educated, psychologically sophisticated professional people to take such positions? As a group they were probably not more devoid of sympathy and caring than other people. As people especially devoted to peace, they probably had considerable empathy for others.

Perhaps because of their own institutional privileges as professors and professionals, they tended to side with authority and hence with the coup; but that did not seem to explain the extent of their rejection of the reformers and freedom fighters. While their reactions undoubtedly reflect more complex motives, two factors seem especially important:

First, many reform-minded "liberal" academics and intellectuals have little appreciation of the principles of either liberty or love. They experience themselves as alienated from American values, but do not possess a sustainable set of alternative principles of their own. They equate liberty with all the failings of American capitalism. They equate love with religion, romance, or other devalued sources. This book is one attempt to remedy this situation by clarifying the values of liberty and love, and their functions in society.

Second, faced with the truly horrible threat of a renewed cold war, the people at the meeting became restimulated on hurt, fear, and helplessness, and thus abandoned the natural human tendency to empathize with and to support victims of blatant oppression. Overcome with feelings of helplessness, they did what so many frightened people do—they identified with the aggressors in the hope of staving off further trouble. Personal Basic Stress Paradigms and learned helplessness took over, blurring their political judgment and their identification with the victims of oppression.

NO MECHANISMS FOR CONFLICT RESOLUTION

While often eager to embrace liberty, members of former communist societies have little or no experience with the peaceful processes for resolving the inevitable conflicts that surface in relative freedom. According to communist ideology, these societies were supposed to be conflict free. As a result, there could be no acknowledged need for mechanisms such as mediation, arbitration, or negotiation. There were no public forums for interest groups to debate or to vie for power. The very existence of contending interest groups was denied in order to perpetuate the myth of solidarity.

Furthermore, there were few community or loving alternatives for conflict resolution. Religion was suppressed and there were few if any other private or voluntary organizations existing outside the government and Communist party realm. Scientific, educational, publishing, artistic, philanthropic, and fraternal institutions were inseparable from the state and the party, bound together more by coercion than by affinity. Whenever people came together for any purpose, they could never be sure they were free of surveillance.

Coercion was the dominant method of conflict resolution in the USSR. Orders came from the top down and resistance was largely passive, taking the form of apathy and resignation. Disputes were handled out of public view within the Communist party apparatus and the outcome was enforced by the state.

Freedom, by contrast, liberates people to express their needs and values, and hence their potential conflicts. Society must provide methods to help resolve conflicts, but liberty *per se* does not seem to adequately do this. Western society itself is grossly lacking in institutions for conflict resolution. In the final chapter we will look at this most difficult problem—how to institutionalize or otherwise make conflict-resolution processes more available.

LIMITS ON THE NEW LIBERTY: INSTITUTIONALIZING FREE ENTERPRISE

Eastern European states are already running into the limits of freedom as a principle. Issues of social justice became apparent from the very earliest attempts to introduce private property and free enterprise. Those in the best position to take advantage of the new freedoms are often the very same people who have a head start by virtue of their connections with Communist party leadership and government *apparatchiks*. In a society suddenly "made free," the original perpetrators are likely to come out on top again. Nothing so clearly illustrates how liberty can degenerate into renewed oppression.

One possible approach involves providing each citizen an equal share in what the government once owned, perhaps through a distribution of cash or vouchers that can be sold, traded, or used to purchase former government property, such as factories, automobiles, and apartments. Efforts are being made in these directions. But a distribution of cash or vouchers will not prevent the rapid reaccumulation of that wealth in the hands of those few who already have the advantages of relative wealth, old-buddy connections, and know-how.

LOVE IN THE SOVIET UNION AND THE EASTERN BLOC

The victims of these totalitarian regimes often managed to maintain close family ties and friendships. Faced with chronic deprivation, generosity became more valued, as individuals shared their limited resources with each other. Family conflict between the generations was considerably muted compared to Western society. People needed each other to survive. In addition, as the churches were suppressed, many people turned more fervently to their spiritual roots. Thus theories that promote a rigid hierarchy of values fail to realize that love often thrives at precisely those moments that people are feeling insecure and deprived of their liberties. The formerly communist societies have a wellspring of love and caring from which they can draw in creating a new community. Their future will be determined in part by their willingness and ability to transform their political system without rejecting their commitment to loving relationships.

Part II: The Cost of Coercing Good Deeds

According to a news report on a verbal exchange between Nikita Khrushchev and Dwight Eisenhower, the Soviet dictator challenged the American president by observing that communism more than capitalism was attempting to implement the Christian values of altruism and sharing. There was some truth to his remarks. Communism, at its most ideal, attempts to enforce love. But so do all forms of modern liberalism and socialism, as well as conservatism. Each has different moral values; but each uses the state to impose its ideals on the society.

DENYING MORE SUBTLE COSTS

The cost of state coercion against its own citizens for supposedly good purposes rarely receives sufficient attention. Most Americans assume that a great deal of government enforcement is necessary not only to suppress crime and maintain defense, but to implement programs for the general good. They want to tax people to pay for public transportation, education, welfare, health services, and the military. They want to control the prices of vital services and to stimulate the economy with various incentives. People may argue about the best approaches and optimal degree of such coercion, but few challenge the principle of coercion itself or look at its negative consequences in any depth.

In their relationships with friends and family, many people more readily accept the need to respect each other's freedom. They wish to develop wholly noncoercive personal relationships. In regard to love, for example, they readily see that it is wrong and self-defeating to try to force their partners to love them. Yet these same people see no potential harm or ethical problem with coercing people for every imaginable "good purpose" in the political arena.

But as already discussed, any use of force in any arena, personal or political, will have negative consequences on the victim and the perpetrator (see chapters 4–6). This means that policing people for their own good—such as preventing them from smoking, drinking, or eating anything they want—has its cost. Similarly, taxing people for their presumed good or the good of others—even for the building of roads, dams, schools, and hospitals—constitutes coercion and has its cost.

Imagine a society in which people feel no financial incentive to work, no pressing need to provide for themselves or their families, and no ability to benefit from their own property and labor. In the USSR and Eastern Bloc nations, years of statism deprived many people of their belief in self-determination. While the widespread lethargy was in part inspired by state terror, it was also produced by crushing individual initiative and the pursuit of self-interest. The former communist societies themselves have, to a great extent, come to this conclusion. While there are differences within regions and cultures, and a considerable amount of skepticism on the part of almost everyone, surveys have shown that most Soviets favor increasing private property and free enterprise. At this moment,

Russia is embarking on radical experimentation with capitalism. Some of the former Eastern Bloc nations are already moving along the free market road with some degree of success.

Of course, the citizens of formerly communist countries are also fearful of these new ideas, but as already noted, freedom must have profound appeal to human nature if they are so willing to consider it after so many years of wholesale indoctrination to the contrary.

CHARITY VERSUS WELFARE

The untoward results of state intervention and coercive social policy are not limited to the extreme example provided by the USSR. At least in the modern industrial society, state centralization of planning has a stultifying effect on individual initiative. Similarly, it is difficult to plan a safety net that does not have some negative consequences on personal responsibility. During a recent trip to Scandinavia, I heard many concerns that young people were no longer willing to work because unemployment insurance paid so well.

On the other hand, the tendency for "government handouts" to make people slothful has been vastly exaggerated. In the United States, where the safety net is much more porous than in Scandinavia, Aid to Families with Dependent Children (AFDC) is the main "welfare" program. It mostly affects families made up of very poor mothers with small children. The malingerers among these mothers appear to be small in number. Mostly, they have their hands full trying to raise children at a poverty level in socially disorganized communities without the help of fathers. Often they work when they can, and most remain on AFDC for short periods of time (Trattner, 1984).

Piven and Cloward observe (1985):

What remains, then, is the minority of AFDC mothers whose life situation has demoralized them, whose experience of unemployment and social disorganization has made them "dependent," whose children may, if these conditions persist, grow up to be "dependent" as well. Welfare is not a good solution for these

*people. It may keep them from starving, but it does not enable
them to reconstruct their self-respect. Eliminating welfare pay-
ments in the absence of other economic and social opportunities
is, however, a worse solution. (p. 4.)*

Unemployment, culturally deprived family life, crime, racism,
inadequate education, and other factors create involuntary poverty
in the larger industrial societies. It is no secret that the inner cities
of America are in many respects like, or even worse than, "Third
World Nations" in regard to poverty, homelessness, violent crime,
infant mortality, inadequate health care, and other measures of
social disintegration.

The problem of poverty cannot be dismissed as laziness, malin-
gering, or the like. Increasing numbers of poor in the United States
cannot keep up no matter how hard they work. Many children are
growing up without the physical health, education, or viewpoints
required for survival or success in modern society. A realistic, loving attitude toward the poor does not allow us to dismiss them as
deserving of their fate.

The great misfortune of modern society is the failure to understand that liberty and love, and not state coercion, is the best
approach to solving problems such as poverty. We would be far
better off if the community could provide charity to its less fortunate members without resort to taxation and government intervention. Then the poor could benefit from both the opportunities
inherent in liberty and the resources of loving community.

The argument is made that the receipt of charity is humiliating,
but it could hardly be as humiliating as the typical experience of
"welfare mothers." Furthermore, charity suggests that someone
actually cares about the individual in trouble. And charity, unlike
government relief, might inspire the recipient to "pay back" by
giving charity to others at a later date. But most important, charity
eliminates coercion, and expresses love.

I am not arguing for an end to the already shredded safety net.
Given the plight of the poor in our callous society, that would be
unspeakably cruel. I am suggesting that we begin to reconsider the
community rather than the state as our source of human kindness.
It would be inhumane to further diminish current levels of aid to
the poor, but we can begin to think about a greater role for love in

the future of society. I will deal further with this issue in chapter 11, but now want to emphasize that liberty and love always provide far better solutions than coercion. Sadly, we seem, as a society, a long way from such a realization. We are becoming an increasingly coercive and loveless nation.

PERPETRATOR OF INVOLUNTARY GOOD DEEDS

Coercion tends to encourage alienation and unrealistic self-evaluations in the perpetrators. Consistent with the perpetrator syndrome discussed in chapter 4, perpetrators, including political leaders and government bureaucrats, become increasingly more grandiose and less sensitive to those whom they are controlling. In a recent public discussion (see chapter 10), former president Jimmy Carter described how dictators frequently, and unrealistically, imagine that they will win popular elections. They consent to the democratic process, only to find that the vote goes against them.

Even democratic leaders exaggerate their public support. In the United States, as confirmed by the small voter turnouts, there is general frustration and apathy about the whole electoral process. Democratic leaders also overestimate their ability to do good. Projects are invented and implemented without regard for their actual outcome or usefulness. Motivated by righteous impulses or the desire to impress the electorate, the benevolent perpetrator is rarely in direct contact with the needs of those he or she seeks to help, and too often, the impact is anything but good.

In order to wield coercive power for the supposed benefit of others, politicians or government agents must first *possess* coercive power. The implications of this are too rarely considered by those who promote the use of force for benevolent purposes. But how do people conduct themselves when they possess coercive power? Are they likely to be more pure than the rest of us—more able to exercise that power in the interest of the relatively powerless electorate rather than in the interest of themselves and their more potent supporters? Or are they likely to be corrupted even beyond the norm by their power and their need to maintain it? The poor and the disenfranchised benefit so little from do-good programs in part because the leaders are first and foremost taking care of themselves, for example, by steadily increasing the strength and scope of their own positions and programs, and their bureaucratic empire. Thus federal projects to feed the poor are more likely to end up feeding an ever more bloated government power structure. State-inspired "conflict resolution" too often leads to conflict generation.

VICTIMS OF STATE COERCION

Victims of state coercion—those who feel oppressed by taxes or government regulations—tend to lose their initiative. We have seen that dramatically displayed in the former communist nations.

The supposed beneficiaries, typical of the coercive dynamic, also tend to become victims. Welfare with its humiliating rules and regulations can discourage people from becoming more autonomous and competent.

As already noted, well-intentioned state activities can be viewed as attempts to coerce love, with all the inherent hazards and contradictions involved in imposing Dynamic III on Dynamic I. We must always beware of attempts to accomplish good ends by means of force. We must move the state from being an institution of conflict generation to one of conflict resolution. Instead of fighting for control over state power in order to enforce their own solutions, people must learn to participate in community—to seek collaborative problem solving without the use of force.

Part III. Hunger, Poverty, and Redistributive Justice

Can the Three Dynamic Theory clarify the issues surrounding specific good intentions, such as the desire to relieve poverty and hunger through redistributions of wealth?

COMPENSATING FOR INJUSTICE BY REDISTRIBUTING WEALTH

Redistributive justice is the attempt to correct earlier injustices and unfair imbalances of wealth. Typically, it motivates taking from the rich in order to give to the poor, for example, to provide special help to the underprivileged in finding employment or seeking education. It epitomizes both the pitfalls and the necessity of coercion in modern society.

Redistributive justice is, by almost any definition, a form of coercion. One group is forced to help another. These implications are rarely considered outside of free market analyses (Von Mises, 1966). Within John Burton's viewpoint (1990), for example, redistributive justice is considered a benign basic need.

At its worst, the impulse to redistribute is motivated by envy. Even if *everyone* ends up worse off, some resentful people want to see society leveled. This is not mere jealousy—the wish to have what someone else has; it is envy—the wish to take away from others. It is born of psychological helplessness: "If I cannot get what I want, no one else will either." In Remnick's article, the young entrepreneur Sterligov identified envy when he said, "Their psychology is all screwed up. They are so used to being equal in poverty that they assume if you have any money, you are a crook." In *Envy* (1966), Helmut Schoeck describes this motivation as the root of socialist and communist programs—the impulse to level anyone who tries to rise above the crowd, even if it means less for everyone.

On the other hand, redistributive justice can be motivated by a very different interpretation of the principles of liberty. Those who have previously been *robbed*—for example, former slaves who were robbed of their freedom and the products of their labor—are now to be compensated by the society that benefitted from the crime. Similarly, Native Americans were exterminated in large numbers, robbed of their lands, and systematically persecuted. Furthermore, both the former slaves and the Native Americans continue to suffer from government policies and social prejudices that suppress their opportunities.

The principle of liberty, which is based on the rejection of force except in self-defense, can thus be used to defend force aimed at redressing past injustices. It is a matter of returning stolen goods and making restitution for past oppression.

Of course, the people compensating former slaves or Native Americans are not the ones who stole from them. Contemporary white people did not use black slaves to earn their wealth. Nor did they steal Native American lands. But Americans in general have benefitted from the capital and other advantages accrued through slavery and the abuse of Native Americans; and, due to continuing racism and prejudice, white Americans continue to benefit disproportionately.

Love also motivates redistributive justice. Through taxation we are made to act charitably (lovingly) toward those who have been disadvantaged. Thus the welfare state can be looked upon as coerced love. Where charity would fail to meet the needs of people, the state enforces giving. But whatever this is, it is hard to call it genuine love or "gifting," or individuals would do it without the threat of the IRS.

CHILDREN AND SHARING

Consider the problem of redistributive justice in regard to teaching fairness to children. If Johnny does not wish to share his toys with Jane, we may encourage him by pointing out that he loves Jane. Or we may explain the practicality of gaining future exchanges in kind from her. Best of all, I believe, we may try to teach him to share through the example of our own generosity toward him and toward others. But only as a last resort would we force Johnny to share his toys. Forcing him to share would, in all likelihood, backfire. It might instead teach him to resent sharing. It may even make him hate Jane. Common sense and empirical research indicate the futility of coercing children in order to make them more generous.

On the other hand, if a child steals from another child, the property must be returned. Redistributive justice, it seems to me, is best formulated in terms of restoring rights and especially returning stolen property. In modern society, where the rich and powerful systematically steal from the poor and disempowered, concern for human welfare supports redistributive justice. But we must set limits on it, and never lose sight of the shortcomings and negative consequences of trying to coerce charity.

Again, what is really needed is a more loving society. Those of us who are more successful must find ways of making the community more livable for those who are not. Ironically, it would be in our best interest to do so. It would require much less financial expenditure to provide charity through private agencies rather than through the government bureaucracy, and even through personal volunteer services rather than through paid bureaucrats. Much more could be done with much less financial burden.

But self-interest is not a sufficient motivation for helping others. In the short run, it is too tempting to grab what one can for oneself. People must, through empathic love, care about the well-being of all members of the community, including those generations who will follow us.

FURTHER JUSTIFICATIONS FOR REDISTRIBUTING WEALTH

As already noted in chapter 3, in order to participate in a competitive, relatively free society, individuals must bring to adulthood a large measure of autonomy and self-determination. This requires certain optimal conditions. Hapless children—raised amid racism, sexism, poverty, starvation, ill-health, and abuse, and without a decent education—have little chance to develop autonomy and to benefit from economic freedom. Similarly, older citizens of Eastern Bloc societies have little psychological capacity to take advantage of the new opportunities. Their more self-determined fellow citizens describe them as lost causes and say in effect, "We can't expect anything from them and we will have to take care of them." If not provided for in their old age by a safety net, they would suffer enormously.

Furthermore, even if all people could reach adulthood more or less autonomous and self-determining, some would still possess overriding advantages. In the United States, for example, those born white, male, wealthy, and in the cultural mainstream are vastly advantaged in competition with equally competent persons born without those attributes. Given the tendency of advantaged people to cooperate with each other to maintain their advantages, the unfair accrual of further advantages seems inevitable. Nor are minority attempts to cooperate with each other an effective counterbalance. Disadvantaged demoralized people are less able to cooperate or conspire on their own behalf, and those in power are often able to thwart their ambitions.

Redistribution of wealth again seems a just policy from this view-point, especially if it is used to support the development of auton-omy and self-determination among disadvantaged children.

Liberty does include the possibility of redistributive justice, but notice that cogent arguments can be made for and *against* it. What tilts the scales? I believe that the balance of liberty and love is critical. For those who empathize with the poor or disadvantaged, the balance will favor helping them out, even if it bends the prin-ciples of liberty.

By contrast, love has *nothing* weighing against it, except the difficulty contemporary humans beings have in feeling it for others less fortunate than themselves. Yet human beings are in-herently loving, and human beings flourish best in loving commu-nity. The problem is twofold: to awaken the idea of love within the hearts of individuals and to find better ways to build loving com-munity.

HUNGER AND POVERTY: DIFFERING ISSUES IN THE U.S.A. AND EMERGING CAPITALISTIC SOCIETIES

Will the poor and the hungry always be with us in our larger industrial societies? Are we doomed to this unfortunate reality? The problem has of course been discussed since the earliest cri-tiques of capitalism and the industrial revolution. The cynicism of Malthus is well-known, as is the greater optimism of Adam Smith. These issues will be framed in terms of the Three Dynamics.

One approach to hunger and poverty is to ask, "How can we resolve the conflict between the rich and the poor, the well-fed and the hungry?" But even though disparities do exist, this is not the central problem in the former communist nations. They don't have enough to go around. For them, the challenge is how to generate wealth. Therefore, the moment freedom blossomed but a little, they became preoccupied with implementing capitalism. In the process, as the press reports quickly indicated, the "rugged indi-vidualist" entrepreneurs initially accumulate their wealth partly at the expense of others who do not know how to compete. That is the price these societies seem willing to pay for Western-style progress.

The problem is not the same in the more successful capitalist countries. In the United States, for example, we already have more than enough *material* resources to eradicate poverty and hunger among our own citizens, and probably enough additional resources to help much of the remaining world as well. My own Montgomery County has for many years been ranked at or near the top in the nation for average family income; and yet we have a growing problem of hunger and poverty. That we do not eradicate poverty and hunger in America—that it seems as if we *cannot*—is not a matter of material or technical capacity.

The extreme free-market position warns that the great engine of economic progress will grind to a halt if some people get a free ride or a free lunch. It is also argued that it is morally wrong to tax one person to take care of another. The "no free lunch for the poor" argument falls apart when the state is already lavishing support on big business and other privileged groups, often to the detriment of the poor (see chapter 8).

There are many other reasons why we have no national mandate to help the poor and hungry. The major liberal attempts to end poverty have not succeeded. Why fail again? Often it seems like a matter of priorities. We consider other problems more important. Class and racial conflict also interfere. The wealthiest among us use their power and influence to maintain their status at the expense of others; and in general the white majority resents helping the underclass, whom it perceives as "different" from them. Sexism plays a role: the poorest and most hungry among us are families with single mothers and children. Clearly, our shameful disregard for the needs of children also plays a role. Patriarchal concepts of superiority, rugged individualism, and competitiveness leave little room for generosity, charity, and empathy for those who are less fortunate.

But whatever conflicts prevent us from eradicating poverty and hunger within America, solving the problem is materially within our grasp, requiring but a fraction of each year's gross national product.

In the Three Dynamic Theory, poverty and hunger can be viewed as a conflict between American society and its large underclass of poor and hungry people. Solving these problems requires a different attitude toward the poor and hungry in America. It means much less coercion, and much more liberty and love. It entails identifying with and empathizing with the less fortunate, helping them to find the means to survive in the short run, and empowering them in the longer run to join as full members of society. In the case of a relatively small number of disabled people, it means being loving enough to take care of those who cannot take care of themselves.

Part IV: Liberty, Love, and the Environment

Liberty is usually considered the enemy of environmentalism. When defenders of the environment look for the chief culprit, it almost always is identified as free-market activities based on self-interest, the profit motive, individual rights, private property, and capitalism. When the lifting of the Iron Curtain disclosed some of the most tragic pollution on earth, pointing the finger exclusively at the free-enterprise system became a little more difficult. Libertarians and anarchists had always pointed *their* finger at the state, and that would have predicted exactly what was found in the totalitarian nations of Eastern Europe and Russia. Now the problem remains: how to revive industry without asphyxiating Eastern Europe.

INDUSTRIAL POLLUTION BEHIND THE IRON CURTAIN

Industrial pollution is so bad in some parts of Eastern Europe and the Soviet Union that the population ages and dies prematurely. But if these industries are shut down in order to protect the public health, the already precarious economies could be tipped over the edge. Meanwhile, the environment and the health of citizens deteriorate with every day that the industries spew forth their toxins. No abstract principle of liberty is sufficient. No general principle of love solves the problem.

Few people realize that the principles of liberty do not support pollution. The principle of self-defense gives every individual the right to prevent his or her body from being exposed to toxin. The offending plants would be closed on the grounds that they were committing aggression against others by polluting their environment and their bodies. Thus, if the right to self-defense were upheld by the state, it would become almost impossible for polluters to exist. Liberty, if properly understood, can become a sword wielded on behalf of the environment.

While escalating the economic crisis, the prohibition of pollution would wipe the industrial slate clean and open the way to a complete overhaul of industry. This could result in a dramatically different kind of society than now exists in the Western world. It could be a step in the direction of smaller, more ecologically sound industrial development. Thus free-market principles provide unexpected support for putting environmental values ahead of industrial development.

INDIVIDUAL AND PROPERTY RIGHTS IN DEFENSE OF THE ENVIRONMENT

The results of applying Dynamic II: liberty to industrial pollution are somewhat startling. Instead of fostering big industry, as free marketeers so often favor, an uncompromising application of free-market principles would close down poisoners of the environment.

In *For a New Liberty* (1973), Rothbard writes, "Government ownership, even socialism, has proved to be no solution to the problem of pollution," (p. 269). He goes on to say: "Note, for example, the two crucial areas in which pollution has become an important problem: the air and the waterways, particularly the rivers. But these are precisely two of the vital areas in society in which private property has not been permitted to function." That is, some of the worst pollution problems involve air and large bodies of water, resources controlled by the state rather than by the free market.

From Rothbard's perspective, if property rights had been recognized, air and water pollution could not have started and could still be brought to a halt. Whenever an industry pollutes the air or any large body of water or any underlying aquifer, the industry offends the rights of *other people*—their bodies or their property. If individuals could sue for damages from air or water pollution, perpetrators would be quickly forced to mend their ways.

However, allying themselves with the industrial revolution, every state in the world has limited the rights of individuals to sue polluters. To protect industry, the state sets the basic standards of *allowable* pollution.

Similarly, if individuals rights were strictly adhered to, there would be little or no danger from nuclear power plants. Until they were safe, there simply wouldn't be any. When the U.S. government first sought to encourage the development of atomic power plants, it became clear that the plants would never be able to obtain private insurance coverage against disasters, because one calamity would bankrupt even a consortium of insurers. So the government intervened and passed legislation to limit the liability of these public utilities. No matter how much damage they might do in the future, the victims will be able to collect only a limited amount.

Without the government setting limits on their liability, nuclear power plants would not have been built until private insurers thought them safe to insure. Perhaps this would never have taken place. Small atomic energy sources might have been safe enough to be insured. Perhaps larger plants might have become safe enough to insure in the distant future; perhaps not. . . . But the landscape would not now be dotted with these behemoths, and the public would not live in fear of them.

Thus, in some cases at least, free-market principles can protect the environment. They are especially effective when individuals can sue to protect themselves from actual or potential hazards. In the arena of pollution, liberty turns out to be a surprising ally. But will Dynamic II principles work when animals and nature, rather than persons, are being exploited and endangered?

CAN THE FREE MARKET PRESERVE NATURE?

Terry L. Anderson and Donald R. Leal have tried to make the case for liberty in *Free Market Environmentalism* (1991) in which they equate the free market with individualism and the pursuit of self-interest. Anderson and Leal are sophisticated enough to add the caveat that self-interest can be modified by concern for "close relatives and friends" and "conditioned by moral principles," (p. 4). But for them, plain old selfishness motivates the world: "Most scientific approaches have implicitly assumed that self-interest dominates behavior for higher as well as lower forms of life," (p. 5).

How can self-interest produce environmentally sound policies? The key, according to free-market advocates, is the desire of people to protect the environment—how much they will pay to accomplish their end. When people becoming willing to spend on behalf of environmental preservation, creative entrepreneurs will find a way to meet their needs, for example, through selling and managing environmental preservations. The Nature Conservancy is a nonprofit organization that identifies and purchases environmentally significant land for preservation. To date, they have saved over three million acres of land (Scheffer, 1991). But as the Nature Conservancy would readily admit, it has thus far been able to save less than a drop in nature's endangered bucket.

Without Anderson and Leal explicitly saying so, it comes down to this: When people care as much about wilderness as about Disneyland, they will pay for the preservation of wilderness the way they pay for Disneyland. This observation has appeal; but it also has shortcomings. Sportsmen pay large sums to preserve game for hunting, but their particular use and enjoyment of nature itself raises moral questions and tends to abuse the environment in other ways. The lead shot used in duck hunting was deadly to the ducks and other birds who ingested the pellets, and by no means all hunters were willing to forsake using it. By contrast, those true "outdoorsmen," the Native Americans, thought of themselves as stewards of the land and its creatures for future generations (see p. 204). Too often contemporary users of the outdoors do not share their reverence toward nature.

Ironically, free-market environmentalism must depend upon love. It must hope that enough people will grow to treasure the environment sufficiently to pay for preserving it, without hope of financial profit from the expenditure. Vast numbers of people would have to love the earth sufficiently to spend large sums of money on its behalf. But the competitive values generated by the free market often mitigate against loving anything for its own sake, especially usable "natural resources."

People will resent paying to save vast areas of air, land, and water, when other people who do not share the cost will nonetheless share the benefits. People generally become willing to sacrifice for a public good only when assured that everyone will be joining in, and that requires coercive state interventions.

Furthermore, not enough people seem willing to take a long-range and even transgenerational view. We must preserve nature not only for ourselves, but for future generations who have no say in what we are now doing. Future generations may not feel very forgiving toward us when told that nature simply had to go because its preservation wasn't consistent with liberty and the free market.

PRIVATE OWNERSHIP OF THE WHALES?

If an animal, piece of land, or other aspect of nature is not owned by anyone, the free market cannot protect or conserve it. Whales and migrating birds, for example, cannot easily be made into property. Furthermore, in a society that promotes free-market values, people are not likely to have an interest in saving anything that they do not own. Yet it is difficult or impossible, and perhaps morally wrong, to establish individual ownership of many natural resources, such as endangered species of whales or migrating birds.

Anderson and Leal look forward to a day when some animals may be electronically tagged and/or fenced in, thereby making it possible to own and preserve them. But this hope is based on a naively atomistic conception of nature. Accustomed to thinking of society purely in terms of isolated individuals, Anderson and Leal tend to think of animals in the same way. The suggestion for tagging endangered species for ownership smacks more of desperation than rationality. We cannot begin to identify every form of life (insects, plants, small mammals, etc.), let alone tag it. As the authors note, even our largest animals, the whales, cannot be easily "owned" and hence protected by the free market.

LESSONS FROM NATIVE AMERICANS

What is needed is not the preservation of individual creatures but of entire ecosystems. In the case of the whale, the ecosystem is the oceans of the world, not to mention their shorelines, the rivers that empty into them, and the air that surrounds them. An individual whale or wolf cannot be saved without saving its habitat, and that habitat can sometimes span across the face of the earth and into the depths of the earth, the air, and the ocean.

Not individual creatures, but whole oceans, vast air spaces, expansive wetlands, great mountain ranges, and immense rain forests must preserved. Even dividing up the earth into "ecosystems" will not ultimately work. Our plans must encompass the whole planet.

Like the Native Americans, we must see ourselves as but a part of a vast, all-encompassing reality (Erdoes, 1989; Weatherford, 1988). This is conveyed by the words of a Hopi, Thomas Benyacya (Erdoes, 1990):

Native Americans have a strong belief that they are responsible for the Earth's well-being. A Hopi elder said in an address to the government: "This land is the sacred home of the Hopi people and all the Indian race in this land. It was given to the Hopi people the task to guard this land, not by force of arms, not by killing, not by confiscation of properties of others, but by humble prayers, by obedience to our traditions and religious instructions, and by being faithful to our creator, Masau'u. (p. 64.)

Wendell Berry (1987) has also expressed sentiments on the spiritual importance of nature:

The survival of wilderness—of places that we do not change, where we allow the existence even of creatures we perceive as dangerous—is necessary. Our sanity probably requires it. Whether we go to those places or not, we need to know that they exist. And I would argue that we do not need just the great public wildernesses, but millions of small private or semiprivate ones. Every farm should have one; wildernesses can occupy corners of factory grounds and city lots—places where nature is given a free hand, where no human work is done, where people go only as guests. These places function, I think, whether we intend

*them to or not, as sacred groves—places we respect and leave
alone, not because we understand well what goes on there, but
because we do not. (p. 17.)*

According to Berry (1987), we not only need to experience nature for our individual spiritual survival and rejuvenation, we must
build communities to a scale that fits within nature:

*If the human economy is to be fitted into the natural economy in
such a way that both may thrive, the human economy must be
built to proper scale. It is possible to talk at great length about
the difference between proper and improper scale. It may be
enough to say here that difference is suggested by the difference
between amplified and unamplified music in the countryside, or
the difference between the sound of a motorboat and the sound of
oarlocks. A proper human sound, we may say, is one that allows
other sounds to be heard. A properly scaled human economy or
technology allows a diversity of other creatures to thrive. (p. 16.)*

From the viewpoint of many environmentally oriented critics of
the free market (Berry, 1972, 1987; Clark, 1989; Ross-Breggin and
Breggin, 1992; Ross-Breggin, 1990), the market is inherently too
human-centered. The environment and its life forms will be exploited and endangered as long as the needs of *people*—even their
individual desires to preserve nature—are the central concern.

Essentially, animals and nature must have their own rights, an
idea that seems preposterous to most free-market advocates.
Whales—and all of nature—must be valued unconditionally. That
means, they must be loved. Perhaps then trees will have "standing" in court, and suits will be brought on the behalf of mountains
and lakes. As Ginger Ross-Breggin has suggested to me, perhaps
the concept of self-defense can be extended to life forms other than
human beings.

A philosophy is needed that focuses on the inherent worth of all
life forms, rather than on the self-interest of individual human
beings as reflected in preserving this or that life form. Consistent
with Native American cultures, humans must live within nature,

and in spiritual awe of it, without attempting to dominate or exploit it.

THE FUTURE OF ENVIRONMENTAL POLICY

Both liberty and love must play a role in the developing attempts to save the environment and the earth itself. It is critical, however, to have clear definitions of the principles of liberty and love in order to understand where each is most appropriate and effective.

Surprising to many environmentalists, greater respect for individual rights and property is one of the keys to saving the air and water in specific locations where people may sue for damages. But when individual rights cannot be so easily defined, we cannot rely on freedom. The profit motive and individual human rights will not protect the inhabitants of the sea or the great rain forests. They require loving interventions by people motivated by their ideals and their identification with nature.

Educating the public and motivating people to take action are crucial to saving the planet. More people must become aware and concerned enough to take action. Every method of public education must be employed, from talking with one's own family and friends, to writing books, lobbying, running for public office, and influencing the mass media.

In my local neighborhood, the county has given official recycling collection boxes to every household. Many people are already recycling on their own. Environmental awareness is growing, but surely not fast enough. There is more hope in a broad-based movement that includes not only environmentalists but those interest in social justice, human rights, peace, and a variety of other closely related reform issues (see chapter 11).

Hopefully the principles of conflict analysis and resolution can help to solve the growing number of clashes between those who would save their jobs and those who would save the environment. On some refrigerators in the United States, there are cartoons depicting the heartless destruction of the spotted owl's habitat by greedy loggers. On others, there are depictions of loggers losing their jobs and their homes because of efforts to save the same creature. Similarly, in the Brazilian rain forests natives struggle to make a marginal living by slash and burn farming techniques that ruin many acres of land. Ironically, the people who want to fight to preserve these rain forests are often the same ones with the most sympathy for poor, indigenous peoples.

It will not be possible to make much progress toward preserving the environment without at the same time meeting the needs of people whose livelihoods depend upon using up those same re-sources. It is difficult to imagining carrying out such large-scale balancing acts without massive government involvement. Yet gov-ernment, rooted so deeply in coercion, has seldom been much help in conflict resolution.

Can love be brought to bear on these problems without turning increasingly to coercive state interventions? There is one way, ex-emplified by Greenpeace and other deep ecology groups who value nature for its own sake and who are willing to risk themselves in its defense, often through civil disobedience.

Recently a sympathetic member of a Congressional staff told me that it was politically dangerous to speak well of Greenpeace on Capitol Hill. Yet the same week, *National Geographic,* an organiza-tion known for its conservatism, sponsored a lengthy TV special in support of the environmental group. Clearly, we are in a time of transition. Civil disobedience, with Gandhi's "loving firmness" as the model, may be the ultimate approach to stopping the destruc-tion of nature (see chapter 11).

UTOPIAN SOLUTIONS AND CONFLICT RESOLUTION

Social scientists, especially ecologically oriented ones (Clark, 1989; Sale, 1985; van Andruss, Plant, Plant, and Wright, 1990) are urging us to develop a new concept of community. Mary Clark's book, *Ariadne's Thread* (1989), is particularly well-informed and enlight-ened about the tragic path humanity is now following, and it offers an alternative consistent with some of the more progressive con-temporary movements of deep ecology and social justice (see chap-ter 11). Her approach allows us to contrast the development of alternative "utopian" models to the *process* of conflict resolution, which is something quite different.

Clark advocates smaller, more tightly knit, and loving commu-nities based on self-sufficient ecological systems. No society, ac-cording to this plan, would use more energy than was available to it. Living within nature, we would fit our needs to those of nature instead of trying to force nature into ours. People would be as connected as possible to their work, and their work would be connected as much as possible to the resources of their own ecosystem.

In Clark's vision, each society would express its own sacred meanings. Cultural diversity would not be expressed within large pluralistic societies but through smaller, separate eco-cultural systems. One's spiritual state would replace one's pocketbook as the measure of personal success. Mutuality and sharing, rather than competition, would be the guiding principle of social relationships. Clark's community is at one with itself and with nature, a true Dynamic I vision of life.

How viable or practical is Clark's vision? Could these or similar communities arise out of the ashes of the USSR and Eastern Bloc nations? There is certainly a tendency for the breakdown and decentralization of the former communist states. But it is hard to imagine that trend reaching the proportions required by Clark's vision.

The long-suppressed peoples of Eastern Europe and Russia want to become more like us, and are bent on adopting capitalism. They may ultimately outdo us in their individualism. And the trend in Western Europe is not toward local community but toward international unity. Furthermore, I will suggest that the global village is a necessary condition for successful local communities, and that it requires free-market industrialization, especially modern transportation and communication (see chapter 11).

Those who promote utopian ideals must be prepared to tell us how we get "from here to there" without the use of massive coercion. While a specific social blueprint may inspire a small group of people, it is not likely to be freely adopted by a whole society. People want to go through their own decision-making processes. That is why the force of a totalitarian state is required to impose any predetermined ideal upon a population. That is exactly what happened in the USSR under Lenin and his successors.

A free people need philosophic and social tools—principles and institutions—that facilitate conflict resolution as they plan and evolve their own communities. Ideals must be generated by individuals, so many individuals that whole communities eventually began to change for the better. In the words of Wendell Berry (1977):

The only real, practical, hope-giving way to remedy the fragmentation that is the disease of the modern spirit is a small and humble way—a way that a government or agency or organization or institution will never think of, though a **person** *may think of it: one must begin in one's own life the private solutions that can only* in turn *become public solutions. (p. 23.)*

Given freedom and encouragement to love, people are likely to surprise us, and themselves, with their creative solutions. Out of liberty and love springs genuine community.

CHAPTER 10

▼ ▼

Resolving International Conflict: The Middle East

I refuse to accept the cynical notion that nation after nation must spiral down a militaristic stairway into the hell of thermonuclear destruction. I believe that unarmed truth and unconditional love will have the final word in reality. This is why right, temporarily defeated, is stronger than evil triumphant.
Martin Luther King, Jr., Nobel Peace Prize acceptance address, Oslo, December 11, 1964

The prophecy of a world moving toward political unity is the light which guides all that is best, most vigorous, most truly alive in the work of our time. It gives sense to what we are doing. Nothing else does.
Walter Lippmann, "Reflection After Armistice Day," New York Herald Tribune, November 12, 1931

The problem of peace and security is indeed far more important than the conflict between socialism and capitalism. Man must first ensure his survival; only then can he ask himself what type of existence he prefers. . . . The struggle for power is equally repulsive, conducted as it is, both here and there, with the traditional dishonesty of the political craft.
Albert Einstein, Einstein on Peace (1968)

As community increases in size, it becomes increasingly difficult to apply any given set of principles to resolving its problems. When large communities themselves come into conflict, the issues become complex beyond one person's comprehension. In this chapter, the principles of liberty and love will be applied to international conflict, using the Middle East as the main example. Clearly, such a task is daunting, and I hope to shed new light on the subject without pretending to solve the world's most threatening and difficult problems.

The attitude of American citizens toward the Gulf war will be given special attention, since America was largely responsible for the dramatic escalation of the conflict. I'm an American, and by focusing on Americans I hope to begin where conflict resolution should begin, with a better understanding one's own role in the conflict.

BASIC STRESS PARADIGMS
AND INTERNATIONAL POLITICS

We have described how Basic Stress Paradigms—hurt, fear, and helplessness—are caused by stress and trauma, and then go on to energize interpersonal and societal conflicts. The same process takes place on an international level. War provides an example.

Love, with its abhorrence of violence against others, motivates people to reject war. But the frustration, anger, and hate generated by Basic Stress Paradigms provide readily available fuel for murderous conflict. I am reminded of an incident during a visit to Israel in the early 1970s when I strayed from the main streets on the outskirts of Jerusalem. I found myself in an alley between partially demolished buildings where Arab children were playing outside the door to their home. Several youngsters, varying in age from a few years old to nine or ten, were using a sharpened stick to torture a puppy to death. One can only imagine what injuries of their own they were revisiting upon the squealing puppy, and with what ease these same injuries might fuel their adult hatreds in the Arab-Israeli conflict. Nor are Basic Stress Paradigms fueling Arabs to the exclusion of Jews. No culture has a monopoly on benevolent childhoods.

Political ideologues and leaders are able to restimulate painful emotion and to channel it into political conflict. During the recent Gulf war, the Israeli leaders used Holocaust images to motivate their citizens and worldwide Jewry. They did so by repeatedly showing footage of Israelis donning gas masks. Few Jews could be wholly immune to such propagandizing. In order to deal fairly with the Arab-Israeli conflict, I have had to overcome the emotional reactions that began in my childhood when I confronted the Holocaust while watching Movietone News. Handling that Basic Stress Paradigm has enabled me to see the humanity of the Palestinians with whom we Jews must now deal equitably. Thus I had to climb down my own conflict tree (see chapters 1 and 9).

While Israel was busy manipulating Jewish feelings of helplessness during the Gulf war, U.S. leaders were manipulating America's post-Vietnam humiliation by promising an overwhelming use of force aimed at a swift, decisive victory. Still playing on shame over Vietnam, they promised to bring the soldiers home quickly and to welcome them as heroes. Thus the Bush administration successfully exploited the energy of America's post-Vietnam Basic Stress Paradigm to motivate support for a gargantuan military assault.

We Americans also sought to *heal* the hurts of Vietnam through reaffirming our patriotism, winning a great victory, and welcoming home our troops. But the perpetrator syndrome (chapter 4) is the ultimate result. Violent victory inflates our egos and distracts us from our inner selves, as well as from caring about others. We become less aware of ourselves and others, and more inured to their pain and suffering. We substitute bravado for justice and mercy. We feel larger, as we become smaller; we feel omniscient as our vision narrows. Superficially we feel less afflicted with helplessness, but in reality we become more deeply mired in it. Basic Stress Paradigms are restimulated but not healed by violence against others. At best, our violence numbs us.

Recently Republican party leaders have lamented how quickly America's morale once again declined after the war, and how quickly President Bush's popularity slid down hill along with the economy. The war's "uplifting" impact was short-lived indeed. Nor does the military victory continue to seem so complete. Saddam is still in power, perhaps more firmly entrenched than before, and the pain inflicted on his people by the war may inflame them to support future wars of revenge. Americans aren't the only ones who will turn to war in order to "heal" the wounds of earlier lost wars.

Basic Stress Paradigms become even greater impediments to peace when they have been inflicted upon each other by the contending parties. Palestinians and Israelites, America's black and white population, women and men throughout the world: Each has so many Basic Stress Paradigms with the other's name on it; peaceful resolution of the conflicts becomes increasingly difficult.

HEALING BASIC STRESS PARADIGMS

Political, religious, and educational institutions—and their leaders—can lend their weight to destimulating societal hurts. They can call for forgiveness and mercy. There are also more direct approaches to healing Basic Stress Paradigms on a personal level. At the 1991 National Conference on Peacemaking and Conflict Resolution (NCPCR) in Charlotte, North Carolina, one presenter, Cheri Brown, conducted what was billed as a seminar on international conflict. In her hands, it became a psychodynamic workshop in the traditions of individual psychotherapy and psychodrama.

Brown believes that generic "painful emotion" derives from childhood hurts and that "Where we are hurting, we are not thinking." Especially, resentment rather than love can dominate us, fueling cultural, racial, religious, and political conflict.

For Cheri Brown, a workshop on political conflict resolution involves feeling, expressing, and working through the painful emotions of individual persons. In terms of the Three Dynamic Theory, as the participants free themselves from hurt, fear, and learned helplessness, they become better able to resolve conflict through the principles of liberty and love.

Of course international conflicts cannot be resolved by holding encounter-group workshops. But it helps when people in conflict become more aware of how their personal hurts help to drive their political outrage.

THE DENIAL OF EMPATHY BY AMERICANS

In talks during and after Desert Storm, Richard Rubenstein of the Institute for Conflict Analysis and Resolution at George Mason University made a singular observation on the prevention of war. He said, in effect, "We will not prevent wars such as the one in the Gulf until we place as much value on the life of a young Iraqi soldier as on the life of a young American soldier." He challenged the values that led Americans to view a kill ratio of 1:1,000 as something to cheer about. Indeed, as the casualty count mounts, including the Iraqi and Kurdish children who are dying of starvation and public health hazards, our *continually growing* kill ratio may exceed 1:10,000.

The U.S. government seemed worried about the potentially inhibiting effects of empathy on public enthusiasm for the war. The military was determined to avoid what it saw as a disastrous mistake in Vietnam: allowing the war to be conducted on television. Seeing the actual violence had stirred the feelings of many Americans. Empathy toward both the Vietnamese and our own soldiers made many TV viewers less willing to tolerate the war.

In the Gulf war, the government and the military succeeded in imposing censorship on the press. As a result, we saw "smart bombs" finding their way into air shafts; but we saw nothing of the hellish strafing of tens of thousands of helpless Iraqis trapped in the traffic jam while retreating from Kuwait. Films of the actual assault on that road of death have never been seen on U.S. television.

The European press permitted one small photographic window into the human cost of the war. Despite the censorship, photographer Ken Jarecke shot a grim and gripping picture along the road of death leading from Kuwait to Iraq where airplanes bombed and strafed nearly defenseless fleeing soldiers. The photo shows in graphic detail an Iraqi soldier, killed by a bomb blast, blackened and mummified, with a fixed grimace on his face, as he struggles to drag himself upright and through the windshield of his truck. The visual impact of the soldier, forever frozen at the moment of the blast, is as dramatic as a Rodin statue, racked with pain.

When Jarecke's photo was published in a British newspaper, *The Observer*, there was an outburst of public resentment, not against the war, but against the picture. Harold Evans, president and publisher of Random House, wrote a defense of the photograph in *The Observer* and, along with the photograph, it was reprinted in the July/August 1991 *American Photographer*. Evans spoke of the need "to redress the elusive euphoria of a high-tech war":

There is something more significant in the protests to **The Observer** *than a proper reticence. They suggest that even now, at the end of the bloodiest century the world has known, even now after the trenches, and Hiroshima, and My Lai, popular culture is still imbued with a romantic conception of war and resents a grimmer reality.*

Americans were equally willing to deny the "grimmer reality"; the photograph was never published in the United States until that memorable issue of *American Photographer*.

PSYCHIATRY IN THE SERVICE OF WAR PROPAGANDA

We have observed that diagnosing people permits psychiatry and the public to perpetrate coercive, inhumane, and physically destructive treatments against mental patients (see chapter 7). The person labeled mentally ill no longer draws our sympathy and concern. Psychiatric diagnosis was also used to obfuscate our violent actions toward Iraq.

A Washington, D.C. psychiatrist, identified as an expert on Saddam Hussein's personality, was called upon regularly by the media during the war to diagnose the Iraqi leader as a madman. The public, long inured to assaults on the "mentally ill," was lulled into believing that the U.S. was going to stop one insane dictator. The cost to tens of millions of people directly and indirectly involved in the conflict was effectively dimmed by the definition of the "enemy" as a single, solitary madman.

When Saddam was not killed or deposed in the conflict—when the U.S. seemingly decided to accept his existence as a counterbalance to Iran—the psychiatrist disappeared from TV. It was perhaps too much for the psychiatrist to proclaim that the war had provided the "shock treatment" that "cured" the madman.

Mental health experts on child psychology also helped us reject our feelings of empathy. Several psychologists commented in the media on the impact of war-induced stress on American children. These psychologists told parents to remind their children that the war was "far away in a distant land" and that there was no chance that it would directly harm them.

But what about the *healthy* tendency of children to empathize with other children? We know that children begin to empathize with each other from very early in life (see chapter 2). Infants respond contagiously to the pain of others and toddlers sometimes extend gestures of sympathy toward other children who are suffering.

Did American children feel no empathy for their Iraqi counterparts? Did they in no way identify with the American soldiers who were being directly exposed to the war? Was love not a part of their distress? Shouldn't it have been? Or do we wish to raise a generation of children who respond as indifferently to the real victims of war as they do to the mass murders in Rambo movies and Sunday morning cartoons?

There was nothing in itself wrong with reassuring children that the war was being fought far away from their homes. It appears that many adult Americans needed the same reassurance, as they stayed away in droves from flying within the continental United States and from taking vacations in places that seemed possible targets of terrorism, like Washington, D.C. and New York City. But after reassuring our children, shouldn't we have *encouraged* their empathy toward other children around the world? Don't we want them to learn that war is harmful to everyone involved, including the people on both sides, and that modern warfare poses risks for the whole planet?

THE DENIAL OF WAR'S IMPACT

Too many adults, including our national leaders, seem unaware that war always has unforeseen negative consequences. In this brief but violent conflict, the cost to the Iraqi people has been beyond calculation. Millions have suffered terrible personal losses in property and in the lives of their family members, both civilian and military. The country's infrastructure has been destroyed, resulting in starvation and epidemic disease. Their bravest youngsters—those who took the opportunity to rebel against Saddam Hussein—have been slaughtered. The dictator may be more firmly entrenched than ever before. The Kurdish people have been uprooted and sustained enormous injury. So have other cultures within the borders of Iraq. The boycott and the flow of refugees has strained surrounding economies. Within Kuwait, the authoritarian government has been reestablished and revenge has replaced justice. The environment has been catastrophically despoiled by oil and by oil-well fires.

In an address at George Mason University on April 8, 1991, James Laue eloquently confronted the catastrophe in terms of lost lives:

*As many as 200,000 of our sisters and brothers are gone forever
from their families and their communities. Iraqis, Kuwaitis,
Kurds, Saudis, Israelis, Palestinians, Americans, Brits. I'm going
to stop for a moment so we all can reflect silently on this incom-
prehensible loss. (p. 5.)*

The public and the press should never again allow censorship to
remove them from the realities of war. They should *now* demand
that realistic films of the slaughter be released and shown to the
public.

A more loving attitude toward all people and a more profound
concern for the planet itself would have prevented the American
public from accepting the attack on Iraq. So would greater confidence in alternative methods of conflict resolution. We return to
the need for the state to become more of an institution for conflict
resolution, and less of an instrument for conflict generation.

THE DENIAL OF PERPETRATION BY AMERICANS

The attack on Iraq should have encouraged a more critical exami-
nation of the concept of liberty, and especially the principle of self-
defense. Instead, typical of the perpetrator syndrome, it led
Americans toward a collective denial of responsibility.

Many Americans would not characterize the U.S. attack on Iraq
and Kuwait as an act of aggression. We want to believe it was
self-defense. We were protecting the Kuwaitis, our own oil supplies, international respect for law and order, and the principle of
liberty itself. We made a necessary preemptive strike against a
dictator determined to control the Mideast, its oil, and therefore
the world's economy. We had to obliterate Hussein's long-range
rocket and nuclear weapon potential before it obliterated others.

If we regard this viewpoint to be true, then we must admit, at
the least, that this particular act of self-defense was very costly to
everyone involved. I've already summarized some of the international costs. At home, we have reinforced our perpetrator syndrome, inuring us further to war, glorifying the results of violence,
and denying the destructiveness of our actions. The war drained
resources and distracted us from more critical domestic problems,

including poverty, hunger, declining health care, a collapsing educational system, continued racism, and catastrophe within the banking system. Instead of encouraging us to conserve energy and to develop alternative sources, the war has bound us even more tightly to Mideast oil. The war brought about the most airtight press censorship in the history of the United States.

It also seems undeniable that the U.S.-led attack on Iraq far exceeded the customary definitions of self-defense. Self-defense is legitimate only if it employs the *minimal* amount of force necessary to prevent further aggression and possibly to coerce just reparations (see chapters 3 and 9). The force used against Iraq far surpassed anything needed to drive Saddam Hussein out of Kuwait and it persisted until the goal of destroying Iraq's military might and overall infrastructure became apparent. The demolition was so thorough that it undermined any hope that the Iraqi economy could generate reparations. Furthermore, it caused incalculable damage to noncombatants, including the earth itself. As in most wars, self-defense became a pretext for a much broader political agenda. Furthermore, it has thus far failed to meet two of its stated goals—getting rid of Saddam Hussein and nullifying Iraq's nuclear capability.

ALTERNATIVES TO THE WAR AGAINST IRAQ

Few people in the West and few governments felt that Iraq's invasion of Kuwait should have gone unanswered. A remarkable worldwide coalition favored sanctions and many observers in the field of conflict analysis and resolution felt such measures were justified. Had the United States intended to prevent further Iraqi aggression and to restore Kuwait, several immediate steps were required, followed by a more long-range solution.

Stopping Iraqi aggression was quickly and relatively easily accomplished by providing military support to Saudi Arabia. This required relatively little military capability and no offensive warfare. Putting pressure on Iraq to leave Kuwait was begun with the United Nation's sanctions. The UN embargo should have been maintained for much longer before turning the Mideast into a war zone.

The problems in the Mideast, including Iraq's attack on Kuwait, have a long history behind them. A glance at the map indicates how carefully the British carved up the area to make sure that Iraq lacked an adequate outlet to the sea. It is well-known that Iraq took the brunt of the war against Iran, while Iraq's backers stayed out of the fighting. It is also clear that the Mideast is too drastically divided into the haves and have-nots.

Serious long-range difficulties stood and continue to stand in the way of peace. Focusing on conflicts among the Arabs, the disparity in wealth in the Middle East is appalling. Countries like Kuwait are rich, while others like Iraq are poor. Within the countries, there are enormous class differences. Any amelioration of conflict would require an increasing generosity on the part of the rich. Dynamic I: love needs more than its customary lip service within the Arab world.

Concern for the well-being of Arab peoples must also play a much greater role in the decision-making of those who are in conflict with them. Unhappily, any increase in Arab unity is seen as a threat to both Israeli and Western interests. A fragmented Arab world seems, on the surface at least, to guarantee Israel's safety and Western access to cheap oil. Thus, the United States was not really interested in ending conflict in the Middle East but rather in preventing Arab unity under Saddam Hussein.

James Laue (1991) has questioned whether this costly war accomplished anything, and urges an approach based on the principles of conflict analysis and resolution:

> *The situation still cries for real solution: mutually satisfied parties, jointly determined outcomes that are mutually satisfactory to all parties, the addressing of the major underlying issues, meeting the standards of justice and fairness, self-implementation by the parties, improvement of the relationships and a commitment to honor the new arrangements voluntarily and permanently. . . . A viable peace plan comes only from a process developed and owned by the parties. (pp. 5–6.)*

ARAB-ISRAELI CONFLICT

The war against Iraq was not caused by the Arab-Israeli conflict. Instead the war was largely the product of conflict between the Arab oil-producing nations and the Western oil-consuming nations, especially the United States. While I am personally grateful for the existence of Israel, it has been too closely tied to U.S. oil diplomacy.

As much as any in the world, the Arab-Israeli conflict exemplifies how coercion breeds and perpetuates conflict. On the one hand, we have the worldwide Jewish community, subject to persecution for more than two thousand years, culminating in the recent Nazi exterminations. Israel, always the spiritual home of the Jews and their religion, became an earthly necessity after the Holocaust. Nor did the threat of extermination wane with the establishment of Israel; it became focused on the population of Israel. Modern Jewish political concerns, including Israeli domestic and foreign policy, is largely governed by the history of persecution and the seemingly ever-present threat of extermination.

But the Arabs, and especially the Palestinians, are themselves the victims of centuries-old oppression, both from indigenous empires and states, and from western exploitation. Since the end of World War II, the Palestinians have been pushed out by uninvited waves of Jews. They have nothing to look forward to but increasing numbers of immigrants into what used to be their country. Nor can they expect any real help from the larger Arab community which is more interested in using them as pawns against Israel and the United States. While Israel has been busy absorbing Jews from the Arab countries, the Arab countries have continually rejected the Palestinians.

Both parties in the Arab-Israeli conflict have legitimate claims. We have a classic example of conflicting claims, each with their own logic and legitimacy. It would be possible to write a seemingly rational treatise justifying either side's position, while vilifying the other's. Indeed, it has been done many times. And so we have two feuding groups, both identifying with the role of victim and both claiming that God, history, and justice are on wholly on their side.

Meanwhile, there is a limited amount of homeland to go around and much of it is sacred to the history of each contesting party. What is to be done?

COERCION IN THE ARAB-ISRAELI CONFLICT

As the Gulf war demonstrated, the Arab-Israeli conflict involves the interests of the entire world. For practical purposes, however, the focus will be on how to approach the conflict between the two most intimate antagonists, the Palestinians and the Israelis. In terms of the three dynamics, what sorts of change in viewpoint do they need to resolve their conflict?

Coercion has of course dominated this stage from the beginning. Even identifying the "beginning" is a matter of dispute, but it is safe to say that both sides feel that the other initiated the use of force. Both sides see the other as the perpetrator and oppressor. Regardless of whoever threw the first stone, after so many years of conflict, both are undoubtedly right about the other. All this is typical of deep-rooted conflict on every level from the personal to the political.

Both sides, or at least the majority of their recognizable leadership, tend to view coercion, including boycotts and military force, as the only solution. The Palestinians want their land back, and believe it will never be relinquished voluntarily. Most Palestinians envision a future in which they will be pushed from the West Bank further into the inhospitable laps of their Arab neighbors. Similarly, the Israelis see their very survival as dependent upon armed might, including an ever-expanding population and land base. From their viewpoint, the surrounding Arab nations, with their enormous superiority in land and population, will attempt to annihilate the entire Israeli nation at the first opportunity. Furthermore, many Israelis believe in a divine mandate to reclaim and settle all those lands awarded by God in the Bible. And so both sides seem almost wholly devoted to coercion as a solution.

Meanwhile, the cost of uncompromising coercion has been devastating to both sides. The Palestinians have lost their homeland and have no place else to go. Some live uneasily in Israel; many are dispersed in exile around the world; and many are penned up with their back against the river Jordan.

How deep is the Palestinian frustration and commitment to violence? In *From Beirut to Jerusalem* (1990), Thomas L. Friedman describes a West Bank toddler walking about carrying a stone, practicing to throw it at the Israelis.

The Israelis too suffer mightily from the cost of their resort to coercion. Their economy is swamped by the cost of the military, their people live in perpetual insecurity, domestic freedoms are compromised, and their coercive tactics against the Palestinians divide them at home and cost them dearly in terms of world-wide support, even among Jews.

TWO PEOPLES UNITED?

The Jews of Israel and the Arabs of Palestine have much in common. They are of course similar in origin, both with their roots in the Mideast. Even their word for "hello" has a similar ring and a common root. In their hearts, both share the same land. In regard to the Jews, it is clear that they are surrounded by a dry sea of hostility. But so are the Palestinians. Palestinians in Israel and on the West Bank (until Intifada) lived better materially than those who fled to Arab nations. Neither Palestinians nor Israelis can expect much help from their immediate neighbors.

THE FIRST PRINCIPLE

The fates of the Palestinians and the Israelis are intertwined. Recognizing this is the first principle for resolving their conflicts.

It seems unlikely that the Jews will expel the great majority of Arabs from Israel and the West Bank. Short of that, Arabs and Jews are going to be intimate enemies for a long time. The alternative of a complete expulsion, while providing momentary security, would only fan still more feverish hatreds. And for ethical reasons, as well as practical political ones, driving out the Palestinians is not a viable alternative. Even in simple economic terms, the continued escalation of hostilities between Israel and the West Bank is too costly to Israel.

Conversely, it seems unlikely that the Palestinians will ever be rid of the Israelis. Driving the Jews into the sea is neither an ethically nor politically sound alternative. The recent resurgence of Russian immigration into Israel, its renewed ties with the United States, the weakening of Soviet power, the escalating U.S. presence in the Middle East, the support of worldwide Jewry for Israel, the might and determination of Israel itself—all suggest that the Palestinians must find a modus vivendi with the Israelis. And there are indications that they are leaning in that direction by modifying their demands for a peaceful settlement, seeking an accommodation with Israel, rather than annihilation of the state.

THE SECOND PRINCIPLE

The second principle, common to most conflicts, is this: the stronger party must reject force and reach toward a settlement.

Israel's might and Palestine's relative vulnerability seem apparent. As by far the superior force, Israel must take the initiative. The greatest obstacle to any conflict resolution is the threat of coercion, and it is up to Israel to foster conditions in which the two sides can begin to communicate in an atmosphere relatively free of coercion and threats. But before doing this, Israel will need to understand the continuing cost of the conflict as demonstrated, for example, by its internal political strife and flagging economy. Recent attempts at peace negotiations are encouraging, but both sides have a long way to go.

Israel's victim mentality, so thoroughly understandable, must be replaced by a greater awareness of Israel's dominant position. Israel cannot, of course, trust its old enemies; but it can trust itself and its own power sufficiently to initiate a more egalitarian dialog. It can start out with a willingness to offer *understanding* of the Palestinian viewpoint. This should not be difficult, since the basic needs of the Palestinians are similar to those of the Israelis; their outcast role in the Middle East, as we have seen, is somewhat similar, including a fundamentally hostile relationship with the rest of the Arab world. The recent assault by the Lebanese army on PLO-controlled areas of Lebanon confirms the plight of the Palestinians.

LIBERTY AND THE LIMITS OF ECONOMIC EXCHANGE

Before Intifada, relations between Palestinians and Israelis were in some ways improving. While the West Bank was by no means an autonomous region, its economic relations with Israel created a free-trade zone between the two communities from which both benefitted. The mutual advantages of free trade between Israel and the West Bank—as well as divided Jerusalem and the Gaza strip—was addressed by Shawn Tully in the May 20, 1991 *Fortune*. In an article entitled "The Best Cause of Mideast Peace," Tully wrote:

What they [those seeking peace] too often ignore are the immense
economic *benefits of peace—and the staggering costs of prolong-*
ing the struggle. A settlement would help bring Israel the invest-
ment capital needed to absorb Soviet immigrants. It would
unleash the Palestinians' formidable business talents, planting a
budding Hong Kong in the Middle East. The result could be a
new generation of Arabs and Jews with a stake in prosperity, not
war. If ever two people could **benefit** *from each other by working*
together, it is the Arabs and the Jews.

Calling for an Arab-Israeli "common market," Tully declares "Any
settlement above all must be built on free trade."

Tully points out that after Israel seized the West Bank from Jordan and Gaza from Egypt during the 1967 war, it opened the
borders between itself and the captured territories. Israeli capital
and technology combined with Palestinian cheap labor resulted in
an economic boost to all involved. In the eight years following the
war, the economy of Israel grew at 7 percent, while the rate in the
occupied territories exceeded 14 percent.

As Israel's economy stagnated in the mid-1970s, it then became
more protectionist, banning many products from the occupied territories. Intifada resulted in the further suppression of trade by
both sides, and then the PLO's support of Iraq against Israel during the Gulf war led to the closing of borders by Israel. While
limited trade and labor exchange has been reestablished, nothing
like the original free trade seems likely to be reinstituted, even
though both sides continue to suffer the loss.

Tully concludes that the occupied territories could become
"booming capitalist enclaves" at the heart of both economic recovery and cooperation between Arabs and Jews. He quotes an Israeli
manufacturer who uses Arab labor: "In our plants and offices, Arabs
and Jews work side by side to make products instead of mischief."
Thus capitalism hopefully leads to cooperation and mutuality.

As useful as it is, something is clearly missing in Tully's analysis.
Psychosocial needs frequently dwarf pure economic interest. So do
other political issues. The desire for political freedom, self-esteem,
and cultural identity motivated the Palestinians to resist the Israelis. Furthermore, despite vigorous trade and the thousands of Arabs crossing into Israel to provide much-needed cheap labor, there

was little impulse on either side for social integration. Arabs and Jews did trade and work together, but they did not make friends with each other. Politically, Arabs were barred from joining the powerful Israeli labor federation, Histadrut. Thus, economic ties that benefitted both did little to bring the two sides closer together.

BACK TO THE FUTURE: JIMMY CARTER AT CAMP DAVID

At the June 1991 National Conference on Peacemaking and Conflict Resolution (NCPCR) in Charlotte, North Carolina, former president Jimmy Carter was interviewed in front of a plenary session by James Laue. With the main topic peacemaking, Carter talked extensively about the Camp David accords in which he brought together Anwar Sadat and Menachem Begin to forge a blueprint for peace between Egypt and Israel. Carter believes that the accords, which were officially endorsed by the Israeli and Egyptian parliaments, still provide the basic principles for an overall Arab-Israeli peace. The Arabs must end the embargo and reject the destruction of Israel, and the Israelis must grant "full autonomy" to the Palestinians and give up Jewish settlements in the Arab territories.

The Arab-Israeli negotiations were unique in that the United States was willing to reward both sides with enormous financial aid, and perhaps to punish them diplomatically if they failed. But in addition to the inducements, and perhaps threats, peace required a complex process of genuine conflict resolution led by Carter.

In analyzing the Camp David success, Carter described the importance of bringing participants together in an inspiring natural surrounding, such as Camp David, and the need for setting deadlines for the negotiations. He talked about the moment when both sides believe that peace is to their advantage, and the importance of a win-win outcome. He helped the process by providing Begin with polls of his own citizens, confirming that they would make concessions, including withdrawal from the newly formed settlements in the Sinai. In regard to Sadat, he emphasized their personal ties and their mutual love and trust. Many of these issues are discussed in Carter's book, *Keeping the Faith* (1982).

Several points stood out in Carter's presentation. One was his conviction that the Arab and Israeli *people,* in contrast to much of their leadership, wanted peace. This confirms the metaphor of the Conflict Tree. Ordinary people are often nearer to their common roots than are their more polarized leaders. Second, although Carter did not emphasize it, I was impressed by hints that the Arab and Israeli people could celebrate each other. This was suggested by the joyous welcome given to Sadat when he made his first visit to Israel. But what interested me the most was the role that love played in the actual negotiations between Begin and Sadat.

At first glance, the assertion that love played any role at all in the negotiations would seem absurd. After all, Begin and Sadat could not get along, and for the last ten days of the negotiations, they never saw each other. And while Carter unreservedly loved Sadat, he did not express much affection for Begin. What impressed me was *Carter's overall loving attitude.* I believe that Jimmy Carter infused love into the whole negotiation process.

Of course, the negotiation and conflict-resolution process involves more than love. Specific conditions must be set up and specific steps must be taken. As summarized in chapter 1, the third party must create a voluntary setting in which power is forsaken as a means of attaining goals; basic needs and vital interests must be identified and rationally addressed by analytic methods; collaborative problem-solving must redefine win-lose conflicts in a way that permits both sides to win; the cost of the conflict must become clear to both parties; and help may be needed in generating alternative mutually satisfying solutions (Burton, 1990).

Most of these processes are related to Dynamic II: liberty. In keeping with the principles of liberty, to begin a negotiation process, the individuals involved must show respect for each other. However, to more fully resolve their differences, they must ultimately collaborate toward understanding and satisfying each other's basic needs. That takes place most thoroughly when motivated by love.

When a third party, such as Carter, intervenes in a conflict, love creates and motivates the forum for conflict resolution. Problem-solving then takes place within the caring context created by the intervener. Ultimately, valued and even loving relationships frequently emerge from the work of getting to know and to understand each other. Richard Rubenstein has pointed out to me that even in bitter political conflicts, such as those in Northern Ireland, conflict-resolution processes can create such rapport between the opposing leaders that they have difficulty being accepted by their constituents when they return home. Thus, there is little or no fundamental difference in the basic process of conflict resolution, whether it involves marital discord (see chapter 6) or national conflict.

At the NCPCR meeting, Carter described the last days of the meetings when he thought Begin would go home without accepting any compromise. As a part of leave-taking, Begin sent over a request for a signed portrait of the American president for his grandchildren. Meanwhile, Carter had obtained the names of all eight of Begin's grandchildren, and he was able to sign individual photos for each of them. When he handed the gifts to Begin, the old terrorist actually cried; and according to Carter, the President did, too. Within minutes after leaving the emotional encounter, Begin made a turnabout and sent word that he would agree in principle to the accords.

Did Carter's astute (if caring) "manipulation" of Begin's emotions bring about the Camp David accords? Of course, a lot more than that went into reaching an agreement: everything from the cost of all the previous wars, to the good intentions of Begin and Sadat, and especially, the political arm-twisting and financial rewards offered by the U.S. government. But I believe that Carter's loving attitude and demeanor played a role.

The anecdote about Begin's grandchildren illustrates an important principle: in the absence of love between adversaries in a conflict, a *loving mediator* can facilitate conflict resolution. The result may not be as thorough as if the parties to the conflict grew to love each other; but the outcome can be positive and pave the way for further gains. I know this to be true from my firsthand experience working with warring couples in psychotherapy, as well as friends, coworkers, and colleagues in my everyday life. It was gratifying to hear it confirmed in regard to warring heads of nations.

THE GREAT LESSON

In concluding this chapter, a fundamental principle of conflict resolution warrants repetition: all people are made of the same biological and spiritual stuff. Individuals born in one culture and raised in another will be the product of the culture that raises them. A child born to Arabs but raised as an Israeli Jew will become one. A child born to Israeli Jews but raised an Arab Moslem will become one. The same can be said of every nationality and religion. It is true of Soviets and Americans, of Chinese and Japanese, of warring African tribes.

When we look across the battle lines drawn on the basis of gender, race, religion, culture, or nationality, we are looking at ourselves. When we know this in our hearts, murderous conflict will be made impossible.

Is there hope that love can become a more pervasive value in the future? Only if people realize that it is the *only* hope for the future.

A potentially unified international movement is evolving from several divergent sources. The final chapter will examine this convergence of values within alternative movements. It could become a worldwide coalition of shared values inspired by the principles of liberty and love. The concluding chapter will also examine what may be the ultimate approach to conflict resolution for the world's most critical problems—Gandhi's "loving firmness."

Part III

▼ ▼

Bringing About Change

▼ ▼

CHAPTER 11

What Kind of Community in Our Future?

Those of us living in large societies automatically assume that without "government" human societies would degenerate into uncivilized chaos. In their lack of "law and order," precivilized societies seem clearly deficient, lagging behind in the linear march of social "progress." What we forget is that our prehuman ancestors were social and formed stable social systems long before they were rational. . . . Strong social bonds, far from being something we create in a calculating, civilised manner, are something we deeply need and cannot help forming. We are not social because of rationally perceived individual benefits, such as economic gain or national security, but because our deepest emotional being does not allow us to be otherwise.

Mary Clark, Ariadne's Thread (1989)

The recognition that all men are persons and are not to be treated as things, has arisen slowly in the consciousness of mankind. It has made its way with difficulty against the recurrent testimony of immediate experience, against sophisticated argument, against the predatory and acquisitive instincts which men bring with them out of the animal struggle for existence. The passage from barbarism into civilization is long, halting, and unsure. It is a hard climb from the practice of devouring one's enemies to the injunction to love them. But in the long ascent there is a great divide which is reached when men discover, declare, and acknowledge, however much they may deny it in practice, that there is a Golden Rule which is the ultimate and universal criterion for human conduct. For then, and then only, is there a standard to which all can repair who seek to transform the incessant and indecisive struggle for domination and survival into the security of the Good Society.

Walter Lippmann, The Good Society (1936)

While no one can predict the future, it seems likely humanity's problems will continue to escalate dangerously unless we develop new and better ways of resolving conflict. We do not know how much time we have left, and we do not know how many years it will take to make the necessary transformations.

Doom has been predicted before. The need for a dramatic change in human attitudes has been announced at least as far back as the Hebrew prophets. The call for a more loving community has also been made many times before—seemingly to little avail.

Even if it is too late for our concerted efforts to prevent ultimate catastrophe—and I do not think that it is too late—I cannot imagine a life well-lived that does not involve trying. To live well, it seems to me, is to act in the world in an empathic and caring manner. Whatever the outcome, each individual can then feel that he or she has made a special effort and a unique contribution.

Life does not ask us to succeed; too many factors outside our control determine that. Life asks us to live ethically and to accept the consequences.

That's the dilemma of life. As individuals we can try as hard as we want, but without community effort little can be accomplished toward social change. The only hope is that sufficient numbers of individuals will transform themselves and their attitudes that community itself will be transformed.

The ultimate solution will require a great awakening of empathic caring throughout the world—an increasing awareness of love in every aspect of our lives, and a willingness to take risks toward implementing it in our own lives and lives of those around us.

TRIVIALIZING LOVE

As Gandhi, Schweitzer, and King will illustrate, political and intellectual leaders have on occasion elevated love to the central position in their lives. More often it appears in folk and pop music. From the Beatles and Bob Dylan to modern pop songs, themes of love abound, most often focused on romantic love, but sometimes directed at the yearning for peace.

The idea of love, as Ginger Ross-Breggin recently reminded me, has been marginalized and trivialized by relegating it to the domain of women. This book seeks to do that which should not need doing; it seeks to legitimize love among thinking people.

Is it naive and even foolhardy to imagine that people throughout the world might someday join in a common concern for each other and their home, Earth? Certainly we have the technological capacity to facilitate such a human community through communication and transportation. We can get to know each other well enough to feel kinship among ourselves. But can the human spirit rise to the occasion? And if so, through what sort of societal institutions?

PLACING HOPE IN RELIGION

It is easy enough to be skeptical and even cynical about religion. For those of us who are Jewish, it is difficult to imagine Christianity as a fountain of love. Historically, Christianity has victimized Jews and other non-Christians, and frequently instigated their outright slaughter. Christianity has also inspired mayhem and murder among competing versions of its own faith.

Nonetheless, the vision of this book has been in part inspired by the Judeo-Christian tradition. I have already cited two Christian psychiatrists, Smiley Blanton and M. Scott Peck, and later in the chapter I will favorably examine the ideas Gandhi, Albert Schweitzer, and Martin Luther King, Jr., three men deeply influenced by Judeo-Christian ideals.

Any Westerner who believes in the efficacy of love is likely to be borrowing from the Judeo-Christian tradition. The Golden Rule is the product of many different religions (Lippmann, 1937, quoted in chapter 2), but it comes to the West through Judaism and then Christianity. The central theme of Christ's teaching is to love God and to love each other. Nonviolence also finds some roots in Jewish and Christian teachings. Clearly many individuals and groups draw inspiration from these ideals.

Churches and synagogues frequently are community centers of caring and charity. American churches have in recent years sometimes spoken out against war and on behalf of the poor. The Catholic Church has been criticized by free-market advocates because of its call for state support of the poor.

On the other hand, organized religion rarely plays a positive role in societal or political conflict resolution. On issues of racism and sexism, for example, it too often reinforces suppressive ideas. Often religious fervor divides Jews, Roman Catholics, and Protestants, and often Protestants feud among themselves. In the political arena, religion tends to motivate and justify violent hatred, and in wartime religion almost always seeks to align God with its particular nation.

Overall, we can hope that Western religion will recall that its true faith is love. If so, organized religion could become a much more benevolent influence in society. Meanwhile, the *ideals* of Judeo-Christian tradition often inspire people to reject the very institutions that are supposed to epitomize and represent them.

PLACING HOPE IN THE STATE

Government-enforced policies cannot solve all of the problems that modern society faces. When government goes too far in suppressing freedom and the pursuit of self-interest, there are disastrous consequences.

Human beings need and want as much autonomy and personal freedom as possible in their lives. They want to determine the course of their own lives, and they resist attempts to thwart that intention. Only when liberty flourishes are people fully able to actualize their own lives and maximize their own chosen contributions to society. Liberty must become much *more* of a reality for all of the world's oppressed, including women and children; the poor, homeless, and hungry; and religious, racial, and ethnic minorities.

Free-market and anarchist critiques are correct in arguing that government should be limited in scope. Not only does the state threaten individual freedom, it frequently becomes the tool of the most oppressive groups in society. Motivated by mixtures of nationalism, racism, religious bigotry, and political ideology, modern governments have routinely become the instruments of violent oppression and unspeakable atrocities.

As described in chapter 9, the state, with its inherent coerciveness, has limits. Dynamic II: liberty is not about to belly up. Nor should it. We need to understand and to define it better; and to recognize the limits of what it can accomplish. We do not need to suppress liberty, but to help people understand the necessity of introducing more loving alternatives as well. We need benevolent ethics that—without suppressing liberty—offer something more. We need a world that respects liberty and promotes love within the context of modern, industrial society.

Government should focus on monitoring and controlling other power concentrations, while the people monitor and control the government. Government should also help to compensate and support those who have been exploited, lack autonomy, or otherwise cannot take care of themselves. Above all else, the state should be transformed as much as possible into an institution for voluntary conflict resolution. In effect, whenever possible, community must replace the state.

Usually, social critics and visionaries turn to the state as their hope for redemption. It is worth repeating that government is based on coercion and is therefore hamstrung when it comes to conflict resolution (see chapters 9 and 10). The state cannot be transformed into an institution for conflict resolution without transforming it into something other than a state. Voluntary, caring community must replace much of what now falls under the umbrella of government.

But how are we to achieve such a transformation, especially if it cannot come through the government itself?

PLACING HOPE IN PUBLIC EDUCATION

In *The Altruistic Personality,* Oliner and Oliner (1988) call for an educational system that will encourage empathy and love, and social responsibility.

Schools need to become caring institutions—institutions in which students, teachers, bus drivers, principals, and all others receive positive affirmation for kindness, empathy, and concern. Participants need opportunities to work and have fun together, develop intimacies, and share successes and pain. Students also need opportunities to consider broad universal principles that relate to justice and care in matters of public concern. . . . In short, caring schools will acknowledge diversity on the road to moral concern. (pp. 258–59.)

But there is a flaw in Oliner and Oliner's proposal. By their own description, it is the loving *family* that produced morally heroic, caring individuals.

Even if schools could fulfill such a basic moral and social function, how is society to develop such schools? Public schools and universities are instruments of the state. They cannot significantly transcend the values promoted by the state, which is itself based on coercion and obedience. For example, whenever a government declares war, it vigorously doctrinates violent patriotism into young citizens through their schools. In Nazi Germany, the educational establishment was quick to support the most vicious anti-Semitism. The educational model suggested by Oliner and Oliner becomes utopian (see chapter 9) because they cannot tell us how to bring it about without first transforming society.

THE NEW HOPE FOR LOVE

Ironically, it is recent international politics that provide the greatest inspiration for a more peace-loving world community. As I began this chapter, the media was filled with encouraging analyses of President Bush's summit meeting with President Gorbachev. The irony was not lost on anyone: from Reagan's "Evil Empire" to "Most Favored Nation" trade status in a few brief years. The Russian Bear that was going to "bury us" was now begging us for charity. As I am finishing the chapter, the USSR no longer exists. Russia, the country we once feared most in the world, is asking to be the recipient of our diplomatic and financial support.

Can there be any doubt about the readiness of masses of people to transform their attitudes from indifference or hatred to friendship and trust? If Russia can succeed in becoming more free, Russians and Americans may one day find themselves the closest of allies.

The earlier irony that our World War II enemies, West Germany and Japan, so quickly became our allies has often been remarked on. But the potential for reconciliation may even be greater between Americans and Russians. My friends and colleagues who visited the USSR regularly believe that Americans have much more natural affinity with Russians than with Germans or Japanese, or almost any other European nation.

Two peoples—whose conflict threatened to obliterate each other, themselves, and the whole world—could turn out to be best friends. Yet a few years ago, most people in both countries would have found such a prospect laughable—or *treasonous*. There have been times when supporting such a rapprochement would have cost you your life in the USSR, and cost you your reputation and your job in the USA.

Consider also the transformation taking place in the individual psyches of the peoples of Russia and other former communist countries. Many of them are rejecting the ideology that was crammed into their heads for so many decades, and calling for much more personal and economic liberty. They are doing so with more conviction than many Americans who remain cynical toward capitalism.

There's an important lesson in these events: dramatic *positive* social change and conflict resolution is possible, involving millions of individuals and whole societies. If today the United States and Russia, why not tomorrow the world? Toward that end, the United States should make every possible effort to support Russia and other newly liberated European nations.

SMALL COMMUNITIES, THE GLOBAL VILLAGE, AND THE MODERN INDUSTRIAL WORLD

What are the ingredients of a good society? Devotion to the principles of liberty is one of them.

As events in the former communist nations underscore, liberty *is* the engine of economic, scientific, and technological progress, at least as we know and define progress in the world today. Only when individuals and corporations are free to pursue their own self-interest, will they innovate at a rapid rate and keep an economy humming. Voices within the affluent nations are being raised in doubt about the wisdom of continued unfettered economic expansion and what they are saying merits attention (see chapter 9). But recent international events have confirmed once again that modern economies flourish only when individuals and groups are in part liberated to pursue their own self-interest.

Utopian solutions that urge a return to small communities often reject the benefits of the free market (Clark, 1989; Sale, 1985; van Andruss, Plant, Plant, and Wright, 1990; see also chapter 9). It is claimed that self-sustaining, cooperative communities could thrive without free-market competition and industrialization. Small communities could live off the land as native peoples have done or develop smaller, ecologically sound industries.

But smaller communities cannot survive outside the context of a peaceful global village, and the global villages requires modern technology, including the free market and industrialization. This proposition is so unfamiliar and yet important, that it requires further analysis.

The well-being of small communities requires peace and harmony throughout their region and even the globe, otherwise they would fall prey to larger, militant societies. Their survival requires a worldwide commitment to humanity as one family with universal respect for the rights of individual persons and each unique culture. Even those who promote small communities, while seeking to limit industrial growth, favor a global community. In *Blue Print for Survival* (1972), the editors of *The Ecologist* (Goldsmith, Allen, Allaby, Davoll, and Lawrence) point out:

There must be procedures whereby community actions that affect regions can be discussed at the regional level and regional actions with extraregional effects can be discussed at the global level. . . . We emphasize that our goal should be to create **community feeling** *and* **global awareness** *rather than that dangerous and sterile compromise which is nationalism. (pp. 40, 41.)*

A world organized around communities will require global awareness and communication.

Without a global village with widely shared agreement on peaceful conflict resolution, smaller communities would be swallowed up and overwhelmed by larger states much as they have been over the last 10,000 years. *But the global village depends upon the free market with its modern industrial achievements, especially international transportation and communication.*

For individuals and local communities to feel as if they are part of a worldwide society, they need contact with the wider world, including sufficient interaction and communication to evolve common ideals and an empathic devotion to each other's well-being. That worldwide contact requires modern industry and technology, especially transportation and communication. This dependent relationship between small communities, the global village, and modern industrialization has been missed by some of the most insightful and imaginative critics of modern society and requires further elaboration.

THE GLOBAL VILLAGE AND MODERN TECHNOLOGY

The global village, as originally proposed by Marshall McLuhan and Quentin Fiore (1967), is a product of modern methods of communication, such as the telephone, radio, and TV:

Electric circuity has overthrown the regime of "time" and "space" and pours upon us instantly and continuously the concerns of all other men. It has reconstituted dialogue on a global scale. Its message is Total Change, ending psychic, social, economic, and political parochialism. The old civic, state, and national groups have become unworkable. (p. 16.)

According to McLuhan and Fiore, not only electronic but print media are key to the global village:

Printing, a ditto device, confirmed and extended the new visual stress. It provided the first uniformly repeatable "commodity," the first assembly line—mass production.
It created the portable book, which men could read in privacy and isolation from others. Man could now inspire—and conspire. (p. 50.)

Although it depends upon modern technology, the global village returns us to a our tribal origins:

We now live in a global village . . . a simultaneous happening. We are back in acoustic space. We have begun again to structure primordial feelings, the tribal emotions . . . (p. 63.)

It is impossible to separate out the necessary technology for a global village from the remainder of the industrial complex. The global village requires telephones, radios, and TVs; photocopying and fax machines; computers and satellite communications; trains, planes, and buses. It requires energy sources and power stations for the production of electricity, and will probably require other fuels as well. We are a long way away from generating sufficient power from the sun, the wind, and the tides; and the development of these sustainable resources will in itself require advanced technology.

In addition to transportation and communication, the global village places other requirements on technology and industry. High-tech medical care is required to permit the free intermingling of peoples. Modern industrial methods of food production and transportation will be required for the foreseeable future for the feeding of populations in upheaval and transition. We cannot continue to ignore the massive loss of top soil and other problems caused by agri-business (Worldwatch Institute, 1990), but neither can we ignore the immediate dangers of famine.

Those who would wholly reject the free market, and hence modern industry and technology, do not realize that they are inadvertently rejecting world community. This reality needs more attention from those who hope for both local and world community. There is an inherent incompatibility between the small, close-knit *local* community and the industry required for a *global* village. The small, self-sustaining local community cannot produce the necessary technology to maintain the global village. The future of a loving world depends in part upon modern industry, as well as upon learning to mitigate its negative impact upon people and the environment.

THE FUTURE OF THE FREE MARKET

Even if it were possible to build a more united world without the extensive use of technology, it is highly unlikely that the next several generations will be willing to discard the advantages generated by the free market and modern industry. Americans aren't the only ones who believe in at least some degree of free enterprise. The trend in the Third World, including the former communist nations, is to want *more* capitalism. Even in Communist China, people were quick to grasp the opportunity to experiment with free enterprise, and like the Russians, were hungry to meet and to learn from Americans (see chapter 10). They did this despite the knowledge that a crackdown might come.

The so-called undeveloped nations will not tolerate outsiders putting a fuel governor on their sputtering engines while the Westernized nations roar along at full throttle. They will not hold back their own economies in the interest of the environment, nor will they limit their armies in the interest of world peace. At least, they will not consider these alternatives until the industrialized nations become willing to make it worth their while and until the people of the world adopt a new ethic.

To implement such a transformation in values will require enormous Dynamic I: generosity on the part of the industrialized nations toward the less developed nations. Ideally America would lead the way in offering incentives to other nations to preserve their environments and reduce their military budgets. This will require a radical shift in values worldwide.

"Small is beautiful" and "self-sustaining ecosystems" remain important ideals. But absent an earth-shaking catastrophe, the implementation of these ideals seems most unlikely on any large scale within the imaginable future. Industrialization is going to be with us for a long time. The goal must be to build more community-oriented values within existing modern society—values that will lead people to *want* to work together to overcome the hazards of the industrial age.

LOVING COMMUNITY

Is there any way to restrain the self-aggrandizing power of government and the monopolistic tendencies of the free market, and at the same time to encourage mercy, charity, and concern for each other and our world? Is there an organizing social principle beyond coercion (the state) and liberty (the free market)?

There is another principle—the energy of human community, love. We must find ways to mobilize the vast resources of love without turning to government or to the free market. Indeed, we must use these resources to help control the excesses of government and free enterprise. How to do that is the most pressing issue of our now and future time. It will require new viewpoints and new institutions as well as increased community involvement at a grassroots and individual level.

There are innumerable ways to mobilize loving community, but to be most effective love must be expressed in its most pure form as defined in the Three Dynamic Theory. It must be unconditional. It must lie outside both the state and the marketplace. It must not be distorted by coercion nor corrupted by the profit motive. By remaining independent of both the state and the market, the love expressed by new institutions could remain true to its essence as a spontaneous, joyful expression of "gifting."

Once people begin to focus on loving community, its expressions will flourish in ways we cannot now anticipate. As possible models, I will describe two potential directions: First, a developing coalition of independent reform groups that share and promote a more loving attitude toward people and the planet; and second, a renewal of civil disobedience in the form of Gandhi's "loving firmness." These two alternatives can embrace both the personal and the political.

LOVING COMMUNITY AND THE THIRD SECTOR

In *The New Realities* (1989), Peter Drucker describes the vast array of voluntary activities that are "non-business, non-government, 'human change agencies,' the nonprofit organizations of the so-called third sector." To illustrate the third sector, he cites the Boy Scouts and Girl Scouts, the Salvation Army, the American Red Cross, American Lung Association, American Heart Association, American Mental Health Association, Urban League, innumerable church activities, a wide variety of cultural activities (museums, symphony orchestras), and community chest activities such as "Meals on Wheels." He does not mention the infinite number of groups that support ethnic identities and the enormous number that support athletics, including Little League. More striking, he makes no note of the great variety of reform-minded or radical counterculture activities (see below).

Drucker points out that "the third sector is actually the country's largest employer," even though it is not reflected in gross national product and labor statistics. One out of every two adult Americans, ninety-million people, contribute to the third sector, most of them in addition to a full-time job.

The third sector, according to Drucker, plays a vital role in building community and bridging the socioeconomic gap between volunteers and less-educated classes:

America's third-sector institutions are rapidly becoming creators of new bonds of community and a bridge between knowledge workers and the "other half." Increasingly they create a sphere of effective citizenship. (p. 204.)

These activities benefit the volunteer as well as the recipients. The new America, which he calls the knowledge society, "needs community, freely chosen yet acting as a bond." Thus the third sector combines what I am calling Dynamics I and II. He concludes in that vein:

It [the knowledge society] needs a sphere where the individual can become a master through serving. It needs a sphere where freedom is not just being passive, not just being left alone rather than being ordered around—a sphere that requires active involvement and responsibility. (p. 206.)

Drucker's analysis is helpful, but the Three Dynamic Theory sheds more light on this vast social activity. The third sector has the *potential* to become loving community, Dynamic I activities that could transform society.

Drucker contrasts the third sector with "business" and with "government." The Three Dynamic Theory helps focus on the basic needs and social relations characteristic of each of these different institutions. What Drucker calls business is actually "free enterprise"—the profit-motivated sector. What he calls "government" is state coercion—the use of organized, legitimized force to obtain certain ends. What he calls the third sector is to a great extent "love"—freely given gifts or gifting as a way of relating.

Drucker characterizes the third sector as consisting of

"human-change agencies." But state and federal governments also support many human-change agencies, including prisons, mental hospitals, museums, art and cultural activities, and innumerable forms of educational and service agencies that aim at human-change, from the public schools to poverty programs. The free enterprise system as well is often involved in human change. It offers alternatives to many government services, including schools, prisons, hospitals, museums, and those services covered by welfare and social security, such as health and disability insurance. The profession of psychotherapy, the epitome of human-change activities, is typically a free-enterprise activity. So are the many management consultants and training programs that aim at transforming both individual managers and their corporations. The difference is that the third sector is based on love—the desire to give gifts to others, to serve for the fundamental purpose of serving, to care for caring's sake. Because it is motivated by ideals, and potentially unencumbered by ties to establishment institutions and to earning a living, the third sector is potentially very radical.

Of course, third sector agencies can easily become distorted or corrupted. Also, those who volunteer may get advantages beyond the joy of giving, such as prestige, useful training experiences, and social or professional contacts. But the basic need and the basic method of social relationship for third sector volunteers is Dynamic I: love.

Drucker calls the third sector "counter cultural" but his reason for doing so is not clear to me. All of the activities he lists are rather conservative in nature, implementing established, time-honored American values. In his brief survey of third sector organizations, he does not include movements that support feminism, civil rights, children's rights, peace, the environment, or other more nearly countercultural groups. This is striking, because a great deal of radical social reform, for better or worse, originates in the third sector, including the whole spectrum from the Ku Klux Klan to the Jewish Defense League and the Black Muslims. Even if they want it, radical approaches usually cannot obtain government or business support. If they do not begin with sufficient Dynamic I energy they cannot survive.

Not every group that falls into the third sector or even the loving community will necessarily express love at its most ideal. Most third sector organizations are likely to be rather limited or focused.

But since they exist outside both the government and the free-enterprise system, their membership is likely to be driven by an ideal of some sort and by a need for community. Even the most cultist and seemingly antisocial third sector groups almost always maintain an intense community experience within themselves, while other people are being excluded or even targeted as enemies. The love shared or promoted by these groups remains corrupted but nonetheless recognizable. The cult often offers the most loving experience in the lifetime of its members, who frequently come from deprived and abused backgrounds. Thus, individuals frequently join hate-mongering groups not only to express their negative emotions, but also to share in the caring community which these groups provide their members.

I am reminded of my shock when, as a young psychiatrist, one of my first clients told me that the most caring and morale-building experience of his life had been in the Hitler youth. Compared to the authoritarian, oppressive family life he had known, the devoted leadership and seemingly high ideals of the Hitler youth became a genuine Dynamic I experience for him.

It is of course commonplace for soldiers of every army to share an intense and often overtly loving experience among themselves, even while they are fighting and killing other human beings. Fear of the enemy facilitates the community among the soldiers, much as it does among cult group members. While acting violently toward others, they allow themselves to become more vulnerable to each other. Men in particular may feel more comfortable in showing and fulfilling their more "needy" feelings when they are, at the same time, "proving themselves" in sports, on the battlefield, or in other seemingly "manly" ways.

Drucker gives us insight into the enormous human energy being poured into the third sector in the United States. As a basically Dynamic I influence, it has tremendous potential to become an energy that uplifts society beyond the institutions of liberty (political freedom and the marketplace) and coercion (the state). To some extent, the third sector already does this, and as Drucker notes, is a great source of community spirit. With so many people willing to donate their time to public service, imagine what might happen if large numbers of them focused their efforts more consciously upon love for *all* Americans and, eventually, for *all* people. The third sector could become the loving community, and the country could quickly begin moving much closer toward the solution of its most difficult problems and conflicts.

BECOMING EACH OTHER'S ANSWERS

In a paper entitled "Becoming Each Other's Answers," Ginger Ross-Breggin has described a number of alternative or minority traditions that have recently begun converging toward a common set of values. All of them are largely third sector or loving community groups. Among these she includes:

1. *Environmentalism*, especially deep ecology.

2. *Conflict resolution*, especially peacemaking.

3. *Feminism*, with its rejection of patriarchy in favor of mutuality, and its growing focus on the male abuse of women and children.

4. *Social justice*, including groups devoted to civil rights and the eradication of racism, children's rights, reform of prisons and the criminal justice system, health care reform, and the amelioration of hunger and poverty.

My own major area of human rights activism has been psychiatric reform, including a great deal of networking with the psychiatric survivor movement (Breggin, 1991). Nearly all the people I work with in reform activities have a strong sense of bonding among themselves and with human beings in general. A high degree of empathic awareness frequently motivates their work.

In the United States, the Native American revival—inspired by growing general appreciation of its philosophy and religion—also holds many values in common with the other groups.

As already noted, the *ideals* of the Judeo-Christian tradition continue to encourage people to love each other as equals in God's eyes. These ideals are the source of much that is positive in this book. The problem is how to bring the institutions of religion up to the standard of their own spiritual principles.

The "shared values" that Ross-Breggin identifies within these alternative movements provide a starting point for a Dynamic I: love coalition. Ross-Breggin has isolated four basic shared values:

1. *Abhorrence of violence.*

2. *Equality of all human beings.*

3. *Inter-connectedness of human beings with the earth.*

4. *The creation of community on both a personal and a global level.*

Each of these values reflect, Dynamic I and can be found in the Three Dynamic Table (see page 261). In addition, Ross-Breggin and I have also discussed in our seminars the emergence of four additional values which cut across Dynamic I: love and Dynamic II: liberty. These are:

5. *Comprehensive thinking and communicating.* Scholars and activists alike are breaking down the traditional barriers between disciplines such as psychology, philosophy, economics, politics, and religion. They are adopting plain English, rather than specialized jargon, and interrelating the various isolated academic disciplines into a holistic conception of humanity and nature.

6. *Personal growth or self-realization as an aspect of political reform.* Personal growth becomes inseparable from making efforts for the common good of humanity and the planet. Personal change leads to societal change and, conversely, working toward the improvement of society improves oneself.

7. *Distrust of statism.* Solutions are evolving through individual actions, small groups, communities, and so-called grassroots efforts. This anarchistic theme is usually unstated and by no means consistent within the reform groups; but individualism and antistatism are closely aligned with the concept of grass roots. It is captured in the slogan of environmental groups, "Think globally, act locally."

8. *Feminism.* Despite the overall emphasis on the equality of all beings, the equality of *women* is by no means a frequent enough theme within the reform movements. But there is increasing recognition of feminism's intellectual

contribution. Patriarchal, hierarchical values of "power over" and competitive exploitation, help explain many contemporary problems, from war and the despoiling of the environment to wife and child abuse.

Many educators, activists, and concerned people from around the world have expressed to us their own sense of a coming together of shared values. Many of the newsletters and journals of these diverse alternative movements are making connections among feminism, peace, social justice, and environmentalism. Numerous critiques of the Gulf war, for example, addressed each of these issues. If this international "Shared Values Movement" could identify itself and draw together in a more orchestrated fashion, it could rapidly discard its minority status. It could become *the* major influence in the course of human events. We could have the potential for a "World Coalition of Shared Values" aimed at educating people and transforming the world into more loving community—Riane Eisler's "partnership future."

The hope for the future lies not only in individual and small-group activities, but in a great coming together of people throughout the world around a common set of values and meanings based on liberty and especially on love.

STANDING FIRM ON LOVE

If the loving community cannot and will not express itself through government or the free market, how will it influence people? In addition to individual actions, education, and other well-known activities, what *mechanism* for change could be used by the loving community, including the proposed "World Coalition of Shared Values"?

The thoughts and actions of three Twentieth Century leaders—Gandhi, Schweitzer, and King—are especially compatible with the Three Dynamic Theory emphasis on both individual liberty and bonding through love. The political and religious principles of these three men especially exemplify the theme of love. Each developed a method of conflict resolution based on love: Schweitzer as a doctor treating African tribal people far from civilization, and

Gandhi and King as political activists through public nonviolent confrontation.

GANDHI'S SATYAGRAHA

Perhaps no one has examined and lived more deeply the issues of severe conflict and its resolution than Gandhi. In *The Conquest of Violence: The Gandhian Philosophy of Conflict* (1988), Joan Bondurant explores *satyagraha*, Gandhi's method of conflict resolution. Of special interest, she focuses her book specifically on Gandhi as a conflict resolver. For Bondurant, Gandhi's major contribution lay not in his overall philosophical, religious, or economic theory, but in his approach to resolving conflict.

What makes Gandhi's vision so important is its spiritual content—the ideal of love—and his determination to be guided by love in confronting life-threatening political conflict. Gandhi gave up his earlier phrase "passive resistance" in favor of satyagraha, which he defined as "the Force which is born of Truth and love or nonviolence," (p. 8). According to Gandhi, God is truth, and "the nearest approach to truth was through love," (p. 18). Conflict is resolved through the search for truth, and the method must be loving.

Satyagraha requires always striving to see the other's viewpoint. The other persons in the conflict must be treated with dignity and they must be treasured.

Satyagraha further requires that every attempt be made to avoid injuring those who are being confronted. The ancient Hindu, Jain, and Buddhist ethical precept, *ahimsa*, means nonviolence or noninjury. Gandhi equates it with love, and Bondurant compares it to Christian charity and Greek *agape*. The refusal to do harm, even in self-defense, became the center of Gandhi's philosophy and methodology. It is love's abhorrence of violence in its more consistent expression. One refuses to *acquiesce* to wrong deeds, and one refuses to *perpetrate* them either.

In conflict, the individual satyagraha may have to undergo suffering, rather than inflict it on others. Through this "self-suffering" the individual hopes to persuade by touching the conscience of one's seeming opponent.

It is a mistake to think of Gandhi as either an inspired idealist *or* a pragmatic politician. He was both. Satyagraha was the highest moral principle, and the *most effective* technique for bringing about the just resolution of conflict.

Because Gandhi was thoroughly committed to civil disobedience, a distinct streak of Dynamic II individualism runs through his philosophy. According to Bondurant, "For Gandhi, society must provide opportunities for the individual, and the final decision as to what constitutes that growth lies with the individual," (p. 162). Bondurant quotes Gandhi, "No society can possibly be built on denial of individual freedom. It is contrary to the very nature of man. . . . Even those who do not believe in the liberty of the individual believe in their own," (p. 162).

Gandhi's moral individualism lent his thoughts and actions, at times, an aura of anarchism or even conservatism. Gandhi did not aim at overturning existing institutions as much as he favored limiting government power and correcting its more grievous moral flaws. Always, however, the ultimate source of morality remained individual conscience. Thus his thought drew upon both liberty and love.

Bondurant identifies the roots of Gandhi's philosophy not only in conscience but in basic needs. For Gandhi, the "criteria of truth lay in the meeting of human needs" and "concern for human needs lies at the core of Gandhian teaching," (p. 193). Thus Gandhi's approach to conflict corresponds very closely with the Three Dynamic Theory.

THE MIRROR LIT WITH LOVE

At first glance it seems surprising to identify Gandhi, as Bondurant has done, as a man devoted to conflict *resolution*. From the viewpoint of the British or the South African government, he was an instigator and provocateur. That is because the British and the South Africans wished to suppress the conflicts that their policies created. From Gandhi's viewpoint as a young Indian lawyer living in South Africa, he was responding to the conflict created by injustice.

It is misleading to think of conflict resolution as a kind of smoothing over of the waters. As Gandhi exemplifies, conflict resolution can be a confrontation of its own: love's confrontation with hatred and strife.

To confront conflict in the light of love is to see it more clearly, more starkly, and more realistically. The person devoted to resolving conflict must first understand its destructiveness and then reflect it back upon the participants.

When a man and woman, for example, have turned their marriage into a battlefield, the loving therapist does not minimize or ignore the hatred and the pain. Instead, the therapist becomes a loving mirror who shows, in all its reality, the pain and hurt that the parties are inflicting on each other. Similarly, when the individual stands up with firmness and love against the evil that others are committing, he or she discloses the evil in its undisguised form.

I am not suggesting that the therapist or conflict resolver leap into the fray to bring out or underscore all its destructive elements. Usually the destructive aspects will come out soon enough on their own. In dealing with people, one must begin at the level of communication the participants can make use of. In therapy or conflict resolution, the task is to help the participants deal with what they are capable of dealing with, while encouraging them to take the next steps as soon as feasible.

If people in conflict seem ready to bolt from the office or the conference table at the first sign of confrontation, or if they seem ready to inflict irreparable damage on each other, of course the immediate goal is to calm everyone down. That may require proceeding as lightly as necessary. But the long-term task remains that of helping the participants recognize the damage that they are doing to each other, while helping them develop new and better principles for nonviolent, loving conflict resolution.

Only the mirror lit with love can accurately reflect the pain that it confronts, while putting that pain within the brighter perspective of future possibilities for liberty and love. The therapist or conflict resolver must be deeply rooted in two realities: the pain that people cause each other when they resort to coercion; and the joy and opportunity they create when they relate through the principles of liberty and love.

ALBERT SCHWEITZER

While Schweitzer was not completely in agreement with Gandhi, he supported the basic thrust of ahisma. In *Indian Thought and Its*

Development (1936), Schweitzer describes Gandhi as moving beyond the proscription of killing and causing hurt or pain. Ahisma in Gandhi's hands became "the complete exercise of compassion." In paraphrasing the principle more to his own liking, Schweitzer declared:

> *. . . that all worldly purposive action should be undertaken with the greatest possible avoidance of violence, and that ethical considerations should so dominate ourselves as to influence also the hearts of our opponents. . . . that only activity in an ethical spirit can really accomplish anything. (pp. 233–34.)*

There is, of course, a sometimes thin line between passive resistance—even with the best of spiritual intentions—and coercion. Bondurant reports that Gandhi himself was concerned about his own tendencies to cross the line. In *Indian Thought and Its Development*, Schweitzer said of Gandhi with a seemingly sympathetic chiding, "He has never succeeded in altogether controlling the agitator within his breast," (p. 232). Schweitzer, of course, was hardly the sort to walk the gauntlet of a rock-throwing crowd or to block the way of police mounted on galloping horses.

Schweitzer would eventually sum up his whole philosophy in the phrase "reverence for life" (see chapter 2). In *My Life and Thought* (1931), he wrote:

> *A man is ethical only when life, as such, is sacred to him, that of plants and animals as well as that of his fellow-men, and when he devotes himself helpfully to all life that is in need of help. (p. 188.)*

He referred to this psychospiritual impulse as "the universal ethic of the feeling of responsibility for an ever-widening sphere of all that lives." (p. 188).

In *The Philosophy of Civilization* (1951), Schweitzer spoke of the will-to-live which he saw operating in all life forms. His observation of this will-to-live led to his ultimate ethical axiom: "Devotion to life resulting from reverence for life," (p. 306). According to Schweitzer:

In ethical conflicts man can arrive only at subjective decisions. No one can decide for him at what point, on each occasion, lies the extreme limit of possibility for his persistence in the preservation and furtherance of life. He alone has to judge this issue, by letting himself be guided by a feeling of the highest possible responsibility towards other life.

We must never let ourselves become blunted. We are living in truth, when we experience these conflicts more profoundly. The good conscience is an invention of the devil. (pp. 317–18.)

For Schweitzer, conflict resolution is an ongoing process of spiritual consciousness in which the individual strives ever harder to be aware of other life and to take responsibility for its furtherance. This is conflict resolution through love.

Like Gandhi, Schweitzer remained devoted to the individual and to liberty. His writings reflect a profound desire to live life exactly as he himself chose to. Consistent with Dynamic II: liberty, in *My Life and Thought* he promoted the Western traditions of "rationality" and "inalienable human rights," (p. 257), advocated "the rights of human personality," (p. 113), and cited his own desire to pursue "an absolutely personal and independent activity . . . to which I could devote myself as an individual and as wholly free," (p. 106).

That Schweitzer and Gandhi chose *service* to humanity should not confuse us about their determination to make their own choices. Nor should their devotion to serving others be understood as a sacrifice. For Schweitzer and for Gandhi, individual freedom, human conscience, and love are inextricable; each *consciously chose* to live a life based on love. They demonstrate the principle that "gifting" is a joy in itself and therefore entails no sacrifice. Thus, love transcends distinctions between selfishness and altruism (see chapter 2).

Schweitzer believed more in individual acts than in political activity as a method of implementing love in society. From political confrontation to tending people in the jungle or raising children in a family, there are many ways to serve, and many ways to devote oneself to resolving conflict.

MARTIN LUTHER KING, JR.

Martin Luther King, Jr. drew upon Gandhi for hope and inspiration. Commenting on "My Trip to the Land of Gandhi" (Washington, 1986), King wrote:

The way of acquiescence leads to moral and spiritual suicide. The way of violence leads to bitterness in the survivors and brutality in the destroyers. But, the way of nonviolence leads to redemption and the creation of the beloved community. (p. 25.)

Using principles identical to those of Gandhi, King described nonviolent resistance as "a courageous confrontation of evil by the power of love, in the faith that it is better to be the recipient of violence than the inflictor of it." By accepting rather than delivering injury, the nonviolent resister "may develop a sense of shame in the opponent, and thereby bring about a transformation and change of heart," (p. 26).

THE FUTURE OF LOVING FIRMNESS

The nonviolent methods of Gandhi and King exemplify loving community: implementing love on a societal level. It is important to explicitly separate loving community from the two dominant institutions of our society, government (state coercion) and the marketplace (the profit motive). Otherwise we fail to identify exactly how we need to proceed. People must become so convinced that love is the best and only hope that they will *voluntarily* and *out of love* band together to express it as a method of conflict resolution. They must *intend* to create a loving community through voluntary relationships among people for the purpose of solving conflicts through love.

Hopefully, the proliferating reform movements that share

Dynamic I values will converge into "The Shared Values Movement." They will be able to speak out against and educate people
about the outrages perpetrated in the name of the state, socialism,
communism, or the free enterprise system. But then, at a critical
moment, there will be a need to take more definitive action—to lay
oneself on the line, so to speak.

Often the decision to act results from personal anguish and outrage over the pain inflicted upon others. An injury against people
or the planet becomes personally unendurable. At that moment,
when words have failed to make a difference, individuals and
groups can turn for inspiration to Gandhi and to Martin Luther
King, Jr. They may wish to help others gather together to witness
the injury and to refuse to participate in the perpetration.

It all begins with personal feelings of empathy and conscience.
What seems to offend me to the core may hardly offend you at all,
and what horrifies you may seem the least among many horrors to
me. Some may wish to stand up with loving firmness against
abuses being directed against themselves within the home by a
family member. Or perhaps they can no longer tolerate the injustices done to them at work or school or in church. Many people
may be more highly motivated by the injuries inflicted upon others, such as a family member, neighbor, or friends; a pet, a local
woods, or park. Still others may feel it most deeply when they
consider the outrages perpetrated against larger groups: battered
women, abused children, the poor, the hungry, the homeless, the
chronically ill, the survivors of psychiatric or penal abuse, racial or
religious minorities, animals, nature, the earth. Some may take
individual actions, others may join groups. Two things can be said
with certainty: there is no end of injuries and injustices inflicted by
people upon each other and upon nature; there is no end to the
need for more action in the name of liberty and love in this world.

SEARCHING FOR BALANCE AND TAKING A STAND

It is not easy to find an ideal interaction or balance among coercion,
liberty, and love. Few people are willing, for example, to wholly
reject coercive state interventions aimed at redistributing wealth
in the interest of caring for the poorest in our midst. Many environmental problems seem to demand government action. We do

conclude, however, that in all areas of life coercion must be kept to a minimum.

Liberty, while not the ultimate value in life, is an important one, and provides the best context for developing love. It also generates what we have come to view as material and economic progress. Whether or not this is positive progress, however, has come under increasing scrutiny; but technological progress seems a necessary component of peaceful global dialog.

Love, the only dynamic that is ethically complete, abhors coercion and violence, takes joy in all expressions of life, and wishes for mutual satisfaction and happiness. Whenever possible, love should be our standard.

Human beings throughout the world need an infinitely more loving attitude toward each other, nature, and the earth itself. Helping ourselves and others to find this love in our hearts is our shared duty. Meanwhile, the ways of going about this are as varied as human relationship and imagination.

Love can be expressed and shared among friends and family, with children, toward animals, in recreational pursuits, in the workplace, in clubs and philanthropic organizations, in the arts and sciences, in schools and places of religious worship, and through groups working toward reform of society. It can be shared and inspired by popular movies and music; and, much too rarely, it can be found in universities and in scholarly publications. I have found it on occasion in the courts, in legislative bodies, and on radio and television. Often I have found and shared it at conferences of people devoted to reform and the improvement of society. Meanwhile, love is always there in nature, ready for the giving and the receiving.

When love is felt and expressed, it can usually be recognized with ease. Some of the basic expressions of love are identified in this chapter in the description of the "Shared Values Movement" and others are listed as short phrases in the Three Dynamics Table. But there is more direct access to love than that—within the place in our hearts that feels joyfully aware of other people, all life forms, and existence itself. We can find love there, and know it by the treasuring, reverence, charity, and forgiveness that it radiates. Then we can encourage it to grow.

When we feel ready as individuals to confront conflict with love, neither the free market nor the government will be wholly on our side. The loving firmness of Gandhi and King may be the only hope. At some point, a sufficient number of people must refuse to participate in the destructiveness that tortures human society, nature, and our earth. In the long run, nothing can substitute for the actions of individuals dedicated to both the preservation of liberty and the furtherance of love. Above all, we need without embarrassment to embrace love as our best approach to resolving conflict and, beyond that, as our way of life.

THE THREE DYNAMICS OF HUMAN PROGRESS FOR INDIVIDUALS, INSTITUTIONS, AND SOCIETIES

▼ ▼

INDIVIDUAL SPIRITUAL STATE	MODE OF INTERACTION

DYNAMIC I: LOVE—THE HIGHEST PRINCIPLE OF LIFE

Beingness	*Loving Affiliation or Gifting*
The Human as a Being or Soul	Abhorrence of Force
Self as Source of Love	Mutual Unconditional Love
Reverence for Self	Treasuring of All People
Acceptance of Self & Life	Peace & Harmony with Life
Spiritual Self-fulfillment	Kindness, Empathy, & Generosity
Equal Worth of All Selves	Concern for Human Destiny
Communality of All Selves	Humanity as One Family
Integrity, Wholeness of Self	Oneness with Nature, God, Life
Devotion to Higher Values	Promotion of Liberty & Love
Love of Truth & Knowledge	Enlightenment

DYNAMIC II: LIBERTY— THE NECESSARY PRINCIPLE FOR PROGRESS

Doingness	*Voluntary Exchange*
The Human as Agent or Doer	Force Limited to Self-defense
Self as Creator of Effects	Control over Physical Universe
Uniqueness of Self	Concern with Personal Satisfaction
Responsibility; Honesty	Contracts & Agreements
Egoism & Self-interest	Competition; Limited Cooperation
Respect for Self	Personal and Business Ethics
Self-direction; Autonomy	Bargaining and Free Enterprise
Reliance on Reason	Scientific & Technical Progress
Individualism	Respect for Rights & Freedoms
Personal Success	Personal & Socioeconomic Progress
Antiauthoritarianism	Open, Pluralistic Society

DYNAMIC III: COERCION—THE MOST DESTRUCTIVE PRINCIPLE OF LIFE

Thingness	*Involuntary Relationships*
The Human as Object or Thing	Arbitrary or Unlimited Force
Self as a Reaction or Effect	Prediction & Social Control
Self-hate & Self-oppression	Hatred & Violence to Attain Ends
Selfishness & Egomania	Envy & Distrust; No Cooperation
Dishonesty toward Self	Lying, Cheating, & Fraud
Out of Touch with Self	Alienation, Remoteness
Anti-individualistic	Adjustment & Survival Values
Biological View of Self	Physical Theories & Therapies
Behavioral View of Self	Behavioral Theories & Therapies
Mechanistic View of Self	Scientism
Personal Failure; Psychosis	Socioeconomic Decline
Authoritarianism	Closed, Totalitarian Society

BIBLIOGRAPHY

▼ ▼

Adler, Alfred. *The Science of Living*, New York: Doubleday & Company, Inc., 1969.

Allport, Gordon. *Becoming: Basic Considerations for a Psychology of Personality*, Yale University Press, 1955.

Anderson, Terry L. and Leal, Donald R. *Free Market Environmentalism*, Westview Press, Inc., 1991.

Andruss, Van; Christopher Plant, Judith Plant, and Eleanor Wright . *Home! A Bioregional Reader*, New Society Publishers, 1990.

Ansbacher, Heinz and Rowena Ansbacher. *The Individual Psychology of Alfred Adler*. Basic Books, Inc., 1956.

Arieti, Silvano. *American Handbook of Psychiatry*. Basic Books, Inc., 1960.

Artiss, Kenneth L. *Therapeutic Studies*. Psychiatric Books, 1985.

Athens, Lonnie. *The Creation of Dangerous Violent Criminals*. Routledge, 1989.

Bastiat, Frederic. *The Law*. The Foundation for Economic Education, Inc., 1981.

Bellah, Robert N.; R. Madsen, A. Sullivan, W. Swidler, and S. Tipton, *Habits of the Heart: Individualism and Commitment in American Life*. Harper & Row, Publishers, 1985.

Berry, Wendell. *A Continuous Harmony*. Harcourt Brace, 1972.

Berry, Wendell. *The Unsettling of American Culture and Agriculture*. Sierra Club Books, 1977.

Berry, Wendell. *Home Economics*. North Point Press, 1987.

Blanton, Smiley. *Love or Perish*. Simon & Schuster, 1956.

Block, Sidney and Peter Reddaway. *Psychiatric Terror: How Soviet Psychiatry Is Used to Suppress Dissent*. Basic Books, Inc., 1977.

Boetie, Etienne de la. *The Politics of Obedience: The Discourse of Voluntary Servitude*. Free Life Editions, 1975.

Bondurant, Joan V. *Conquest of Violence: The Gandhian Philosophy of Conflict*. Princeton University Press, 1988.

Boulding, Kenneth E. *Beyond Economics: Essays on Society, Religion and Ethics*. Ann Arbor Paperbacks, 1968.

Boulding, Kenneth E. *Ecodynamics: A New Theory of Societal Evolution*. Sage Publications, 1978.

Bowlby, John. *Attachment and Loss Volume II: Separation Anxiety and Anger*. Basic Books, Inc., 1973.

Branden, Barbara. *The Passion of Ayn Rand*. Doubleday & Company, Inc., 1986.

Branden, Nathaniel. *The Psychology of Self-Esteem*, Bantam Books, 1969.

Breggin, Ginger and Peter Breggin. "Feminist Paradigms and Conflict Resolution." *ICAR* Newsletter (Institute for Conflict Analysis and Resolution, George Mason University) Spring 1992.

Breggin, Peter R. 1964. "Coercion of Voluntary Patients in an Open Hospital." *Arch Gen Psychiatry* 10:173–181, reprinted with a new introduction in Edwards RB (ed), *Psychiatry and Ethics*. Prometheus Books, 1982.

Breggin, Peter R. *Electroshock: Its Brain-Disabling Effects*. Springer Publishing Co., 1979.

Breggin, Peter R. "Evaluating Human Progress: A Unified Approach to Psychology, Economics, and Politics." In Konstantin Kolenda, ed., *Organizations and Ethical Individualism*. Praeger Books, 1988.

Breggin, Peter R. "How and Why Psychiatry Became a Death Machine." Paper presented at *Medicine Without Compassion*, a conference on the history of medicine during Nazi Germany, Koln, Germany, 1988.

Breggin, Peter R. "Iatrogenic Helplessness in Authoritarian Psychiatry." In Morgan RF (ed), *The Iatrogenics Handbook*, IPI Publishing Co., 1983.

Breggin, Peter R. *Psychiatric Drugs: Hazards to the Brain*. Springer Publishing Co., 1983.

Breggin, Peter R. "Psychiatry and Psychotherapy as Political Processes." *American Journal of Psychotherapy*. 29:369–382, 1975.

Breggin, Peter R. *The Psychology of Freedom*. Prometheus Books, 1980.

Breggin, Peter R. "Psychotherapy as Applied Ethics." *Psychiatry: Journal for the Study of Interpersonal Processes*. Vol. 34, No. 1, Feb., 1971.

Breggin, Peter and E. Mark Stern (Eds.). *Psychotherapy of the Psychotic Patient*. Haworth Press, in press, 1993–94. Will also appear as a volume of the journal, *The Psychotherapy Patient*, in press, 1993–94.

Breggin, Peter R. "Sex and Love: Sexual Dysfunction as a Spiritual Disorder." In Shelp EE (ed), *Sexuality and Medicine*. D. Reidel, 1987.

Breggin, Peter R. (1992–3, in press) "The Three Stages of Human Progress." *Review of Existential Psychology and Psychiatry*.

Breggin, Peter R. *Toxic Psychiatry: Why Empathy and Love Must Replace the Drugs, Electroshock and Biochemical Theories of the "New Psychiatry."* St. Martin's Press, 1991.

Breton, Denise and Christopher Largent. *The Soul of Economies: Spiritual Evolution Goes to the Marketplace*. Idea House Publishing Company, 1991.

Brown, Charles J. and Armando Lago. *The Politics of Psychiatry in Revolutionary Cuba*. Transaction Publishers, 1991.

Brown, Phil. *Transfer of Care.* Routledge, Chapman, and Hill, 1988.

Buber, Martin. *I and Thou.* Charles Scribner's Sons, 1958.

Burton, John, ed. *Conflict: Human Needs Theory.* St. Martin's Press, 1990.

Burton, John. *Conflict: Resolution and Provention.* St. Martin's Press, 1990.

Burton, John. *Resolving Deep-Rooted Conflict.* University Press of America, 1987.

Burton, John. *Separation: Anxiety and Anger.* Basic Books, Inc., 1973.

Carnegie Council on Adolescent Development. *Turning Points: Preparing American Youth for the 21st Century.* Carnegie Corporation of New York, 1989.

Carter, Jimmy. *Keeping the Faith.* Bantam Books, 1982.

Chesler, Phyllis. *Women and Madness.* Doubleday & Company, Inc., 1972.

Clark, Mary E. *Ariadne's Thread: The Search for New Modes of Thinking.* St. Martin's Press, 1989.

Clark, Ronald W. *Einstein: The Life and Times.* Avon Books, 1984.

Coate, Roger A. and Jerel A. Rosati, eds. *The Power of Human Needs in World Society.* Lynne Rienner Publishers, 1988.

Cohen, David, ed. "Challenging the Therapeutic State: Critical Perspectives on Psychiatry and the Mental Health System." The Journal of Mind and Behavior. Vol. 11, Nos. 3 and 4. Also in book form. Haworth Press, 1990.

Coleman, Lee. *The Reign of Error: Psychiatry, Authority, and Law.* Boston: Beacon Press, 1984.

Costello, Judy. "Beyond Gandhi: An American Feminist's Approach to Nonviolence." In Pam McAllister, ed., *Reweaving the Web of Life: Feminism and Nonviolence.* New Society Publishers, 1982.

Cousins, Norman. *Albert Schweitzer's Mission: Healing and Peace.* W.W. Norton & Co., 1985.

Csikszentmihalyi, Mihaly and Isabella Selega Csikszentmihalyi. *Optimal Experience: Psychological Studies of Flow in Consciousness.* Cambridge University Press, 1988.

Dalai Lama. *Ocean of Wisdom: Guidelines for Living.* Harper & Row Publishers, 1989.

Daly, Herman E. and Cobb, John B. Jr. *For the Common Good.* Beacon Press, 1989.

Davies, James Chowning. "The Existence of Human Needs." In Roger A. Coate and Jerel A.Rosati, eds., *The Power of Human Needs in World Society.* Lynne Rienner Publishers, 1988.

de Waal, Frans. *Peacemaking Among Primates*. Harvard University Press, 1989.

Dewey, John. *Freedom and Culture*. Prometheus Books, 1989.

Drucker, Peter F. *The New Realities*. Harper & Row Publishers, 1989.

Dyal, James A. *Education for Survival: The New Security Paradigm*. Paper presented at the annual meeting of the American Psychological Association, August 19, 1991.

Egeland, Byron and Martha Farrell Erickson. "Rising Above the Past: Strategies for Helping New Mothers Break the Cycle of Abuse and Neglect." *Zero to Three*. 11(2), 1990.

Eisenberg, Leon and Leo Kanner, "Early Infantile Autism, 1943–1955." In Charles Reed, Irving Alexander, and Silvan Tomkins, *Psychopathology: A Source Book* Harvard University Press, 1958.

Eisenberg, Nancy and Janet Strayer. *Empathy and Its Development*. Cambridge University Press, 1990.

Eisler, Riane. *The Challice and the Blade*. Harper & Row Publishers, 1987.

Ellis, Havelock. *Studies in the Psychology of Sex: Volume II*. Random House, 1937.

Erdoes, Richard. *Crying for a Dream*. Bear & Company, 1989.

Erikson, Erik. *Childhood and Society*. W.W. Norton & Co., 1963.

Etzioni, Amitai. *The Moral Dimension*. Free Press, 1988.

Fausto-Sterling, Anne. *Myths of Gender*. Basic Books, Inc., 1985.

Feather, Frank. *G-Forces: The 35 Global Forces Restructuring Our Future*. William Morrow and Co., 1989.

Fireside, Harvey. *Soviet Psychoprisms*. W.W. Norton & Co., 1979.

Fischer, Louis, ed. *The Essential Gandhi*. Random House, 1962.

Fisher, Roger and Scott Brown. *Getting Together: Building Relationships As We Negotiate*. Penguin Books, 1988.

Fossey, Dian. *Gorillas in the Mist*. Houghton Mifflin Company, 1983.

Foucault, Michel. *Madness and Civilization: A History of Insanity in the Age of Reason*. Vintage Books, 1965.

Frank, Leonard. *The History of Shock Treatment*. Available from L. Frank, 2300 Webster Street, San Francisco, CA 94115, 1978.

French, Marilyn. *Beyond Power: On Women, Men, and Morals*. Ballantine Books, 1985.

Freud, Sigmund. *The Problem of Anxiety*. W.W. Norton & Co., 1936.

Friedman, Thomas L. *From Beirut to Jerusalem*. Doubleday & Co., Inc., 1989.

Fromm, Erich. *The Art of Loving*. Harper & Row Publishers, 1956.

Fromm, Erich. *Escape from Freedom*. Farrar and Rinehart, 1941.

Fromm, Erich. *To Have or To Be?*. Harper & Row Publishers, 1976.

Galbraith, John K. *The Affluent Society*. Houghton Mifflin Company, 1958.

Galbraith, John K. *Annals of an Abiding Liberal*. Meridian Books, 1980.

Gandhi, Mohandas K. *Gandhi: An Autobiography*. Beacon Press, 1957.

Gelles, Richard and Murray Straus, *Intimate Violence: The Causes and Consequences of Abuse in the American Family*. Simon & Schuster, 1988.

Gilligan, Carol. *In a Different Voice*. Harvard University Press, 1982.

Goffman, Erving. *Asylums: Essays on the Social Situation of Mental Patients and Other Inmates*. Doubleday & Company, Inc., 1961.

Goldsmith, Edward; Robert Allen, Michael Allaby, John Davoll, and Sam Lawrence, eds. *Blueprint for Survival*. New American Library, 1972.

Goodall, Jane. *The Chimpanzees of Gombe*. Harvard University Press, 1986.

Gould, Stephen J. *The Mismeasure of Man*. W.W. Norton & Co., 1989.

Green, Arthur. "Physical and Sexual Abuse of Children." In Harold Kaplan and Benjamin Sadock, eds., *Comprehensive Textbook of Psychiatry*. Williams and Wilkins, 1989.

Hanh, Thich Nhat. *Peace Is Every Step: The Path of Mindfulness in Everyday Life*. Bantam Books, 1991.

Harris, Adrienne and Ynestra King. *Rocking the Ship of State: Toward a Feminist Peace Politics*. Westview Press, Inc., 1989.

Hart, David K. "Management and Benevolence: The Fatal Flaw in Theory Y." In Konstantin Kolenda, ed. *Organizations and Ethical Individualism*. Praeger Books, 1988.

Hart, David K. "Public Administration, the Thoughtless Functionary, and 'Feelinglessness.' " In Robert B. Denhardt and Edward T. Jennings, Jr., eds. *The Revitalization of the Public Service*. University of Missouri–Columbia Press, 1987.

Haworth, Lawrence. *Autonomy: An Essay in Philosophical Psychology and Ethics*. Yale University Press, 1986.

Hayek, Friedrich A. *The Counter-Revolution of Science: Studies on the Abuse of Reason*. Liberty Press, 1952.

Hayek, Friedrich A. *The Road to Serfdom*. The University of Chicago Press, 1944.

Helgesen, Sally. *The Female Advantage: Women's Ways of Leadership.* Doubleday Currency, 1990.

Hertz, J.H. *The Pentateuch and Haftorahs.* Soncino Press, 1960.

Hess, Karl. *Dear America.* William Morrow & Co., 1975.

Hoffman, Martin L. "The Contribution of Empathy to Justice and Moral Judgment." In Nancy Eisenberg and Janet Strayer, eds., *Empathy and Its Development.* Cambridge University Press, 1987.

Horney, Karen. *Neurosis and Human Growth.* W.W. Norton & Co., 1950.

Horney, Karen. *Our Inner Conflicts.* W.W. Norton & Co., 1945.

Hudson, Michael C. *The Palestinians: New Directions.* Center for Contemporary Arab Studies, 1990.

Hunt, Morton. *The Compassionate Beast: What Science Is Discovering About the Humane Side of Mankind.* William Morrow & Co., 1990.

Jaffe, Peter; David Wolfe, and Susan Wilson. *Children of Battered Women.* Sage Publications, 1990.

James, William. *The Principles of Psychology.* Vol. I & II. Henry Holt & Co., 1890.

James, William. *Varieties of Religious Experience.* The Modern Library, 1929.

Jenkins, Bruce. "Einstein Institution Delegation Discusses Civilian-Based Defense with Lithuanian Officials." *Nonviolent Sanctions: News from the Albert Einstein Institution,* Vol. II, No. 4, p. 4., Spring 1991.

Karon, Bertram. "Psychotherapy Versus Medication for Schizophrenia: Empirical Comparisons." In Seymour Fisher and Roger Greenberg, eds., *The Limits of Biological Treatments for Psychological Distress,* Lawrence Erlbaum Associates, 1989.

Kaufman, Gershen. *The Psychology of Shame.* Springer Publishing Company, Inc., 1989.

Kaufman, Les and Kenneth Mallory, eds. *The Last Extinction.* MIT Press, 1986.

Keirsey, David and Marilyn Bates. *Please Understand Me.* Prometheus Nemesis Book Company, 1984.

King, Jr., Martin Luther. *Strength to Love.* Pocket Books, 1963.

Kohn, Alfie. *The Brighter Side of Human Nature: Altruism and Empathy in Everyday Life.* Basic Books, Inc., 1990.

Kohn, Alfie. *No Contest: The Case Against Competition.* New York: Houghton Mifflin Company, 1986.

Kolenda, Konstantin, ed. *Organizations and Ethical Individualism.* Praeger Books, 1988.

Kropotkin, Petr. *Ethics: Origin and Development*. Dial Press, 1924.

Kropotkin, Petr. *Mutual Aid: A Factor of Evolution*. Porter Sargent Publishers, Inc., 1914.

Kruegler, Christopher. "A Bold Initiative in Lithuanian Defense." *Nonviolent Sanctions: News from the Albert Einstein Institution*. Vol II, No. 4, p. 1, Spring 1991.

Laing, R.D. *The Politics of Experience*. Ballantine Books, 1967.

Lamont, Corliss. *The Philosophy of Humanism*. Frederick Ungar Publishing Co, 1977.

Lee, Dorothy. *Freedom and Culture*. Waveland Press, 1959, reprinted in 1987.

Leifer, Ron. *In the Name of Psychiatry*. Science House, 1969.

Lennon, Randy and Nancy Eisenberg. "Gender and Age Difference in Empathy and Sympathy." In Nancy Eisenberg and Janet Strayer, eds. *Empathy and Its Development*. Cambridge University Press, 1987.

Lepp, Ignace. *The Psychology of Loving*. Helicon Press, Inc., 1963.

Leritz, Len. *No-Fault Negotiating: A Practical Guide to the New Dealmaking Strategy That Lets Both Sides Win*. Warner Books, 1987.

Lerner, Gerda. *The Creation of Patriarchy*. Oxford University Press, 1986.

Liebert, Robert; Rita Wicks-Nelson, Robert Kail. *Developmental Psychology, 4th edition*. Prentice-Hall, 1986.

Lippmann, Walter. *The Good Society*. Little Brown and Company, 1937.

Mack, Phyllis. "Feminine Behavior and Radical Action: Franciscans, Quakers, and the Followers of Gandhi." In Adrienne Harris and Ynestra King, eds., *Rocking the Ship of State: Towart a Feminist Peace Politics*. Westview Press, 1989.

Mahler, Margaret S.; Manuel Furer, and Calvin F. Settlage. "Severe Emotional Disturbances in Childhood: Psychosis." In Silvano Arieti, ed., *American Handbook of Psychiatry*. Basic Books, Inc., 1959.

Marx, Karl. *The Economic and Philosophic Manuscripts of 1844*. International Publishers, 1959.

Maslow, Abraham H. *The Farther Reaches of Human Nature*. Viking Press, 1971.

Masson, Jeffrey Moussaieff. *Against Therapy: Emotional Tyranny and the Myth of Psychological Healing*. Atheneum, 1988.

Masson, Jeffrey Moussaieff. *The Assault on Truth: Freud's Suppression of the Seduction Theory*. Faber and Faber, 1984.

May, Rollo; Ernest Angel and Henri F. Ellenberge, eds. *Existence: A New Dimension in Psychiatry and Psychology*. Basic Books, Inc., 1958.

McAllister, Pam. *Reweaving the Web of Life: Feminism and Nonviolence*. New Society Publishers, 1982.

McLuhan, Marshall and Quentin Fiore. *The Medium is the Massage: An Inventory of Effects*. Bantam Books, 1967.

McConnell, James V. *Understanding Human Behavior*. Holt, Rinehart and Winston, 1989.

McCullough, Christopher and Mann, Robert Woods *Managing Your Anxiety*, Jeremy Tarcher, 1985.

McKibben, Bill. *The End of Nature*. Random House, 1989.

McKnight, Gerald. *Verdict on Schweitzer*. The John Day Company, 1965.

Merton,Thomas, ed. *Gandhi on Non-violence*. New Directions Publishing Company, 1965.

Mill, John Stuart and , Harriet Mill Taylor. *Essays on Sex Equality*. University of Chicago Press, 1970.

Miller, Alice. *Thou Shalt Not Be Aware*. New American Library, 1984.

Millett, Kate. *Sexual Politics*. Ballantine Books, 1978.

Mitscherlich, Alexander and Fred Mielke *Doctors of Infamy: The Story of Nazi Medical Crimes*. Henry Schuman, 1949.

Montagu, Ashley. *Touching: the Human Significance of the Skin*. Harper & Row Publishers, 1978.

Morrison, Andrew P. *Shame: The Underside of Narcissism*. The Analytic Press, 1989.

Mosher, Loren and Lorenzo Burti. *Community Mental Health: Principles and Practice*. W.W. Norton and Co., 1989.

Muller-Hill, Beno. *Murderous Science: Elimination by Scientific Selection of Jews, Gypsies, and Others, Germany, 1933–1945*. Oxford University Press, 1988.

Naisbitt, John and Patricia Aburdene. *Re-inventing the Corporation*. New York: Warner Books, 1985.

Nock, Albert Jay. *Our Enemy the State*. Free Life Editions, 1973.

Norton, David L. "Social Organization and Individual Initiative: A Eudaimonistic Model." In Konstantin Kolenda, ed., *Organizations and Ethical Individualism*. Praeger Books, 1988.

Nozick, Robert. *Anarchy, State, and Utopia*. Basic Books, Inc., 1974.

Okin, Susan Moller. *Justice, Gender and the Family*, Basic Books, Inc., 1987.

Oliner, Samuel P. and Oliner, Pearl M. *The Altruistic Personality, Rescuers of Jews in Nazi Europe: What Led Ordinary Men and Women to Risk Their Lives on Behalf of Others?*. The Free Press, 1988.

Oppenheimer, Franz. *The State*. Free Life Editions, 1975.

Ouchi, William G. *Theory Z: How American Business Can Meet the Japanese Challenger*. Avon Books, 1981.

Pavlov, I.P. *Experimental Psychology and Other Essays*. Philosophical Library, 1957.

Peck, M. Scott. *The Road Less Traveled*. Simon & Schuster, 1978.

Peters, Thomas J. and Robert H. Waterman, Jr. *In Search of Excellence: Lessons from America's Best-Run Companies*. Warner Books, 1982.

Phillips, Kevin. *The Politics of Rich and Poor: Wealth and the American Electorate in the Reagan Aftermath*. Random House, 1990.

Piven, Frances Fox and Richard A. Cloward. *The New Class War: Reagan's Attack on the Welfare State and Its Consequences*. Pantheon Books, 1985.

Plutchik, Robert. "Evolutionary Bases of Empathy." In Nancy Eisenberg and Janet Strayer, eds., *Empathy and Its Development*. Cambridge University Press, 1987.

Podvoll, Edward M. *The Seduction of Madness*. HarperCollins Publishers, 1990.

Rand, Ayn. *Atlas Shrugged*. Random House, 1957.

Rand, Ayn. *For the New Intellectual: The Philosophy of Ayn Rand*. Random House, 1961.

Rand, Ayn. *The Fountainhead*. The Bobbs-Merrill Company, 1943.

Rand, Ayn. *Introduction to Objectivist Epistemology*. New American Library, 1979.

Robitscher, Jonas. *The Powers of Psychiatry*. Houghton Mifflin Company, 1980.

Rogers, Carl R. *On Becoming a Person: A Therapist's View of Psychotherapy*. Houghton Mifflin Company, 1961.

Ross-Breggin, Ginger. "Becoming Each Other's Answers." Unpublished, 1990.

Rothbard, Murray N. *The Ethics of Liberty*. Humanities Press, 1982.

Rothbard, Murray N. *For a New Liberty*. Macmillan Company, 1973.

Ruskin, John. *Unto This Last and Other Writings*. Penguin Books, 1985.

Ryan, William. *Blaming the Victim*. Vintage Books, 1976.

Sale, Kirkpatrick. *Dwellers in the Land: The Bioregional Vision*. Sierra Club Books, 1985.

Scheffer, Victor B. *The Shaping of Environmentalism in America*. University of Washington Press, 1991.

Scheflin, Alan and Edward Opton, Jr. *The Mind Manipulators*, Paddington, 1978.

Schmookler, Andrew Bard. *Out of Weakness: Healing the Wounds That Drive Us to War*. Bantam Books Inc., 1988.

Schneider, Isidor, ed. *The World of Love*. Volumes I & II. George Braziller, 1964.

Schoeck, Helmut and James Wiggins, eds. *Scientism and Values*. D. Van Nostrand, 1960.

Schoeck, Helmut. *Envy: A Theory of Social Behavior*. Harcourt, Brace & World, 1966.

Schweitzer, Albert. *Indian Thought and Its Development*. Henry Holt & Company, Inc., 1936.

Schweitzer, Albert. *The Philosophy of Civilization*. The Macmillan Company, 1951.

Schweitzer, Albert. *My Life and Thought: An Autobiography*. George Allen & Unwin Ltd., 1933.

Scott, William G. and David K. Hart. "The Moral Nature of Man in Organizations." *Academy of Management Journal*. June, 1971.

Scott, William G. and David K. Hart. *Organizational America*. Houghton Mifflin, 1979.

Scott, William G. and Terence R. Mitchell. "The Problem or Mystery of Evil and Virtue in Organizations." In Konstantin Kolenda, ed., *Organizations and Ethical Individualism*. Praeger Books, 1988.

Seeley, Robert A. *The Handbook of Non-Violence, Including Aldous Huxley's An Encyclopedia of Pacifism*. Lawrence Hill & Company, 1986.

Seligman, Martin E.P. *Learned Optimism*. Alfred A. Knopf, 1991.

Sharp, Gene. *The Politics of Nonviolent Action* (3 volumes). Porter Sargent Publishers, 1973.

Shelp, Earl E. *Sexuality and Medicine: Volume I: Conceptual Roots*. D. Reidel Publishing Company, 1987.

Shipler, David K. *Arab and Jew: Wounded Spirits in a Promised Land*. Penguin Books, 1986.

Shivers, Lynne. "An Open Letter to Gandhi." In Pam McAllister, ed., *Reweaving the Web of Life: Feminism and Nonviolence*. New Society Publishers, 1982.

Sites, Paul. "Needs As Analogues of Emotions," In Burton, John, ed., *Conflict: Human Needs Theory*. St. Martin's Press, 1990.

Skinner, B.F. *Beyond Freedom and Dignity*. Alfred A. Knopf, 1971.

Smith, Adam. *The Theory of Moral Sentiments*. Liberty Classics, 1976.

Smith, Adam. *The Wealth of Nations*. Penguin Books, 1982.

Spencer, Herbert. *The Man Versus the State*. Mitchell Kennerley, 1916.

Spitz, R.A. "Anaclitic Depression," *Psychoanalitic Study of the Child*. 2: 313–42, 1946.

Spooner, Lysander. *No Treason: The Constitution of No Authority (1870)* and *A Letter to Thomas F. Bayard (1882)*. Ralph Myles Publisher, 1973.

Stone, Merlin. *When God Was a Woman*. Dorset Press, 1976.

Sullivan, Harry Stack. *The Interpersonal Theory of Psychiatry*. W.W. Norton & Co., 1953.

Thompson, Ross A. "Empathy and Emotional Understanding: the Early Development of Empathy." In Nancy Eisenberg and Janet Strayer, eds., *Empathy and Its Development*. Cambridge University Press, 1987.

Thoreau, Henry David. "An Essay on Civil Disobedience." *The Portable Thoreau*, Carl Bode, ed. Viking Press, 1980.

Tolstoy, Leo. *The Kingdom of God Is Within You* (1894). University of Nebraska Press, 1894.

Tournier, Paul. *The Meaning of Persons*. Harper & Row Publishers, 1957.

Trattner, Walter I. *From Poor Law to Welfare State: A History of Social Welfare in America*. The Free Press, 1984.

Von Mises, Ludwig. *The Anti-Capitalistic Mentality*. Libertarian Press, 1972.

Von Mises, Ludwig. *Human Action: A Treatise on Economics*. Contemporary Books, Inc., 1966.

Von Mises, Ludwig. *Omnipotent Government: The Rise of the Total State and Total War*. Arlington House, 1969.

Von Mises, Ludwig. *Planned Chaos*. The Foundation for Economic Education, 1947.

Wachtel, Paul L. *The Poverty of Affluence*. New Society Publishers, 1989.

Walker, Lenore E. *Terrifying Love: Why Battered Women Kill and How Society Responds*. Harper & Row Publishers, 1989.

Waring, Marilyn. *If Women Counted: A New Feminist Economics*. Harper & Row Publishers, 1988.

Washington, James Melvin. *A Testament of Hope: The Essential Writings of Martin Luther King, Jr*. Harper & Row Publishers, 1986.

Waterman, Alan S. "Psychological Individualism and Organizational Functioning: A Cost-benefit Analysis." In Konstantin Kolenda, ed., *Organizations and Ethical Individualism*. Praeger Books, 1988.

Weatherford, Jack. *Indian Givers: How the Indians of the Americas Transformed the World.* Fawcett Columbine, 1988.

Weaver, Henry Grady. *The Mainspring of Human Progress.* Foundation for Economic Education, 1947.

Weaver, Paul H. *The Suicidal Corporation: How Big Business Fails America.* Simon & Shuster, 1988.

Wilson, Edward O. *On Human Nature.* Harvard University Press, 1978.

Wolfe, David A. *Child Abuse: Implications for Child Development and Psychopathology.* Sage Publications, 1987.

Worchel, Stephen; Joel Cooper, and George R. Goethals. *Understanding Social Psychology.* Dorsey Press, 1988.

Worldwatch Institute. *State of the World.* W.W. Norton & Co., 1990.

Wyatt, Gail Elizabeth and Gloria Johnson Powell. *Lasting Effects of Child Sexual Abuse.* Sage Publications, 1988.

Yllo, Kersti, and Michele Bogard. *Feminist Pespectives on Wife Abuse.* Sage Publications, 1988.

ABOUT THE AUTHOR

▼ ▼

Peter R. Breggin, M.D., a Harvard College and Case Western Reserve School of Medicine graduate, and former teaching fellow at Harvard Medical School, was full-time consultant for the National Institute of Mental Health before going into the private practice of psychiatry in Bethesda, Maryland, from 1968 to the present. He is the director of the center for the Study of Psychiatry and Professor (Adjunct) of Conflict Analysis and Resolution at George Mason University, as well as the author of numerous books and articles dealing with psychiatry. Dr. Breggin frequently lectures and gives seminars to lay and professional audiences and appears on national television as an expert on psychiatric and conflict-resolution issues. He has been a consultant in landmark and federal legislation on behalf of patients' rights and psychiatric reform. Dr. Breggin's most comprehensive book on the subject of psychiatry is entitled *Toxic Psychiatry: Why Therapy, Empathy, and Love Must Replace the Drugs, Electroshock, and Biochemical Theories of the "New Psychiatry"*, and is also published by St. Martin's Press.